MW01003130

Life Lessons of a Legend

Captain Tony Tarracino and Brad Manard

Cover Photo by Rob O'Neal

ISBN: 1-4392-0222-2
ISBN-13: 9781439202227

Visit www.booksurge.com to order additional copies.
Proofreader: Cindy Ballew, Precisely Write

OCEAN KEY

RESORT & SPA

KEY WEST, FLORIDA

12-8-14

A little island distraction
to help you along
your journey to
full recovery.
Until we get a chance
to share one in Key
West together, A "virtual"
beer at the Hogs Breath
always helps.
Slainté   Hugh

To all of my family with love.

And to my wife, Marty.

In the dictionary, beside the word compassion, should be Marty's picture. Through her I have learned, lived, and loved, and from her I have become a better person.

And to my friend, Shel Silverstein, who told me books are forever.

— Captain Tony Tarracino

Author's Statement

Captain Tony is a man of history, a man whose story is important to know, and a man who offers many exceptional qualities as well as many flamboyant characteristics. The life he has lived has been his own and the thoughts, actions, and beliefs he shares in this book are his and do not necessarily reflect those of the author nor are his actions strictly condoned or advocated by the author. What is important are the life lessons learned from Captain Tony's experiences. These are of incredible value and reflect his true qualities.

As a writer, I am cautious in considerations of censorship, yet as an educator and parent I understand the importance of guiding our children and monitoring their learning. While Captain Tony's lessons are valuable for all ages, the way he learned some of the lessons is most appropriate for mature readers. Therefore, I would encourage parents to read *Life Lessons of a Legend* and make their own decisions regarding the appropriateness for younger readers.

– Brad Manard

Acknowledgements

Little did I know that purchasing a book for a birthday gift would have such an impact. Before passing it on, I read a few pages of Jimmy Buffett's *A Pirate Looks at Fifty*. Tapping into the curiosity it evoked, I bought a copy for myself. Though I did not know it at the time, that moment was the birth of *Life Lessons of a Legend*.

Buffett's book was like a reflection of my opposite being, a person whose life was filled with adventure and exotic fun. Reflecting, I wonder if, as a younger man had I ventured onto sunny, white sand beaches releasing my writing creativity in song lyrics and learned to play guitar with acoustic soul, might I have become Jimmy Buffett? That vision was in stark contrast to what my life had become as a small town school superintendent in the heart of conservative Iowa. Inspired, I decided to embody the spirit of Jimmy Buffett, joined the Parrotheads, and took one fateful trip to the land of margaritas–Key West–where I met the living legend Tony Tarracino.

Through it all, my parents Jim and Maxine Manard were concerned I had joined some colorful, feathery cult until they met Captain Tony. Along the way, my friends got nauseous being subjected to the constant steel drum rhythm of Buffett music until, absorbed in the fun, they slowly began to understand, appreciate, and encourage my playful discovery. In a special way, all of those who experienced my journey have played a role in the writing of *Life Lessons of a Legend.*

I offer a heartfelt thank you to all who have contributed to the madness. The manuscript benefited significantly from the reading and rereading by my wife, Denise, and the deft-line editing of my sister Claire Seely. To Key West's Wendy Tucker, Captain Tony's official biographer, for her thoughts, insights, and appreciation, and Albert Kelley, Tony's legal advisor and friend. Gratitude goes out to Rob O'Neal of the Key West Citizen for sharing his photographs of Captain Tony. Thank you to Randy Christ, the former manager at Captain Tony's Saloon and a fellow Iowan, for added color, support, and icy cold libation in the midst of tropical temperatures.

Through the writing process, a unique and charitable group of friends offered ongoing support, encouragement, and enthusiasm. The members of the Isle of Iowa Parrothead Club in Cedar Rapids, IA embrace *Midwest Latitudes and Caribbean Attitudes,* and have guided me on an adventure into the rediscovery of my own untamed spirit. Special thanks for the heartfelt friendship of club members Doug Rassler, lead singer of the Cedar Island Band, and his wife, Deb, for sharing their talents throughout, particularly on one fine night in Key West's hidden treasure, the Chart Room.

Capt. Tony's family was more than charitable with their time, always expressing love and appreciation for their husband and father while speaking genuinely to his character and history. Two that I owe particular thanks to are Tony's wife Marty, who from the moment we first spoke became a cherished and lasting friend, and Tony's oldest son, Louie, who always brings Italian enthusiasm to the party making him a kindred spirit as the day fades into the soul of a Key West night.

There is a group of friends that must be acknowledged, friends who embraced my enthusiasm for this project, and individuals who have made a lifetime commitment to our friendship. Particular thanks to my brother Tim Manard, sister Jana Dingeman, son Wayne Rogers and daughter-in-law Lindsay, and a future guitar player whose smile can christen any day – my grandson Jonas.

Tom and Deb Cox have been life-long friends always toasting my silliness and appreciating that willingness to leap. Mark Johnson is a true friend, who, on our annual RAGBRAI bike rides across Iowa continues to impress upon me the importance of Bob Marley's influence. Terry and Susan Koertner have discovered their own spiritual journey and eternally opened their doors and arms with love. Finally, Bob and Janel Lesan laughed all along the way as they allowed me to guide them to the Caribbean where, during one night of high spirits and confidence on a quiet Jamaican beach, our everlasting friendship was cast in the glow of radiant sunset. They have and will always be a source of support.

Prelude

I don't know why Tony took such a liking to me, or what drew me to the crusty old sea Captain. Our worlds were from the opposite reaches of America. Captain Tony was an 86 year-old gambling hustler from New Jersey who had turned into a womanizing, gun-running boat captain in the predominately gay island of Key West, Florida. I was an educator born and bread in Iowa, living conservatively comfortable in the corn and Bible belt of America's heartland. I'd been faithfully married to the same woman for 18 years, while there were eight different mothers to Tony's 13 children. While I liked to believe I was an open-minded individual, I'd had very little contact with those outside of my safely heterosexual existence in middle America, quite the opposite culture to Tony's life experiences. The only parallel was leadership. Tony had been the Mayor of Key West, and I was a school district superintendent.

There was nothing special in the way we'd met. It was the way the legendary Captain Tony meets hundreds of people each day, yet somewhere in our brief conversation, he leaned in closer, lowered his sandpaper voice, made that way from sixty years of filterless cigarettes dangling between his lips, and began to whisper his stories to me. With his words there was wisdom in his clear blue eyes and orneriness in his happy grin framed by a white goatee that gave him a sincere, drawing, yet devilish look. His face would brighten with lucid memories from a half a century before, and his arms would swing about with enthusiasm as if living the excitement of the actual moment once again. He was a man of bars, a listener, advisor, and a storyteller that kept the patrons coming back for more lively libation to take away the day.

Smiling with that great big grin of enthusiasm that just took you over, Tony's arms spread to the full length of their skinny, flaccid ability, "our worlds are like this," showing they were as far apart as his eagle spanned wings would go. "Prairie thinkin' superintendent." He'd point at me. "Conch Republic pirate." He'd point back to himself. Then he'd add with a daring wink and a mischievous grin perfected during his life as a hustler. "I'm going to bring you into my world."

Before we met, I had pictured him to be a muscular and rugged man, powerful in his laughter at the dangers of the sea, stout like a biceped boxer ever ready for a brawl. When I found him, so many years had passed, so many years since he had sailed the seas as captain of the Greyhound, an arduous vessel stout with balance breaking headlong into the mounting waves of September, deep in the heart of the hurricane season. So many years he had been known as The Captain, famous for his catch of massive tiger sharks and tons of goliath grouper, a man of legends born from the secret missions of the Cuban Revolution, memorialized in the songs of tropical singers, and a lover of women, aged

Scotch, and his thirteen children. He was a living legend, the last living pirate at the end of America.

When I found him, it was much by accident. On a Key West vacation with my sun-loving wife Denise, we sat soaking in the tropical heat of a late June day, drinking from the plastic souvenir cups holding a volume of libation and the image of a grinning Captain Tony on the side. We were intrigued watching travelers who had come to the island and been captured in the history of the Captain Tony's Saloon.

It was the bar with his name, the bar famous for its age, its music of the lifestyle, and the early times when Hemingway had graced its stools, but most of all, famous as the home of the sea-bearing Captain Tony. Turning innocently, I had scanned the room adorned with his image. It was a room of history, of the past. Then I saw the smile and the ocean blue eyes, clear and bright, and I knew. With the eyes of Newman, the boldness of Hemingway, and the spirit of his surrogate son, Jimmy Buffett, he sat holding court in the corner of Captain Tony's Saloon.

Without time for thought, I stepped away from the scarred wooden bar and moved across the dingy concrete floor to greet the living legend. In an upward glance, his smile grew as did the youthfully clear blue in his friendly eyes, tired only on the edges, and he reached his hand to greet me as he greets everyone with a jovial smile, bright attentive eyes, and a firm, warm handshake.

"Captain Tony," with nervous wonderment, I stumbled even those words, "Captain Tony. It's an honor to meet you."

"Thank you." The magnetism shone from his growing smile and the gruff strength of his voice. "You too, young man, you too. What's your name?"

"My name's Brad." I answered, giggling like a school-boy though I was well beyond half of his 86 years and nowhere near young.

"Brad," he held our handshake with firmness and the power that his small, elderly body no longer hinted at, "it's nice to meet you. Is that your wife over there?" His hand released as the wrinkled and slight curl of his long finger pointed toward Denise who'd turned looking for her lost mate. "The beautiful one."

"It is." I answered, not stuttering those simple words.

Again with his grin, he waved her to us as if he were drawing a bee to honey.

Looking up, sure and confident with the wisdom of time, he said. "I love beautiful women." His smile grew in orneriness with a slight curl at the left corner, and he winked with all of the spirit a legend could muster. "Let me tell you a story about another gorgeous woman. There have been so many in my life."

That is how we met, Captain Tony and Brad Manard, the wild womanizing legend of the Conch Republic and the cautious small town school superintendent. His had been a life lived teetering on the edge, seeking balance where it was most difficult to balance. It was a teetering cliff above treacherous hurricanes and high-spirits, wild women and betrayal, and guns and wars. Having somehow kept from falling off the unrecoverable cliff where he would have been swept away in the gale of a raging storm, he lived his life now in a reflection of his past, true stories from the edge like a cheap romance novel gone wrong.

Five months past my first escape to the island, I returned to the freedom of saturated sunshine, thick salty air, blended icy drinks, and tropical sea breezes far from my humdrum Midwest. Stepping into the saloon, Tony was once again perched on his stool in a fog of smoke swirling like his sea-bearing, bar spirited life. I slipped into the line behind the autograph seekers, waiting patiently to greet my grandfatherly friend of four hours from five months before. Nervously, I waited my turn, wondering if the magic of storytelling would still be the current between us. Finally, as the filled space cleared, I stepped to him, reaching out my uneasy hand and said, "Hello Tony. Do you remember me?"

The Captain's eyes rose until they met mine, the blue brightening as a grin spread across his thin, leathered face, and he asked, "Where's Denise?"

Thus, part of the legend, that Tony is the Casanova of Key West.

During my tropical escape, Tony shared more stories, stories of the many friends he'd known. Stories of his close relationship with the famed treasure hunter Mel Fisher, of his love for the young Jimmy Buffett who grew to be a legend in his own right, and people in his life that had touched his heart in friendship like Tennessee Williams and Shel Silverstein. His pride glowed as he shared stories of the native island folk unknown to the world, his people. They were the people who had created depth in his life giving the quality of friendship, and from them new tales were born enhanced by his own aging memory.

We talked for a time, and I spoke of my idea for this book, to share his stories, and learn the wisdom of a lifetime grown into a legend. I wanted to write of his life of experiences and share his hard learned lessons with others. He liked the idea Captain Tony did, and encouraged me saying, "write whatever you want." Then with his black pen, he wrote his home address and telephone number on a business card. Taking my hand in a grip of warmth, his eyes locked on mine like friends parting with an unknown future.

"Call me," then he added with a wink and heartfelt grin that made me believe, "you and I, Brad, we're going to do things together."

Over the next couple of months I called and left messages, instructions to call my cell phone, my home, or write to my email address. I made every effort to have him reach me, yet I heard nothing. Then in late February in the middle of a small dinner party of plum red wine and Iowa beef tenderloin steaks the telephone rang.

"Brad," he said. "I'm sorry I haven't called back."

"Captain Tony." The words burst from me both surprised and excited, and I heard a dinner guest say to the others *He really knows him. He really knows Captain Tony.*

"How're you doing?" I asked with the equal excitement of my eighth Christmas.

"My friend died, and I was in the hospital." His voice was slow, gravelly, as if it was a challenge to put the breaths of a sentence together. "Had pneumonia and they had to put a pacemaker in too. They got me on oxygen, damn thing's running tubes up into my nose. I'm not going to be alive forever, Brad. Let's write that book. You've inspired me. Let's tell people what I think." Despite the Captain's enthusiasm, his breaths were labored, short, and wheezing. "I've lived a full life, an amazing life. I've got a lot to teach, and I won't live forever. Let's write that book. Let's tell the world about my philosophy."

And, of course, I answered. "It'd be my honor, Tony."

So this is the book. It is a book of lessons shared by a living legend. I know that the charm of Captain Tony is the energetic wit from which the tales come. Many find his blatant honesty refreshing and amusing while others find his vocabulary offensive, yet when he speaks, there is no doubt as to his meaning. While his life is not one I would emulate, his spirit inspires many, yet others are appalled with the contradiction of his philandering behavior. He will be the first to tell you he is a true paradox. He is both extremely honest and a great bullshitter. With tremendous pride he'll tell you he's both. I have learned there is great truth in that statement.

What is truth and what is fiction is only for us to decipher, but all of it, every story is of the real legend that is Captain Tony Tarracino. So this is our story, *Life Lessons of a Legend* based on tales told by Captain Tony to teach a middle-aged, mainland educator the lessons of his life as we hung out together in Key West. They are stories shared from a lifetime of experiences and the wisdom born from them with some wily sea captain bravado thrown in for flavor. This is the legend of Captain Tony.

CHAPTER 1

Duval Street in Key West is like Bourbon Street in New Orleans with fewer clothes. When you step onto the main street of Key West in the heart of the Conch Republic, you step into a different world. For me, there is a refreshing honesty on Duval Street with the mixture of tourists and locals. There are the talented street musicians, singing and playing for change to feed a homeless body, sun-loving girls striding down the street in clothes they love but would never wear back home, skimpy-thin outfits that reveal more than they hide. There is the entrepreneur selling pictures to be taken with his live parrots, iguana, or massive snakes that live comfortably around his neck. It's a lively street carnival.

The bars have a mixture of acoustic entertainment from classic Buffett melodies to raunchy comedy set to the tune of hit songs. Music is what helps make the transition, singing to the tropical tunes, laughing at the bawdy jokes you would never share at work, and becoming engrossed in the fun that keeps the crowd roaring in their escape from the mundane to this Caribbean paradise. All is intermixed with a kind of genuine spirit not valid in the tourists' real lives, but certainly authentic in the untamed spirit of their soul. As the saying goes, you may be Andy back in Mayberry, but in Key West, you're just another Otis. That is the honesty of Key West. It is the "ville" in Jimmy Buffett's margarita.

Two doors west of Duval on Greene Street is where you'll find the *Salt of Key West*. In a building you would expect to be old, like the name and image on its plywood marquee, the color is bright yellow like his optimism while the dinginess inside hides the secrets of a life lived on the edge. The *Salt of Key West* has always pushed the edge, an edge that is far beyond any cliff you and I have ever dared to step near or lean over for fear of falling to become a pile of broken bones gone array. Stepping through the yellow doors into the saloon of beer-stained floors and rough wood beams decorated with a million business cards and dozens of ornamental bras, you will find the legendary captain. He is Captain Tony, the *Salt of Key West*.

I had come to Key West seeking the legend and to learn more of his spirit, motivated to understand how a man with a shadowy past could capture the hearts of those in the present. With a wink of the eye and a knowing nod, people will tell you that Captain Tony is the father of 13 children by eight different women, only three of whom he married. I wondered how today in this world of equality, he still managed to be revered? A legend yes, but how would this speak of the quality of this man's character? The tales expand to his exploits as a gun-running revolutionary, a spy for the U.S. Government during the Cuban revolution.

Again, there is the question of character versus legend. His buddy Jimmy Buffett certainly has legendary qualities, but he too lives with his own untamed spirit. So how could this person, Captain Tony, a Casanova crusader of women, gun-running escapades, and deep into the night saloon exploits be elected mayor of Key West and honored with that title for life?

How, at 87 years old the *Salt of Key West* Captain Tony Tarracino was still active and impacting the lives of the people of an island that he loved as his own be revered despite his past. I know that legends are not born so much of acts, but from the quality of the individuals who perform them. Who, I wanted to know, was the man that the legend of Captain Tony had been born from? I sought not the legend, not the morally questionable escapades, but the quality of his character.

I found Tony where I'd first met him one year before, sitting on his stool in his autograph corner of Captain Tony's Saloon. He had his arm around a 30ish woman with short-cropped brown hair and bright green eyes who was wearing a provocative bikini top.

Tony's eyes squinted as he pointed to her. "I remember you. We had an affair."

"No Captain Tony," she blushed, "we never had an affair."

"Well," he patted her shoulder tenderly, ornery as they come, "we should have."

Beside him was a grocery sack with an oxygen tank and plastic tube, the life breath of his 87th year. He was not smoking his standard Lucky Strike cigarette and I wondered if, after a lifetime of habit, he had traded in breathing smoke for breathing oxygen.

As he looked up at the sight of me, his face jumped with excitement, his eyes grew large as his mouth fell open in a happy smile on the verge of laughter that life was so good.

"Brad," he exclaimed as he recognized me, "it's good to see you."

I was amazed once again at the strength of his firm handshake, so contradictory to the small, frail body from which it came. Standing slightly unsteady with bowed legs and the gentle rounding of his back, the brightness in his eyes was that of a teenager's. Surrounded by a white goatee and mustache, charisma flowed from the smile of this wiry man whose arms still hinted at the strength of an able sailor. His hair was full, thick and white as the breaking Atlantic Ocean waves, the antique remnants of what once had been Italian jet black. His enthusiasm was infectious, and I immediately felt my own spirit lifting.

Captain Tony, a man with the spirit of the sea and the attitude of a sailor on leave, had never changed. He had been on shore leave for 87 years, living life as if he had to pack every ounce of fun, every daring experience into one exact moment, the moment of immediacy. With his head slightly tilted, his eyes happy with large bags, full and puffy, hanging like tiny water balloons below his eyes, he smiled his greeting.

"We're going to write a good book, you and me," he looked straight into my eyes, staring honesty. "I'm a great bullshitter. But honestly, I don't have to lie. I don't lie if I can help it, but I might exaggerate. It's the way I tell stories." Already his arms were waving about, his voice clear with his own anticipation of the stories. "They're colorful, my stories; truthful, but colorful. I want you to believe these stories because what I'll tell you is the truth. You can't make up these stories. They're too amazing. I'm going to be honest with you." Then his eyes shifted just a bit. "But I might throw in a little bullshit just to dress them up."

I believed him. What I knew of Captain Tony was this. He is honest. He's not afraid of the truth, so he says it bluntly, unabashedly, and with enthusiasm. Tony tells the truth about the important things in life, the things that matter. He tells the absolute truth as he knows it, and all intertwined within the truth of the important things is a great big bunch of colorful, fun loving bull.

Feeling a small crowd growing behind me, I stepped to the side allowing the next admirer to shake the hand of the *Salt of Key West*. Tony's attention immediately brightened with an uplifting smile as if it was his great honor to meet the next tourist.

"Captain Tony," a tanned man with sandy brown hair and a large, full body reached to shake his hand, "my name's Jamie Prentice. I'm a fifth generation Conch. My grandmother was Gladys Burgett."

"No shit." Tony talks like a sailor on leave too, 'shit' and greater words of color flowing from his vocabulary like most people say 'heck' and 'golly'. But would you expect less from the *Salt of Key West?*

An east coast transplant turned shrimper, Tony was raised poor in New Jersey and still lived with the influence of 1935 when gambling and the mob were his way of life. He is a throwback to a different time, a time of black and white films and saloon doors bursting open as the fighter is flung onto the hard dirt street. Standing up he curses as he brushes himself off, dust flying from his weathered clothes, and he lowers his head marching right back into the saloon.

Tony reached again to shake the younger man's hand. "I knew your grandmother. She owned the Brown Derby. It's the Green Parrot Bar now, but before it was the Brown Derby."

Jamie was proud to know that Tony remembered, giddy like a boy meeting his idolized sports hero. "Before that it was a morgue," Jamie tells us, "few people know that."

Tony lifted both hands excited with the memory, his hand shaking up and down as if playing mariachis to the beat of his life.

"It was a morgue!" his voice rising, emphasizing 'was.' "It was really an ice house, but one day they put a body in there to preserve it. With that body on ice, nobody wanted to buy ice anymore, so it became a morgue." Tony's eyes narrowed, quiet for an instant searching through the clutter of his memory for the right moment, the time of Gladys Burgett. "She used to wear a Brown Derby all the time, wore it to promote the bar."

"That was my grandmother." Jamie was almost bouncing, a full-bodied man of maturity excited at the connection. "When I was a boy, I used to skip school, and I'd hide on your boat. I'd crawl under the life jackets, and I'd stay there until we were out in the ocean. Then I'd come up from under the life jackets and spend the whole day out on the boat with you fishing."

Tony's mouth burst open, his burly eyebrows lifting, stretching his face longer. "That was you?" He pointed, gripping his hands into fists of excitement until they clapped together. Then Tony reached out his hand to the boy grown into a man.

As they grasped hands once again, Jamie's face grew flush red with excitement. "I'm a ship captain now, Tony. Captain James Prentice."

"No kidding." His eyes burst wide with a big smile, looking to me as he pointed with wonder at his grown up protégé.

Jamie nodded, a boy come home to tell his hero, to tell the man who had shown him the sea, that he had grown to be much like his boyhood idol. Captain James Prentice, Jamie all grown up, glowed heartfelt emotions as he gripped the hand of his mentor. They talked more then, sea talk, ship captain talk, tales and technical language, and stories that delight those who share the ocean. Through it all, it was as if Jamie had fulfilled a promise to himself, a promise to return to Key West and thank Captain Tony for his guidance to live life upon the sea they both loved.

The conversation ended as most conversations with Tony do. Jamie shaking his hand, telling him what an honor it was to see him, stepping one step away then stopping to repeat words of adulation, another step, his hand lifting to wave again, words of good wishes and health flowing from him to Tony. He didn't want to leave the Captain. Few do, so that is the way most conversations end. Slowly, respectfully, one step at a time as admirers edge away with their hands reaching back, waving, not wanting to disconnect.

In the moment of Jamie's final goodbye, I eyed the pictures decorating Captain Tony's Saloon. Blown up images, there were photos of Tony's past with his good friends Shel Silverstein, Jimmy Buffett, and others. Seeing their smiles reflecting back, I could not help but see that so many admired him. Turning to the legend, I asked Captain Tony where the description the *Salt of Key West* had come from. With honest sincerity, he explained as if this was just another typical description in a long list of adjectives.

Years ago there was an article in the New York Times that described the 12 most intriguing people in the United States. They talked about those people you know, famous people like Elizabeth Taylor. The twelve most famous people in the whole country, and I was on the list. Captain Tony, they wrote, Captain Tony, the

Salt of Key West. I was one of the 12 most intriguing people, and they described me as the Salt of Key West.

There was so much I wanted to learn from this man, so much that there must be to know. A throwback to a time long gone of dusty backroom card games, wooden ships of the sea, and kitchen bound women, he is lost in the progressive sophistication and digital world of the 21st Century. He was the last of a generation that could be described as swashbuckling, a hard born seaman that spit on the caution of OSHA. Too many rules, he certainly must believe, too many rules.

His life was of backbreaking work on high seas that made him feel proud and capable and of wild times with free women before women had burned the bras of freedom. Tony was of hard driving acoustic ballads and shots of scotch burning harsh in his throat. He was a man of JFK conspiracy intrigue having slipped into the inner circles of the Cold War. *The Salt of Key West* was a man unafraid to live a life from which legends are made.

This was the man I had come to know and learn from.

A pretty girl in her mid-twenties stepped forward, handing Tony a souvenir tee-shirt to autograph. Tony looked up buoyant with happiness like a little boy who'd just gotten a great compliment from his teacher. Taking the tee-shirt, he pulled the cap off his black Sharpie pen.

"What's your name?" He asked kindly.

"Nicole." She answered as her husband leaned curiously on the counter behind her.

I thought of my own experience of a year before as I had done much the same. My wife Denise had captured Tony's attention. Dressed in untypical attire complimenting Caribbean humidity, she wore a hip slimming lycra mini-skirt and matching bikini top. I remember thinking that he'd forgotten I was even there as I'd leaned on the counter much as Nicole's husband did now. But then he had turned to me and begun to tell one of his stories.

As Tony signed the shirt, he asked her. "What do you do?"

Nicole, with her pretty blond hair pulled back into a sun bright bun, beamed a brilliant, dazzling smile. "I'm a nurse." She shared proudly.

"Oh. A nurse," he glanced to me winking, "you know, of all the women I've slept with, and there's been a lot of them, I've learned that nurses and stewardesses, they're the best lovers." With a teasing point of his hand, and a slight wink, he said. "I bet you're a great lover."

From beneath her husband's straw hat, curled at the edges like a bull riders trophy, he grinned slyly as if she surely didn't wear her hair in a bun all the time. During the day, the heat kept it up off her shoulders, but at night, at night it hung fully down over her shoulders like the flailing tail of a wild filly.

When Nicole gave Tony a playful, tender slug in the arm, her husband's two-day stubble of vacation ruggedness only grew fuller with his smile.

He had captured her, and her husband knew it. In the few moments of their conversation, Tony had read her and seized her fancy as she found herself flirting with the salty sea captain. Tony and nurse Nicole fell naturally into a dialogue about his zest for life, his recent operation and the pacemaker now residing in his chest.

Her husband stood beside her taking it all in as I had watched from near Denise one year ago. This is how it happened one year ago. As he had flirted with my wife, I had connected with the *Salt of Key West*.

"You and I, Brad, we're going to do things together."

I had stood by as Tony signed autographs and flirted, smoked and signed, shook hands graciously, thanked each and every one of those who had waited to greet the legendary *Salt of Key West*. All of this had been done with Denise at his side, she charming him as they each fell under the others' beguiling spell. They had talked and teased until, with great pleasure, she disappeared through the growing crowd surrounding the worn wood bar to get Tony another glass of ginger ale. As the last in line of autograph seekers stepped away, Tony had waved me in.

"What brings you to Key West?" He had asked, waving his fingers for me to come closer as smoke swirled from his cigarette drifting upward between us.

"I told my wife it was for our anniversary, eighteen years together this week," I had leaned in closer, my own orneriness whispered quietly, "but truth is I'm a Parrothead."

"Really." He'd straightened at the connection, his own voice quieting with the secret.

"We went to a Buffett Concert in Chicago last night, then flew to the land of Jimmy Buffett this morning." I shrugged slyly. "For Denise it's a great anniversary present. For me, I've come to Margaritaville."

"I've been to Chicago, the Tweeter Center." Tony shared with his matter-of-fact enthusiasm. "My favorite place for a concert is Alpine Valley in Wisconsin. I used to go to a lot of Jimmy's concerts, but with my health." His hand flipped the ultimate gesture of displeasure. "I don't get to see Jimmy as much as I used to." With that, Captain Tony grinned, slipping back into a time of fond memory as he talked on.

Years ago Jimmy came in here like all the other musicians. We were big then, Captain Tony's Saloon. One of those big trendy magazines had called Captain Tony's "The Great American Bar." Everybody wanted to come to Key West and play guitar here. Jerry Jeff Walker, Eric Clapton, David Allan Coe, everybody wanted to play Captain Tony's in the late 60s and 70s. Jimmy came in like any other musician, a kid with a guitar wanting to play Captain Tony's. He bugged me and bugged me until one day I told him he could play when the regular guy was on break. I paid him $10 and three Budweisers to play for ten minutes during the breaks.

Excited to be on the island of Buffett's inspiration with a Parrothead hero hearing one of the ultimate Parrothead stories, I asked. "What'd he play?"

"You know," Tony eyes locked onto a busty blond with a Devil's Canyon cleavage as she sauntered in to a goggling reaction from all the boys, "everybody asks me that, what Jimmy played the first time." The bosoms turned toward him, and he opened his arms for a hug. "Hell if I know. I was over by the door hustling a gorgeous woman."

Tony welcomed the beauty into his arms, shrugging slightly as if Jimmy playing had really been no big deal. At the time, it probably wasn't. Buffett was a struggling country singer back then. A penniless guitar player having bombed out in Nashville, he found himself in Key West looking for work and wanting to gain exposure by playing in Captain Tony's Saloon.

I liked Jimmy, and he stayed in Key West, hung around the bar. We became friends. One night a few of us were sitting over by the fireplace. Over there in the corner having a few drinks, and we probably had a fire going as it was late in the evening. It was winter when it gets just a little cool down here at night. We were just a few friends sitting around talkin' and drinking beer.

Anyway, music was the topic because Jimmy was trying to figure out how to get his career going again. He'd recorded some stuff, done an album up in Nashville, but it hadn't gone anywhere, and his career had come to a screeching halt. Key West was at a peak back then, but nobody was writing songs about it, so someone said "Jimmy, why don't you write songs about Key West?" He must have liked the idea because he wrote "Margaritaville," "Changes" and he put them on his "Changes in Latitude, Changes in Attitude" album. As they say, the rest is history.

Captain Tony had leaned over the corner of the souvenir counter so I was face to face with the legend listening intently to his soft-spoken memories. I'd found myself in that altruistic moment when one legend shared a real life story of another legend. I had been given a private moment hearing his intimate words not shared with the typical tourist. I was in Parrothead paradise.

When Denise had returned, Tony had gripped my arm with a kind hand then turned his attention back to the new line of autograph seekers. As he did, we drank out of our Captain Tony plastic souvenir cups, waiting for the crowd to thin again. When the crowd broke, I had stepped up to thank Captain Tony.

"I do a little writing, Tony," I shared. "Could I write of this visit and send you a copy of our words? A memento if you will?"

Tony reached his hand to my shoulder and eye-to-eye as my grandfather had done years ago, he said. "You write anything you want. I'd be honored." Then he added with a wave of disgust. "Screw that copyright stuff. You have my permission. Write anything you want." His arms fluttered in irritation at the legalities, still a throwback to simpler times. "You and I, Brad. We're going to do things together. I've got that feeling."

Winking, he had taken Denise in his arms and pulled her tightly to him, kissing her cheekbone as his free hand squeezed her firmly.

With her gentle touch to his face, Denise's eyes had been true to his. "Thanks Tony."

"You like that?" He had laughed like the ladies man he knew he was and squeezed her one more time.

I'd never seen another man get away with that. I'd never seen another man so bold and brash as to pull my wife close, firmly holding her as he smiled into her eyes.

I'd never seen it happen until Captain Tony did it, and I certainly never expected to see appreciation in my wife's illuminating smile. Sly old sea dog, he could get away with anything.

As I thought back on that day one year ago, realizing I was standing once again with the *Salt of Key West*, I could not help but wonder how my life would change in the course of the next several days. Can we not help but grow from time with a legend? How would the salty sea captain of the Conch Republic change my life as a conservative educator from the cornfields of Iowa? What lessons would I learn?

When Tony began to say goodbye to Nicole and her husband, he reached down, slightly patting her slender, youthful figure. Just as with Denise, it made her smile that this old man was flirting so unabashedly, and her husband didn't even blink. The things an ornery old man can get away with. Maybe that's part of the charm.

As they stepped from the door, Coral, Tony's daughter pulled her car up to the curb on Greene Street. Tony waved, and turned in a slow shuffle with a slight jerky motion, picked-up his portable oxygen tank, and slid small steps toward the door. When he did, I stepped with him down the two steps to the car and greeted Coral. We had met during my October visit, and I'd found her to be a caring daughter with a good heart, someone that Tony admired greatly. As Tony slowly made his way into the passenger seat, we confirmed our plans for the next day, and I felt the warmth of honor that the *Salt of Key West* had chosen me to share his story.

Well into the evening, the heat still hovered around 80 degrees. I found myself wandering down Duval Street, wandering toward my temporary home in a historical guesthouse not far from Old Town. Intent on getting back to my room, tired from the travels of the day and focusing on my own middle-aged weariness, I was surprised to be drawn to the music flowing from Irish Kevin's Saloon.

The guy playing acoustic guitar was as much a high-priced entertainer, as he was a wizard of finger rolls and changing chords. The bar was full of people, most looking young but legal, of course. I listened for an hour, listened to the sound of people at play, and I allowed my hips to begin to sway. This was the genuine me, the guy who loved acoustic music, loved to dance and sing with the band. This was the me they seldom saw in Iowa, and I began to feel myself melting into the crowd.

I became engulfed in the crowd swaying to the music and allowed the mystique of Key West to invade my mind. I was in this land working with this man to write this novel about a life lived opposite of my own. Tony had lived life teetering on the edge unafraid of taking the risk of fun. He was a gambler and it had shown in everything he did. Tony's only expectations had been to be true to himself. Tony was right. Our worlds are so far apart. Further then I had sometimes imagined, yet here I stood in Tony Tarracino's world.

I raised my beverage in a toast to the man playing guitar as he sang Buffett's *Changes in Latitude, Changes in Attitude,* and I allowed my soul to slip into the mysterious adventure of Captain Tony Tarracino's life.

CHAPTER 2

Tony and I sat across from each other, him sipping his morning coffee, sweetened and creamy, and me my morning carbonated fizzy Diet Coke, the different choices of two men generations apart. He was bright-eyed this morning wearing a long sleeve shirt, slacks, and black slippers to shuffle along in. His oxygen was beside him, but he didn't need it yet, fueled by his own enthusiasm to talk about his life. In his left hand he fiddled with his nicotine inhaler, empty of the nicotine, but after 70 years of having a cigarette in his hand, he needed something to fiddle with.

"So." Sensing his desire to talk, I pressed the recorder button.

"Brad," his face turned to mine, a gleam in his eye, "we're worlds apart." His arms spread to their farthest reach on each side of him, with a serious stare to match his grin. The full bags under his eyes and the slight sag of his deep-wrinkled face showed sharp wisdom like a pricking sliver of acute awareness. "Iowa and Key West. Prairie thinking and the Conch Republic. 1935 and the 21st century. Married, educator." He pointed at me, then back to himself. "Captain, bar owner, and lover of many, many women. We're two different people, but I'm going to educate you whether you like it or not. I'm going to bring you into my world."

Feeling like I had changed roles, moving from the educator of my daily routine to the student in Captain Tony's university of life, I wondered about learning from a man who'd lived on the edge. I had seen the edge from a distance, but never ventured close enough to truly look over. My greatest adventures had been vacation packages to exotic locations surrounded by people just like myself enjoying their all-inclusive cocktails. Tony was the buccaneer challenging the winds, high seas, and pirate perils while searching for the treasure hidden somewhere within the islands.

Grinning at my own naivety, I ask Tony. "What is your world?"

That twinkle in his eyes gleamed again, pulling the past from the depth of his memory. "My world started out in New Jersey where the mob ran the show, and they were our heroes. That's how we thought back then, thought of mobsters as our heroes. They had money, power, and fancy cars. But you didn't cross the mob. I came to Key West on the run from the mob. I had $12 in my pocket and the clothes on my back. But that's another story."

Tony crossed his legs, his back slightly hunched. As he leaned forward, his nicotine inhaler between his fingers, he lifted his hands to rest on his chin as his head moved slightly up and down. His chin had grown longer with time, his hands wrinkled with a yellowish tint to his clean and trimmed nails. There was a depth in his gaze as he searched back to find the right words, the words to educate.

"I," he hesitated, looking up with a slight morning ruffle of his thick, white hair. "I've known gorgeous women in my life, many, many wonderful women. Women made me. They taught me how to treat people, taught me about compassion. I've got so many friends, had so many friends both men and women. Not just friends like Jimmy Buffett or Tennessee Williams. They're wonderful people, but I've got so many friends who are just regular folks. Regular like you and Denise. They're what's truly valuable in my life. All of those friends who are just plain, ordinary, real people." Leaning in, he closed the gap between us with a slight thoughtful pause lingering in the air. "I think it comes from growing up poor in New Jersey. Those were the best years of my life, those years in New Jersey with ordinary people. The people next door, down the block, the people struggling to make a buck and raise their children to be good and kind." Straightening so his full weight rested against the wicker chair, he nodded knowingly. "Those were the best years of my life. We were poor, but we had great connections with people. I lived surrounded by poor people with wonderful hearts. As I look back now, I know that I learned so much from people of poverty."

I can't get away from that, from my youth, from the poverty I grew up with in New Jersey. Poverty gave me the strength to fight injustice, to fight the self-serving of the world who try to run over the less fortunate. Because of that poverty, I was always a hustler. We learned how to hustle to survive and take care of each other.

Back then as young boys in New Jersey, my three brothers and me, we'd buy a hundred pounds of peanuts, a penny a pound.

Another penny a pound to have them roasted, that's two cents a pound. Then we'd buy these little paper bags that were real cheap. We'd put the peanuts in little bags, and go out by the stop light on Highway U.S. 1. The light would turn red, and we'd run out among the cars.

"Peanuts." We'd call out. "Peanuts, a nickel a bag." And we'd sell peanuts.

We'd go out when the big air ships would come in and sell peanuts. I was there, a block away selling peanuts the day the Hindenburg caught on fire. Big event, world event, history; I was there selling peanuts for a nickel a bag. That's how we made our living as kids, selling peanuts for a nickel. If I made a dollar, I'd give my mother seventy-five cents, and I kept a quarter. That's what we did to survive.

Reflective like Harry Reasoner, Tony sat comfortably in his chair, legs crossed with the next thought already well formulated in his mind.

"My family's Italian, but I grew up Jewish. It was a Jewish neighborhood, and all my friends were Jewish. My father never spoke English, but he was a proud man. He had four sons. For an Italian, having four sons made him like a king. He was so proud. Sal was the oldest then came me, Joey, and Louie. I named my first son after my brother Louie. Louie was the anchor in our family. Sal did great things in his life, a gay man who wasn't afraid of who he was. Joey, he was a great musician. Louie was a barber, but it was Louie who we always went to when we needed help."

"We were poor but we didn't know it." Tony paused with this slight smile as his mind drifted through his childhood. "My mother died when I was 11. She had a stroke, and for a time my father took care of her. She was always in bed, couldn't get out of bed, and my father, every night he washed her sheets by hand." Tony's eyes grew distant going back in time. I envisioned a small, well-kept house with shutters and a large oak front door. "I'll never forget my father…" Tony raised his hands as his father would have, instructing, telling. "I told him, *Dad, you don't have to wash her sheets every night*. He looked at me with those intense Italian eyes. *It's your mother*. He said. *Nothing's too good for your mother*. So every night, my father washed her sheets by hand, scrubbing, making them clean. I've never forgotten that compassion, the compassion that my father showed for my mother as he hand washed her sheets."

The island guesthouse room grew quiet as Tony sat silently, and for the longest time nothing was said. His eyes cast downward there was gentleness in the still moment contrary to the image of a man known as the *Salt of Key West*. He stared at the table between us, but his thoughts were of a different time and different place, of his mother and how his father had cared for her with such deep compassion. Then, as if it were time for my first lesson, he raised his eyes to meet mine. His hand lifted, his finger coming outward to teach. His blue eyes were intense as he nodded with such surety.

"It's the only word in the dictionary that means anything. You can throw all the other words away. The only important word is *compassion*."

"I remember two other influences in my life, great influences from my childhood. They were people of compassion but in different ways. Still, I learned much from them, and they guided me out into the world." Captain Tony sat back relaxed now, leaning into the round back wicker of my guesthouse chair as if gazing out over the ocean to chart his course. "There was my teacher and my priest."

"Good people to learn from." I said.

Tony's grin flickered as the corner of his mouth turned upward toward the twinkle in his eyes. "You haven't heard the stories yet."

Adjusting himself slightly in the chair, settling in for the comfort of a long story, he looked at me with serene calmness as the slight knowing smile of a hustler grew to greet the story of his teacher and his priest.

"When I was in eighth grade." Tony spoke like a grandfather telling a simple tale of years past when life was not so complicated. "I had an affair with my school teacher, my first sex."

Watching him, knowing what I did of Tony Tarracino and his womanizing past, the calmness of this bold pronouncement didn't surprise me. In some ways I expected it. Renowned as much for his sex drive as his heroic adventures, he was like a little old rabbit scurrying around sniffing for fluffy little bunnies. The great joke of his life, his unrestrained prowess for a soft touch, tender lips, and firm, round breasts must have begun with some sordid tale of youthful misadventure. Now the parable was being told. I wondered had he lived the *Summer of '42* long before the summer of '42?

Aged with the knowledge of experience, his eyes were framed by bristly white eyebrow shards and pockets of skin that hung full below them. From those eyes came a grin that was both unshakable and charming. "My teacher told me, *Tony, you belong out there, you belong to the world.*"

She was a woman of about 35, a voluptuous, glamorous blond. She and her husband had a beautiful home down on the New Jersey shore. One day my teacher asked me, "You want to come down for the summer, cut the hedges, help out around the yard. I'll give you ten dollars a day." Ten dollars a day on weekends? That was good money for a 14 year-old kid back then.

Her husband was a producer of plays, and worked weekends with the performances. My teacher and me, we used to go down to her beach house on Friday night, come back on Sunday. I did a lot of work around the house. She fed me and all that, and I made $10 a day. It was a great set-up for a 14 year-old kid, but it got even better.

She was a heavy drinker, my school teacher, and on one of those beautiful summer Saturday nights, I came in and she's there on the couch smoking a cigarette, a scotch and water in her other hand. Sultry in the heat like a saloon hooker, she's laying across the couch in a summer dress and one of her breast is almost tumbling out. It was like a picture over a bar, you know, one of those saloon images of the seductive woman daring men to come to her.

She invited me to come over and sit down. I didn't know what to do. I'm 14 and she's my teacher. So I did as I was told, and I sat down next to her, and we began to talk. My teacher is drinking, and she's talking about life and how we need people. I don't remember the details of what we talked about. I was confused and aroused, and I just remember talking and like a kid in a candy store, thinking about her breast that was nearly falling out. I was 14. That's what I remember.

The next thing you know we're having sex. I was an inexperienced kid, and it just happened. One minute I'm trimming hedges, the next minute I'm having my first sex with my teacher. I could almost say I was raped. What I didn't know then is I'll sleep with anybody, so it couldn't have been rape. But it happened so quickly. One minute I'm talking to my teacher as she swirls the ice in her highball glass, the next we're naked together. Anyway, that was my first sex, with my eighth grade teacher on the couch at her beach home. Scotch and cigarettes on her breath, voluptuous and beautiful, she was teaching skinny little me about sex.

So during the two months of summer vacation, every weekend I would go with her down to the house on the shore and have great sex. She still paid me $10, so call me what you will, but I was getting the education of my life. I can't explain it, but we were together all that summer. She was a full-bodied woman with an odor about her that was supple, sexy. It was so unique. I'll never forget that smell. And she taught me so much about sex. It was a great adventure for a boy. At that age, you'd crank me up, and I'd go for hours. I was like that rabbit with the battery. She loved it, and I was living a boy's fantasy.

That was my first real love. To this day, it's hard to explain. At the end of the summer, school's about to start, and she says to me. "Anthony, you're much older than you think mentally and physically. What happened between you and me was a very beautiful thing. I needed you Anthony, and at your age, I think maybe you needed me, but I know I needed you. I want to thank you."

I was in love with her, my first love built on lust, but she said to me. "Anthony, you belong to the world. There's nothing you can learn in school anymore." Remember, this is around 1930. We looked at school differently then. So she says to me. "I don't know what's going to happen to you. I don't know where you're going to go or what you're going to do, but Anthony, you belong to the world."

I thought she was trying to talk me out of going back to school because we'd been having sex and she'd get in trouble, but it had nothing to do with that. "Anthony." She told me. "You belong to the world."

It was such a different time them. Sex with my teacher and her trying to convince me to quit school, but it was a different time. A formal education wasn't so important, so I quit school and went out into the world.

To this day, she is my escape. I still turn to her often to be my cocoon. I know she's dead and gone. She was thirty-five when I was 14, but I still use her as my cocoon. You know a cocoon, the protection for caterpillars becoming butterflies. If I've got a problem, real heavy stuff, I'll go to her, go to my cocoon like I'm in the womb, and I'll be protected while I think out the problem. She's

*been that for me all my life. All my life my teacher's been there.
She's my cocoon today.*

The quiet of a fond memory seemed to linger in the
air. I watched him, watched for signs of sadness, concern,
manipulation, or betrayal, but I only saw the calmness in
his memory. His eyes looked past me, distant but happy,
and there was this slight smile growing on his face, the
smile of a distant memory that has come back to greet you
like a long-lost friend, and in the greeting is a warm hug, a
touch that reminds you of why you have missed the friend
so much.

"That's quite a story, Tony." I spoke delicately as I stood
and moved across the room to the miniature refrigerator,
hesitating before it. "Do you think she meant to be your
cocoon?"

His smile almost became a laugh. "I think she needed
some compassion in her life, someone to hold her and make
her feel wanted." Shifting slightly, he looked across the
room to me. "I understood that, and it felt good to me too,
to be held."

"These are different times now." I told him, reaching
into the coolness for another Diet Coke.

Tony nodded his understanding. "We've drawn better
lines to protect the children. We should do that, protect
the children. But, yes, those were different times." Tony
shrugged matter-of-factly as he did to so many things in
his life, things that were only matter-of-fact if you had
actually lived them and moved on to legendary status. "But
if you think about it, in the long run I was able to draw

an understanding of compassion from my teacher. What was so wrong with her life that she spent her weekends alone at the shore with a 14-year-old boy to keep her company? She needed me at the time whether I knew it or not. Back then I probably couldn't look past the sex. I was a 14-year-old rabbit, but there was compassion between us, one to the other. As she said, we needed each other, and I know now from her loneliness that on some level she was desperate. I must have given something to her, something she needed."

"Do you think you're better for it today?" I sat back down before him, searching for his honesty.

"That's hard to say." Tony smiled calmly, at ease with the question. "We don't know how my life would have been different had my teacher not been there to tell me *You belong to the world.*" He took a sip of his coffee, a slight warmth still steaming upward through the opening in the insulated cup. "We only know what my life has been like. I can find great value in my experiences with my teacher because of the compassion and the lesson that I *belong to the world.*"

I struggled with this, listening to the values of a time not like mine. Without a doubt, Tony had been taken advantage of, but from that he had gained something. Maybe it was because it was so soon after his mother had died. Maybe the cocoon was that protection his mother had given him, lost when she had died three years before. Or maybe I was over analyzing. Maybe it was just a 14-year-old boy's sexual awakening. I did know his teacher had been right. This 87 year-old version of Tony Tarracino most definitely did *belong to the world.*

Tony pointed his inhaler my way. "Soon after my affair with my teacher, my priest Father Anthony returned from a trip home to Italy. We all went to welcome him back. He was a great man, a good man, and he saw something in me." Reflective in his thoughts, Tony leaned closer, his forearms resting on his slender, atrophied thighs. His eyes lifted upward like a prophet, a man of age and wisdom. "My priest said to me *The world owns you, Tony.*" Suddenly, his eyes burst open as if surprised by the priest's words. "To me it was the same thing my teacher had said."

Leaning backward, his gaze seemed to turn soft with a slight turning smile.

"I believe," Captain Tony said, "I believe there is a jewel in every person. Sometimes you just have to search to find that jewel. I believe my teacher and my priest saw that jewel in me, the way I communicate and connect with people. That's why they told me I belonged to the world." Tony reached his hand forward, repeating their words. "*You belong to the world.*" He turned his hand over to show the similarities. "*The world owns you.*" Nodding at the parallels. "The same meaning."

He grinned at the memory, and I thought of his words spoken to Jimmy Buffett. Why he kept on doing all that he was doing, kept on sharing with people, expressing his views, and encouraging others. Why would a man 87 years young spend most evenings sitting in a bar greeting people? Tony would probably joke and say something about his ego, but I had watched him, observed the connection, documented the conversations, and visited with those who greeted him. They came for the legend, but always left with a little something else, some slight connection or word of encouragement, something that lifted them up beyond that moment in time. We are all people in search of something, and Tony gives to those in need. While Buffett had described it in the song lyrics of *Last Mango in Paris*, Tony had shared with me that he had actually told Jimmy, *there's still so many things I need to do*. I guess belonging to the world has its responsibilities even 70 years later.

"So," Tony, once again leaned in comfortably like one friend sharing his story with another. "I went out into the world and, like most people, I started working; working hard." His hand flipped in the air, the inhaler between his thumb and index finger as he waved nonchalantly. "I did what most people do. I started a career, eventually got married and had children. While working, I learned that I was a great organizer. I had this insight into how to do things better, more efficiently, and how to manage people to do the same thing. I became an Efficiency Expert for Atlantic Stock and Nut. My life was right on track. Good job, good company, I was married to my first wife Mimi, and we had three kids. Louie, Tonia, and Richard. Then the war came along. It changed a lot of things for a lot of people, but for me, well, wartime was different. Atlantic Stock and Nut, they put me on loan to Boeing to help with a problem they had with one of our products Boeing used building planes. I was sent to Seattle where I supervised hundreds of people."

I had already learned that nothing with Tony was simple, and each story was sure to become more than you might have expected. So I asked the question.

"Why was wartime different for you?"

Tony only shrugged, glancing down as if reluctant, hesitating to tell the story. Then he spoke.

"It's when my life began to change. I was sent to Seattle to work in the Boeing plant. There were 5,000 women and me working in this plant. The men were all overseas, and I was working with 5,000 women, supervising many of them, and my wife and family were on the other side of the country. I think, I've always thought that I had some kind of breakdown in Seattle. Things changed for me there. Seattle was hard. I was away from my family, the work was tough, and I was hanging out nights in a casino. I played a lot of black jack, did a lot of gambling, even helped as a night manager of the place for a while. Something happened to me there."

Once again, just for a moment, he became distant. He sat before me quietly staring at his hands as they rested in his small lap. He was white and wrinkled with his lips pressed together as his mind drifted back to a lifetime ago.

"Beautiful women." He said, slowly lifting his eyes. "They have always been my weakness, and in Seattle I was overseeing 5,000 women. With 5,000 women and no men, I began to pick up the slack." Tony nodded a sly wink, a slight curl in the corners of his mouth as he chuckled to himself. Shrugging as if saying 'that's just the way it was back then.'

I met a girl in the factory, an Eskimo girl named Naomi. She was so beautiful with her dark skin and little Eskimo nose. Naomi became pregnant, and she had a baby. It was my Eskimo baby, a beautiful little girl. Then Naomi's mother up in Alaska got sick, and she took our baby and went home to take care of her mother. She just disappeared. I couldn't find her. Didn't know where she was. I never saw her or our baby again. That was tough, a confusing time. Baby somewhere up in Alaska, a wife and children back home, so many women, and gambling every night. Something happened to me in Seattle. Something that wasn't so good.

I come back from Seattle, back to my wife and family in New Jersey, and my life was pretty much in the toilet. I don't know if I had a nervous breakdown or what, but Seattle was tough on me. The way I lived, the things I did. I came back, and things weren't working with Mimi and me. The war was tough on everybody, and being away for so long had been tough on both of us, so we divorced. But back then, 50 some years ago the whole thing was pretty devastating.

Divorced and all screwed up, I was living in my brother Louie's cellar. My normal life, family, job, everything had gone to hell. I'm living in the cellar, got a little cot and a little television. Nothing else. I'm doing some gambling, playing the horses, and trying to figure out what's going on in my life. The mob and gambling had always been very influential in my Italian family. I learned to add with a pair of dice so turning to gambling was natural.

One day I've got the TV on, you know, one of those little RCAs with the tiny black and white screen. I'm jiggling the channel changer around. The only channel we got in those days was New York, maybe something from Connecticut, a couple of channels with weak signals. So I'm jiggling the changer trying to get some reception, and I hear a guy say, "This is the feature race of the day which we'll be broadcasting for the next 40 days." There's no picture, just static fuzz, but I turn the volume up, and I can hear Garden State Park right outside of Philadelphia. They're broadcasting the feature horse race everyday at 4:30. There's no picture, but I'm picking up the volume as clear as can be.

My brother Louie's a gambler, so I call all my brothers together, and the next day they stay home from work. At 4:30 I turn on the TV, and there it is "This is the feature race from Garden State Park, and they're off!" Holy Christ, we're hearing the race live. Unheard of back then.

So we make a plan. The next day my brother Joey stays at home, Louie was at a phone booth near his bookie's, and I've been inside the bookie joint since 1:30 in the afternoon eating sandwiches and peanuts and making small bets. At 4:30 I look out the window.

Joey's at home listening to the TV. He picks up the phone and calls Louie at a phone booth around the corner from the bookie's. Louie has a cop friend of ours put a sign in his car window '$300,' and he drives by the bookie joint. I see $300 and boom, I quick put a bet on the number three horse. Bang, instant winners.

This is going on and on, and we're being very careful, different signs, different ways of communicating the number, and we've got about 15 days left. We're getting big enough, got enough money that we go to Newark to a bigger joint, bigger bookie, to up the bets. Nobody's ever questioned us, and we're looking for some real big money. I mean we got something going, and we're ready to cash in on some big winnings.

What we don't know is at the bookie place in Newark there's an overlay scam going on. An overlay means you've got a favorite. Say he's 2:1. He's the favorite, a real heavy favorite, so what happens is these guys start playing some long shot, a real long shot. They're spreading the word and everybody's betting on this other horse. So now with these bets on the long shot, the favorite goes off at 15:1 cause everybody's been playing this "hot tip" on a different horse.

I don't know this. So I put a big bet on the favorite that we know's already won, and should have been 2:1 only he goes off 15:1. Damn, that's a lot of money. So when I go to collect our money, the guy says, "You know Tarracino, I think you gave me that bet a little late."

I puff up my chest and say, "You took my bet. I want my winnings." So there's a big scene, him arguing with me and me giving it right back. I gotta stand-up for myself, otherwise he knows something's up. In the meantime I'm shitting cause this is the mob I'm messing with.

He says, "Look, you come to Gleeman's Bar and talk to Gleeman about this. I'm not going to argue with you, but I'm not going to pay you either. It's up to Gleeman." This is bad, me having to go see this mob boss, but what can I do. If I don't show up they know, and they'll come after me. I'm in deep either way.

So that night I get two big beefy college guys to go with me. Big guys with chests, muscles, real beefeaters, and I give them each five bucks and all the beer they could drink to be my bodyguards.

With them on each side protecting me, we go to Gleeman's Bar to collect my money.

We stand there a while drinking and waiting, and I'm getting more nervous. Finally, Gleeman comes in, and he walks up to me. "Tarracino," he says. He's this big guy, heavy ethnic look about him. Round chest and belly, slick black hair, and dark eyes. When he looks at you, he squints. Got tough guy written all over him. He says. "Tarracino?"

I say, "Yeh, I'm Tarracino."

He tells me, "Stay right here. I've got to go in the back to make a phone call."

While he's in the back these two gorillas come in the bar. I mean gorillas. They're so scary they should've been in a zoo. They've got these thin, black collared Chesterfield overcoats on that make these massive gorillas look even bigger. I'm a little guy, a hundred and thirty-five pounds. I'm not even half of one of these gorillas, so it's like four guys coming at me.

They walk right up, and I turn and look and my bodyguards are gone. I don't know where they are. I look around. "Where are my bodyguards?" Gone. My beefeater college boys had run out on me, leaving skinny Tony to take on these bulking mob tough guys. Now I know I'm in deep shit.

These two gorillas picked me up, one on each side lifting me under the arms and carry me out to this big black limo. It's just like in the movies today. Two gorillas, a skinny little hustler with his legs running on air, and a black limo, and we all know how the scene ends.

They drove me to where the Newark Airport is now. Back then it was the city dump. Not a nice landfill like today, but a true city dump. Piles of crap everywhere. They pulled me out of the limo, and they beat the crap out of me. I mean they beat me all over hitting, kicking, punchin'. Broke my jaw, ribs, battered me black and blue, and I'm laying a bloody mess of bruises and broken bones on the ground in the filth of the Newark city dump.

I'm lying there barely conscious, and I hear one of the gorillas says to the other. "Should I finish him off?"

The other guys says, "Why worry about it? The bulldozers will cover him in the morning."

I didn't breathe. I just laid there playing as dead as I could play.

I laid there all night, laid in the dump bleeding and beat up with a broken jaw and four broken ribs. They'd really done a job on me sending a message about cheating the mob. Finally, the next morning I made my way out and somehow got back to my room in Louie's cellar. My brothers are afraid I'm not going to make it, so they get a doctor to help fix me.

I was in pretty bad shape, but my brother Sal stayed by my side and nursed me back to health. Down in that cellar, he got me well again. As I healed I was safe hidden in the cellar, but the mob had left me for dead. To them that's the way I wanted to be because if they found out I wasn't dead, I'd be that way soon. I knew I couldn't live in New Jersey anymore, couldn't even show my face or I was a dead man. I had $10,000 from our previous betting, so I decided to head for Florida.

Now think about this, me going to Hialeah Park in Florida with $10,000 in my pocket. Man, that's like a Jewish guy going to Israel. A gambler with lots of money and a race track. It's like a dream.

I remember going to Florida. The first oranges I saw, I stopped the car. There were coconuts and fruit to be had everywhere. This is *back when people didn't travel so much, and Florida was a dream. We didn't have travel shows or just jump on airplanes to fly places. No Internet to see these distant locations. We didn't know what Florida looked like except the way people may have described it. To me, Florida was a dream.*

That dream lasted about a month until I lost my ass at the track. I was down to nearly nothing. I had the clothes on my back and about $12 in my pocket, so I go to the bus station not knowing where I can go on $12. I'm destitute. I see this sign says 'See Key West.' I ask the bus clerk, "What's Key West?"

He says, "Oh, it's like the Barbary Coast, man. Big Navy town, whores, gambling, wild place."

"No kidding." I say. It sounds perfect. "What's it cost to get there?"

"Six bucks to go the hundred miles, but you just missed the last bus." So he tells me this. "For 50 cents you can take the bus to Homestead, and you can always hitch a ride from there."

Tony is laughing to himself, laughing with this big grin. He's been sitting back in his chair for the last 15 minutes, oxygen pressing life into him as he'd shared the story. He wore the grin of somebody who can look back now and smile, smile because he lived through that time, overcame it, and was better for it. It's a smile not so understandable to us today. We who have lived distant from poverty, not experienced a depression, not been destitute without money, a home, or food. I cannot fully understand the expression, but I can appreciate the slight nod of his head, the ways his eyes cast downward with some satisfaction that his past is only in his memory.

"So." He looked back up with a satisfied grin. "I hitchhiked from Homestead to Key West on a milk truck with $12 in my pocket." Tony drew a long line out with his fingers as he spread his arms though the air between us. "In those days you could go from the top of the Keys to Key West and only see a light here and a light there. At night it was like a string of pearls stretching out over the ocean. And the drive, you couldn't drive without getting a couple of flat tires. All the land crabs." His hands were in front of him bouncing along like the car on a crab-covered road. "Crunch, crunch, crunch. Land crabs everywhere."

"I spent my first night in Key West down on Mallory Square Dock sleeping in somebody's 1929 Plymouth. $12, divorced, on the run from the mob, and I'm on an island at the end of America. That's the night I found myself. On that lonely night stealing sleep in the backseat of some stranger's Plymouth, I said to myself, *Tony, from now on, if you're going to fuck-up, do it first class.* If I was going to make mistakes, and we all do, it was time to start making mistakes for the right reason."

I watched the small, almost ancient man with the insight, orneriness, and experiences of his life lived on the edge. The history that brought him to Key West explained much. Now, some 50 years later, I knew that he had not messed-up much since then, but when he did, he had accepted it and gone on. Making mistakes *first class* means you make your decision for the right reasons, for the good of people and a betterment of those around you. Then, if it all turns out bad, you accept your mistakes and move positively beyond them.

"People have told me I'm so crooked that when I die they'll be able to screw me into the ground. But I was always honest. I made myself the image of a hustler, the real sharpy, the New York mafia type. I did that deliberately. But I was always honest." When he spoke, there was calmness, a sense of inner peace that seemed to be exposed. "You see, Brad, your reputation precedes you, so I made sure I had a good one preceding me."

Laughter grew with the connection between us, friends sharing an image that had created his reputation. It was a legend telling his secret; for without a reputation, there would be no legend.

I understood Tony better now. I understood his childhood, the loss of his mother, and his mistakes and lessons learned hard. I understood the strange twist of events that had guided him to Key West and set his sails on a course never plotted, never anticipated. He sat before me, the dexterous little man who had pulled off a life that left most of us with our mouths hanging wide open. That life had created a reputation that had been guided by compassion and built upon by daring deeds, an excessive weakness for women, and a decision to make mistakes *first class*. His inspired grin told me how proud he was of the reputation, the legend, and the real life he'd lived.

It had been a couple of hours, and I could tell that the stories had tugged energy from Tony. He had talked much of the time through the oxygen flow, but more so, there was the emotion of reliving a time long ago. He was tired. His body slumped a bit more, his head not held quite so high. It was time to wrap up the morning, to pull our talk together in a nice little ending.

"So," I smiled at the old man as he looked up with his thick white beard nicely highlighting the wrinkles of time. "What's the purpose for this Tony, for you and me and this book we're writing?"

Without hesitation, he waved his hand in the air. "You know I'm dead. I'm a dead man trying to get my house in order. I'm 87 with a pacemaker and living on oxygen. Thank God I've got a tremendous ego that keeps pushing me to do more because if I stopped, I'd surely die. This book is all about my ego. My friend, Shel Silverstein once told me books are forever. I want to live forever. My ego's so bad. I know I won't live forever, not unless we get this book written. That's how Shel's living forever, through the books he'd written. It's my out-of-control ego. I want to live forever." His grin brought my own out, and we laughed at his self-centered confession.

As we both quieted, Tony reached up, motioning me closer with his long, narrow finger as if to share some great secret. "I'm not the cheater and the hustler everybody thinks, but I played the part well. See, the truth is life is just people. The truth is I want the people to know what this little WOP thought in life. If that can help just one person, isn't that enough?" Shrugging slightly, his hands lifting between us. "Ego aside. Isn't helping one person enough?"

I leaned to Tony, exploring more, a little bit deeper. "So what does this little WOP think about life?"

Captain Tony nodded as if I'd finally asked the right question. "There are some things that still confuse me. And," he added, "there are some things I know, things that don't confuse me."

I watched his eyes. "What doesn't confuse you?"

With his head moving up and down, that clear nod of understanding brought from a lifetime of testing himself and knowing, he answered.

"I know that compassion is the most important word in the dictionary. It's what we must live by if life is truly about people. I know there is a jewel in every person. Sometimes we have to search to find that jewel, but there is a jewel there. In every person there's a jewel. And I know that the simplest good thing we can do for each other is to always say a nice thing that will make the other person feel better; a simple word of kindness." He looked up, sharing a nod of acknowledgement. "That's what I've learned since I arrived in Key West 50 years ago with $12 in my pocket and the clothes on my back."

"Those are pretty good lessons."

"Yes," Captain Tony said. "I hope just one person can learn them. That's enough to make this all worth while."

Like a father to a son, Tony pointed to himself then moved his hand reaching forward to me, the lesson flowing from the Captain to the educator.

Grinning with the kind eyes of a teacher smiling into my own eyes, he repeated. "Just one person."

That afternoon I wandered alone along the streets of Key West looking at the architecture, the 100 year-old homes remodeled into magnificent guesthouses and private residences. As I walked, the quiet seemed to be protective in some melancholy way.

Admiring the care given to century-old homes refurbished into a museum of a town, Tony's lessons kept filtering through my mind. For a moment, I stopped to admire the different trees, the palms and fruit trees and the large Banyan trees reaching out beyond their trunks. A man stepped from his front door onto the white pillars porch of the home I stood admiring. I waved a friendly greeting.

"Beautiful home." I called to him.

He stopped suddenly, looking to me. "Thank you." He called back.

"You've done a magnificent job of restoring it." I pointed at the newly painted shutters.

"It's been a chore," he answered then glanced over his shoulder at the front of the house, "a labor of love."

"The best kind of labor." I called back to him.

"Yes," he stood with his hands on his hips watching me, "it's been rewarding."

Waving as I began to step on down the sidewalk, I yelled back. "Have a wonderful day."

"Thank you," he waved too, smiling as he did, "I will."

It was a simple moment, a simple word of kindness to a stranger. That was important, I reminded myself, to connect with people through kindness. I walked on with the calm fulfillment of satisfying self-reflection.

CHAPTER 3

Tony called about 10 o'clock excited for another day of my attendance at the Captain Tony University of Life. He had an appointment at 11:00 and invited me to meet him afterwards at the saloon where we would slip away for lunch.

"Before we meet," he instructed, a serious, unequivocal voice, "go to the Mel Fisher Maritime Museum. It's on Front Street a couple of blocks south of Duval, a beautiful old red brick building. You should learn about Mel, learn to understand his optimism and the determination in believing that *Today is the day.*"

"I'll try." I told him, glancing down at the task lying before me. "I'm working on some school issues right now."

"Nothing serious, I hope."

"Important for 95 kids and four teachers." I answered. "I'm manipulating a four teacher 3rd grade budget to satisfy a five-teacher need."

His voice was spry, quick with a solution. "It's all about the people, so finish the math to benefit the children, then take some time at Mel's Museum." Shaky and gravely in his natural tone, the voice was of many, many years and tough times, yet he spoke like a grandfather concerned for his children. "But don't focus on just the information. Learn about Mel as a person. That's what's important."

"How well did you know him?" I asked, wondering about his life connection to the celebrated treasure hunter.

"He was a good friend, a pal of mine that I learned much from." Tony shared in that raspy, empathetic voice. "Just go to the museum."

I looked at my budget manipulations and divided the total by five. Grinning satisfied, I answered. "Okay, Tony. I've got to call our elementary principal with some good news, and then I'll go to the museum. I'll see you about noon."

"Learn about Mel." He insisted.

"I will." I answered.

Just after noon with the sun tall in the sky burning down upon the island, my stomach was gurgling for a fresh seafood lunch. Tony and I found ourselves sitting in the far back corner of a quiet restaurant, a block north from Captain Tony's Saloon on Greene Street. Tony had chosen this place for two reasons. Of course, he was friendly with the owner, a long time Conch who he knew would only serve the freshest of seafood. It was also large enough to slip in quietly and get an isolated booth to visit undisturbed. I better understood the need for isolation having just walked, or strolled easily along at Tony's shuffling pace, a block down Greene Street with the legendary Captain, Key West's Mayor Emeritus.

In that one block stroll, there was the store manager who stepped out onto the sidewalk to hail him with a cheerful greeting and warm handshake. A few steps later a large, attractive thirtyish woman with a bright red and white smile came bouncing from a bar to bear hug Tony like a long lost friend she hoped to devour. She had worked at the saloon, Tony explained, gazing into her rich eyes. "You're a great lady. It was an honor to have you working for me." With that her eyes perked up, her smile grew more lively, and she gave the Captain another massive hug. His kind words had made her day. *Share a word of kindness.*

Not too far beyond, a homeless man of street dirt and stench reached up to shake Tony's hand. Grungy with tattered clothes, no shoes on his crust embedded dry and calloused feet, and two yellowed teeth, we stood above him looking down at the burning concrete he called home. Tony greeted him by name, asking anxiously how he was doing. The destitute man gave a dignified nod reassuring Tony that he'd found a nice place to sleep hidden in some swamp water bushes near the Naval Base. It was not a brief moment of cordiality, but a conversation between two men mutually respectful of each other, a kind gesture of time given sincerely by Tony to the man living on the blister hard sidewalk from where he always looked up at the world passing by.

At the restaurant several people waved to Tony from the bar, their hands excitingly flinging in the air like a high school cheerleader waving to her all-too-proud mom in the stand. Tony waved back, his hands like thin white sails rising up above the ocean as he stopped to share a hearty hello, a few words of encouragement, and a warm smile. We found our way to a back booth of red vinyl and dim lighting where a manager of Caribbean complexion welcomed us, and Tony did his introductions.

"This is Brad Manard." He told him. "He's a famous writer doing a book on me. We're going to be interviewing, recording, that sort of thing." I fought the embarrassment at being called a *famous* writer knowing a dream was not the reality of the moment, but then again, just by saying it, Tony made me believe the dream could be true. "We'll need a little quiet time back here." He added with a tenuous handshake and toothy grin.

With Tony's kind request, the manager waved to the waitress snapping his fingers like Sinatra had just joined the Gambino family for pasta, and she magically appeared before us with crab emblazoned menus offering anything our seafood loving pallets might desire.

"You seem to get along with everybody." I pointed toward the bar where a middle-aged couple gawked our direction, words whispered back and forth to each other. "Everybody either knows you or wants to know you."

"When you've been alive as long as I have," Tony waved his hand, an explanation in itself. "You understand how important people are in life. My life has been a collection of friends and good people. Not like a collection of stuff, but a collection of experiences and memories of hearty connections. What is life without people? That's what life is, it's the people."

"I know." When I looked up, he was watching me closely, and I found my eyes diverting from his intense blues. "This book is such an exciting time for me, but so is coming to Key West. I needed some separation to reconnect with myself. The tasks of the past few years have been absorbing, and, quite frankly, I'm soaked."

Tony just smiled. "Reconnect with yourself?" He fiddled with his oxygen tank checking the level. His hands were atrophied with thick ridges as he adjusted his glasses to see the dial better. When he looked back up, he spoke clearly. "Sounds to me like you've been spending too much time with yourself, too much time on tasks. What you need is to reconnect with others. Brad, you're a smart, caring person who likes people, but I see a resistance in you, a hesitation to be you. Maybe you're what you're missing, that you that's a people person."

"Yes." My confident browns reflected back into his blues. "You may be right. Connecting with people is what made me successful at what I do. Maybe I am what I am missing."

Tony gave a little tap to the table between us, his finger driving into the dark oak tabletop. "It's all about the people. The best way to reconnect with yourself is to connect more with others."

"Have you always believed that?" I asked.

"It's how I grew up." Tony answered, his voice raspy with age. "An Italian in a poor neighborhood, we didn't have money or anything special. We only had each other. It was the best time of my life, but I learned a lot too. I learned that the way we treat people defines us."

When I was a young boy, we had a Jewish family who lived next door. Paul was my best friend. He was my age, about 12. Paul Binder and me, we always wanted to be Boy Scouts. I always wanted that. We'd see the Boy Scouts walk by our house, 12 kids in a troop with their little American flags waving high, and Paul and me, we wanted to be Boy Scouts like them. We'd be so proud to be able to march and wave our own flags.

It cost $12 to join, so we saved our money, nickels, dimes, and pennies. We sold newspapers, helped out the neighbors, anything we could do to earn that $12. Finally, we had enough money, so we went to the Boy Scout headquarters on Saturday. It was in the back of a grocery store, so we went to the back, Paul and me, and we knocked on the door. A man answered and asked nicely, "What do you two gentlemen want?" I said, "Well, we want to join the Boy Scouts." "Yes." He said. He was very nice. "You know it cost $12?" We held out our hands and showed him our money, our nickels and dimes and pennies. We showed him all the money we'd saved.

He asked, "What is your name?" I told him Anthony Tarracino. "And what is your name?" He pointed to Paul. My friend said, "Paul Binder." The nice man pointed at me and said, "You're Italian." I said, "Yes." Then he asked Paul. "What about you?" Paul said, "My family's Jewish."

The man nodded and went back into the grocery store. Leaving the door open, he's talking to another man, the scout leader I'd guess. I couldn't see him, but I heard him. I'll never forget what the other man said. He said, "We don't want no Italians and no Jews in our troop."

Never have I forgotten that. I don't even know what the guy looked like, but he taught me the pain of prejudice and a good lesson of the deep hurt that a lack of compassion can cause.

Tony looked up from his memory. There was a long held and unyielding sadness as he spoke to me. "Do you know your power as an educator, the power you have over children's lives? Every day you influence them. Every day you have the chance to touch them and teach them right or wrong, good or evil, prejudice or acceptance. You're a very powerful man."

"In a sense, yes," I told Tony, "as long as I keep my focus on what is best for children. That's my only job, doing what is best for children. That's the challenge when you're balancing individual expectations and too little funding."

Tony looked at me for a long moment, quiet as he watched. I wasn't sure if he was lost in thought or clear in his understanding. He just stared at me as if clarity had come to him. "You know that successful leaders spend most of their time connecting with people, or, as an educator, with children. That's what this world is all about, that's what leadership is all about."

It's the people.

"For instance," he looked up over his menu, pointing at the soft-shelled crab and tapping his finger with an emphatic guarantee, "sometimes people think I'm prejudice against gays, against minorities, against women because I say what I believe. The truth is I respect all people, but I'm honest. That honesty is part of how I connect with people. I might tell someone that gays confuse me. Not because they're gay, my brother Sal was gay, but because of how they portray themselves. They become flamboyant and then want special treatment. You see, I think of what's good for all. Too many people band in their little special groups and only think what's good for them."

"It's similar in education, the constant battle between what's good for all children versus what's good for the individual." I lifted my shoulders only to sag them.

"Exactly what I mean." Tony said. "Here in Key West most gays recognize that, but there are some who only want what is good for the gay community, and to hell with the rest of Key West. That's what I have a problem with. It shouldn't be what's good for this group or that race and to hell with all others. It should be what's good for all of us. You can teach that, you know. That's your power as an educator, and that's the truth about life. Life is people. How we treat each other is all that really matters." He paused for a moment closing his menu and placing it on the table before him. "The only way a leader can help people recognize that is to be compassionate in their actions. That can't be done if you don't connect with those you lead." A big knowing grin broke within his white beard. "It's the only way to be a successful leader."

"And being a successful leader in a political system," I smiled to my friend who smiled back, "which is what schools have become, is a high wire balancing act when each decision should so obviously be what's best for all children. Trouble is that's a hard thing for some people to agree on."

Tony smiled placing his hands on top of his own menu mirroring my conviction. Speaking to me as a good father would, he said. "Brad, if I'd only sailed calm waters, I'd never have known where my boat was capable of going."

Reading our minds, the petite waitress reappeared at the table, pen and pad in hand. Tony ordered fried soft-shelled crabs sharing that they were his favorites. On his recommendation, I ordered the grouper sandwich with all the fixin's. While we waited for the food, Tony sat across from me as an old man bursting with spirit and an internal drive to keep living, wanting to talk, share, and never cease the lessons. Where had it come from, I wondered, the source of the internal spirit hidden in his history?

"Tony. Take me back to your early days in Key West." I asked. "How'd you become a shrimper?"

As he started the story in his slow, thoughtful manner, I began to realize the calm trust blossoming between us. Tony wasn't just the legend that had awed me a year before with his local celebrity status. Something in the way he spoke, his insightfulness, and his straightforward challenge of my leadership had been an awakening. It was the way he now reached toward me with a light touch of explanation, the fragileness of his learned fingers resting in emphasis upon my hand. Within that caring act, calmness spread through me like the warm Caribbean waters.

"Over 50 years ago I found my utopia." He said as if the words were so important. "It didn't start out so special, being flat broke and sleeping in the back seat of somebody's

1929 Plymouth, but it became my utopia. When I fell in love with the people, that's when it became my utopia."

It wasn't the birds, flowers, sun, or warm weather. It wasn't the ocean views or palm trees. It was the people, and it all started with my first job, a job I took because I was destitute, desperate for money and a place to live.

When I woke up in the Plymouth that morning, I heard singing. 'When you're old and you're feeling blue...You don't know what to do...Remember me...I'm the one who loves you.' I've never forgotten that song. It was like birds in the morning, to wake up and hear beautiful singing.

I crawled out of the back seat and looked through this big hole in the wall, and there was all these Conch women, Key West natives, heading shrimp. Those beautiful women are all gone now, but they were wonderful people standing over the table pulling the heads off shrimp.

One of the women points at me and says, "You want to work." I said, "Sure." I didn't know what was going on, but I needed a job.

Tony pointed off over my shoulder. "So they gave me a job heading shrimp down by the docks. It's where the Schooner Wharf Bar is today. Nice little bar that says a lot about Key West. We should go there sometime this week. You'd like it. Mel Fisher used to hang out there in the mornings, just one of the locals doing what locals do. It's down around the docks from the Conch Republic Restaurant. That's where I worked."

I go in and this woman's got me on this big table, and I start heading shrimp. You're pulling the heads off, holding the tail, and ripping the heads from the bodies. A pile of shrimp filled each table, and we'd be pulling their heads off in the process cutting our hands on the razor sharp shells. One after another, very monotonous, pulling heads off hundreds of shrimp. With the hard slicing shells, the cuts got worse and worse as my hands turned from soft to raw. They're all swelled up, and the infection was terrible, puffy, infected hands, and no OSHA in those days. Just swollen, bloody hands.

To fight the infection we would stick our hands in a bucket of Clorox. I'd take my bloody, cut, and swollen hands and plunge them raw into a bucket of sterilizing Clorox. The burn, it hurt so bad that you wanted to scream, to beg for forgiveness, but when the Clorox seeped into the swollen cuts, it killed the infection, protecting our hands. I felt sorry for these people, the Conch women working so hard, their hands cut up and swollen fighting the pain with pure Clorox seeping into their raw open flesh. They had to physically torture themselves to do their jobs.

Twenty-five cents a bucket for the heads, that's what we were getting, pathetic wages for a dismal job. After working there a while I found out that in Georgia they were paying twenty-five cents a bucket for the bodies. The bodies are a lot bigger, so it took fewer shrimp to earn twenty-five cents. I learned that the body of a shrimp was twice the size of a head. Here in Key West, they were paying half the rate as they did in Georgia. They were taking advantage of the ladies working there, the true people of the island.

The company had a little card they provided for each worker. They used to pin it on you. When you filled a bucket, you'd dump the bucket of heads, and they'd put a punch in the card to show *you had another twenty-five cents coming. So I went to the five and dime, and I bought the same punch, identical to the one used by the bosses. Every once in a while I'd wait until the bosses were gone, then I go around to all the Conch women and put an extra punch in all the worker's cards. It was my effort to provide fair wages. After all, they were paying twice as much in Georgia. What was an extra punch here and there? Well, it meant a lot to those poor Conch women.*

That was my first job in Key West. That's when I began to fall in love with the people, heading shrimp with the Conch women. They were beautiful people, and I'd found my utopia here on this little island at the southern tip of the United States.

"Hanging around the docks where I was working, I got a job with Captain Bernie McCracken." Tony smiled fondly, drifting back to that time. "Talk about a guy with compassion. I told him I was an experienced shrimper, and after ten minutes on the boat, Bernie knew I didn't know anything about boats or shrimping. I didn't even know if I was going to get seasick. I was wearing these pointed leather New Jersey shoes with soles that would slip slide across the wet deck as I was trying to figure out what the hell to do. I was like the mob's version of Gilligan's Island, and I was an incompetent Gilligan. Didn't have a clue, so Bernie made me cook and said, *Someday, Damn Yankee, you're going to be a good fisherman.* He never called me Anthony. It was always Damn Yankee. Bernie took this land-loving Damn Yankee out on the ocean and taught me to be a shrimper."

Bernie didn't like to fish on Sunday, the Holy day, but one Sunday we got caught out on the ocean. I was setting the table for us to eat, and Bernie yells down to me, "Tony, I want you to set a place for the Third Man." I called back up, "The Third Man?" Bernie looked down into the galley at me and preached, "All the years I've shrimped, we've lost a lot of men, we've lost family. Every fisherman's a part of our family, and he has family back on shore too. When the sea takes them, she never gives them back, so on Sunday, no matter where we are, there's always a place for the Third Man, an honorable place at the table for those left to the sea."

As Bernie told me, I shrugged at his silly superstitions, and did what I was told. I set a plate for the Third Man.

You've got to remember that we're on the shrimp boat. It's not like land where things are calm and cozy. On the boat, the waves are crashing, the boat's rolling, and the pots are banging together. It's a pinball ride on unforgiving seas. You never really sleep when you're out on the ocean. After four or five days, you're strung out like a violin string ready to snap. You can't sleep below because the smell of the bilge is terrible, like the docks after a massive fish kill in summer. I was cooking, but I was feeling the affects of so many days on the water and the smell. The smell was more than a conditioned nose could stand.

That night, we'd been out for eight days, and I was so thankful when Bernie said we could start heading home, so we set our bearings for Key West. Bernie told me to throw the net over, and we'd drag on the way home. He couldn't waste time, couldn't waste an opportunity to net more shrimp.

I was tired, just beat. I hadn't been able to sleep below, the smell and affects of the waves, so I'd been sleeping on the deck. No mattress, no blanket, just in my clothes on the damp hard wooden *deck, the waves rolling us like a cheap carnival coaster. After seven nights of that, I was so tired, exhausted from throwing and pulling nets, fighting to balance against the waves, and calming my stomach from the stench of a thousand dying shrimp. But Bernie was the captain, so I threw the net over just as Bernie had said. He was the boss, and I did what I was told.*

Back then on the watery deck, the boat's got a fifteen-inch beam holding a light above you. One light shining down in the night and that's all you have for as far as you can see, one little light shining down on you. I can see the captain inside the Pilot House, but I'm alone on the deck of this little beat-up boat needing sleep, needing to be home while I'm watching the net for signs of being full.

It was one of those dark nights, black ocean nights, when it happened.

Tony looked up for a moment, looked up and his eyes captured mine. Blue like the sea, they were clear yet haunting as he said. "Every time I tell this story the hair rises up on my arms, the back of my neck. Look there." He pointed at the raised white hairs on his slender forearms, static tall from his skin.

It was one of those black nights when you can feel the darkness, feel it surrounding you, closing in like a creaking dungeon door. I'm under my little light in the middle of the dark, and I'm hauling the net in, pulling hand over hand the enormous weight of the full catch. As I get it onto the deck, barely visible in the meager light, I pop the net, and everything from the sea comes tumbling out. Crabs, shrimp, sponges, baby sharks, debris, they all fall out scattering littered over on the wooden deck. I go to work, pushing the garbage, the stuff we can't use to one side and the shrimp to the other side, separating the good from what's going back into the ocean. Middle of a black night, I'm sitting on a little stool with the single light raining down on me as I separate the latest catch.

As I sat there, I felt like there was somebody on the port side. That feeling you get that somebody's watching you. You don't know. You can't see them, but you have this eerie feeling.

I said to myself "Come on Tony. You're tired, your beat, you're full of it." I don't know. It was a feeling I had, but it was silly, so I sat there talking myself out of it. I looked up to the Captain, and Bernie is in the Pilot House steering the boat, cigarette dangling from his mouth as smoke swirls creating a foggy shadow as he's staring straight ahead into the black ocean night. I knew we were alone, but as I sat there the feeling wouldn't go away, the feeling like there was someone else there, and the hair began to rise on the back of my neck.

I was afraid to look because Bernie was at the helm, and I was the only other one on the boat. When I finally got the courage to look up, there he was, a man standing on the stern, his arms crossed, staring straight ahead. It scared the shit out of me, and I can only describe him one way. Many years ago, there was a radio program "The Shadow Knows." All you could see of his face was the shadow of his nose. With the light on me, he was like the Shadow, and I could only see his nose. It's strange, a silly comparison, but that's what I saw.

I kept looking up at Bernie to see if he saw him too, but he never looked at me. He's doing his job guiding us home. Except for my little light, it's black night on the ocean. I don't know how long it was before I looked back again. It could have been a minute. It *could have been a half hour. I was so scared that time was not in my control.*

I finally looked up again, and he was still there. The slicker the man was wearing had gotten damp from the salty night sea. His hat was there with just the shadow of his nose visible, and he was still looking straight ahead.

I was so scared that I jumped up and hauled ass for the Pilot House. I ran in the door, a scared kid from New Jersey trapped with a ghost on a fishing boat in the middle of the ocean, and Bernie says "What's the matter with you Damn Yankee, what's the matter?" I looked up all pale and scared and said, "It's just the smell of the sponges. The smell of the sponges got to me. I had to get the hell out of there."

I didn't go on deck again until it was daylight, and by then Key West was in sight. I told Bernie "You know Bernie, Mae's pregnant." I was starting with my excuses. I was married again, married to a girl from New Jersey, and I started using her as my excuse. I wasn't going back. There was no way I was going back on that boat in that ocean. "She don't like to be left alone. I think I'm going to take a break from fishing for a while so I can be closer to my wife while she's pregnant."

Bernie says, "God damn it Tony, I give you a good share of what we make. I love working with you. You're a damn good fisherman for a Yankee. You're going to be a hell of a captain someday."

I said, "I can't leave Mae alone." I wasn't going back out, and I was persistent that I wouldn't go. I was afraid, but I wouldn't tell him why. I kept using my wife and her pregnancy as an excuse.

Bernie looks at me. I've never forgotten this. He looks at me, and I could see that he wasn't accepting my excuses. He kept watching me, his eyes on mine. Then Bernie hesitated and looked me dead in the eyes. He says, "Did he have a rain slicker on?"

I froze staring back at Bernie, and he says to me. "Always set a place for the Third Man."

I know Tony's a story teller, but as I listened to him, as I watched him tell the tale of the Third Man, when I saw the hairs on his arms rise, I believed him. Whatever had happened that night with Captain Bernie McCracken out on the dark ocean, it was all very real to Tony.

The haunting story was something he had lived. Like his life, the story was filled with compassion. There was the compassion of Bernie to bring the Damn Yankee on in the first place and train him to be a shrimper, the compassion of Bernie to always set a place for the Third Man, and the lesson learned by Tony and taught to me of the importance of compassion in our lives. Real or imagined, only the shadow knows.

"Mel Fisher was a man of great compassion." Tony interrupted my haunted thoughts.

"I did go to the museum this morning." I said, shaking away the image of the Third Man knowing that Tony truly believed this unbelievable tale. "A great adventure, to be a treasure hunter. It's like living a kid's dream of sailing the seas searching for the gold and silver hidden where X marks the spot. I bought the book *Fatal Treasure*."

"A very good book!" Tony stated. As I nodded, he added, "Before you call treasure hunting a great adventure, read that book. It's true to life, and it tells both of the adventure and the years of toil, tragedy, and optimism treasure hunting demands. Treasure hunting for Mel Fisher wasn't a kid's game. Maybe a kid's dream, but it was serious, dangerous, and costly in dollars and lives."

"You've read it?" I asked, wondering if this man of knowledge had too gained insight from literature.

Tony nodded, his eyes happy with my recognition. "It's a story of a great man who believed in a dream, but Mel Fisher was also a man who loved his family dearly, a man of compassion. While he achieved his dream, I'm not sure he's confident that the dream was worth the cost."

In my visit to the museum, I had learned much about both the adventure and the tragedy. Mel Fisher had dedicated his life to searching for the sunken Spanish Galleon Nuestra Senora de Atocha, described in Spanish lore as one of the richest shipwrecks still undiscovered. Throughout the 17 years of the search, he had always remained optimistic. His favorite saying was *Today is the day!* It was what he believed, that today is the day he would find the hull of the ship and the mother lode, the preverbal X. Despite financial setbacks, tragedy along the way including the death of one of his sons, and intense court battles with a greedy government, his optimism finally paid off.

In the summer of 1985 Mel's team of divers happened upon the X at the bottom of the vast sea and discovered the mother lode. Their long sought treasure, covered in sand and barnacles, turned out to be a bounty of $200 million worth of silver and gold having sat for three centuries on the ocean floor. Included were 127,000 silver coins, 900 silver bars nearly 70 pounds each, over 700 high quality emeralds, 2,500 other precious stones, and 250 pounds of gold bars and jewelry. Mel Fisher had remained the eternal optimist whose personal belief that he would find the X that marked the spot finally paid off in a way Black Beard had never imagined.

"I helped Mel and his family out when they first came to Key West." Tony was chit-chatting now, just visiting. "Great people, and we became very good friends. On July 20, 2003, I received the greatest honor of my life when I was awarded the Mel Fisher Lifetime Achievement Award."

Tony was smiling with his chest raised high, remembering his close friend. "I remember the day they discovered the mother lode. Two hundred million dollars worth of silver brick settled like a pyramid on the ocean floor, some gold and gems thrown in as a tip. I thought that would change Mel, all the riches, but I should have known better. Mel was a great optimist, a great person of compassion, and he understood that life is all about people. That was the jewel in Mel, his optimism, his compassion, and his connection with his family. He realized he could find thousands of emeralds on the bottom of the ocean, but if you didn't search for the jewel in people, the rock hard gems were worthless. Unless you knew Mel and understood him, you can't have understood how much this award meant to me. This is what I said about Mel when I received the Mel Fisher Award. It went something like this."

To describe Mel is very hard, to truly know this person. He had a great love for family, his wife and children. But you know, he found the mother lode. He really found it! All them years he said, "Today's the day" until one day, today was the day. "Today's the day." Such great belief. Such wonderful optimism.

Mel and I became good friends when he first came to Key West, Mel and his wife Deo toted their kids and a dream along to the island. I helped the family some, and we became buddies. We'd travel together, hang out in the bar. We did our share of drinking. We did what friends do, pals.

Then he finds the mother lode. The newspapers are full of stories of the discovery. Four hundred million, five hundred million dollars, estimates of amazing wealth, figures you wouldn't even imagine. I couldn't believe it. I thought, my gosh, what's this going to do to Mel. I knew he was a man seeking to discover, and I thought 'what's the next mountain he can climb' because if you don't have a mountain to climb, boy, you're stuck. So I was worried that this would be Mel's greatest mountain, and how would he exceed this? I was worried that with this mountain climbed, the wealth would overtake him.

But a great thing happened. You know, in our world today if you've got a lot of money you build a giant house with 25 rooms and 15 toilets. You know how many toilets you have, that shows how big you are. It's one of the ways we measure wealth today, by counting toilets. I was worried because Mel and his wife, Deo, were living in a little house in Key Haven, and I was thinking, boy oh boy, two hundred million dollars. He's going to have one of those giant houses with 15 bathrooms. Count 'em. Fifteen bathrooms.

I should have known better because I knew Mel. I should have known the number of bathrooms he had didn't matter to Mel. Mel was the same man with the same heart and optimism whether he was rich or poor. He understood that all the money in the world can't make you wealthy. It's the people that make you wealthy, the quality of your connection with family. While he was a treasure hunter, he knew that true wealth comes from your relationship with others.

Every morning, Mel'd wear that big gold chain, his favorite piece of treasure. He'd put it on and walk down Greene Street right past Captain Tony's Saloon, a million dollars hanging around his neck and no bodyguards, no armored vehicles for protection. He'd walk down Greene Street like he always had, and he'd have breakfast at one of our little restaurants or stop in to visit friends at the Schooner Wharf.

In the evenings, Mel would sit at the bar in Captain Tony's and have a few drinks with that big solid gold chain hanging around his neck. People would come by, and he'd pose for pictures with them. People from all over the world could walk into the bar, and there sat the richest treasure hunter in the world. He was just a man, just an ordinary hard-working man who pursued his dream until he discovered it. But he didn't keep it to himself. He didn't hide in a 25-room mansion with all those toilets. He didn't care how many toilets he had as long as he had one.

He gave the people their dream when they could talk to him. He'd take his gold chain off and put it around their necks, and have their picture taken with the man whose "Today is the day" *had happened when he found the mother lode. He lived every man's dream. But he didn't hide it in a big mansion with 15 toilets. Mel understood his dream was the dream of so many, so he shared it with everyone, everyday ordinary people he met on the street.*

These are the things I've never forgotten about Mel. He had that one great word I always use. Compassion.

"You see, Brad." Tony stared across the smooth tabletop. Sometime in the conversation he had slipped on his oxygen tube unnoticed. Breathing comfortably, the passion from which he spoke of his friend had been too consuming to be aware of details like oxygen. "Mel Fisher understood things about people that few others do. He had $200 million, but saw himself no differently than he saw down and out street people."

This theme kept emerging from Tony, from back in his history in Elizabeth, N.J. where life had not been so grand, where life was not of becoming a legend but of living day to day, selling peanuts to survive, and scraping pennies, nickels, and dimes together in a dream of becoming a scout. Tony was clearly shaped by a life in which wealth was not part of the experience.

"Today we treat street people like they have cholera, any excuse to throw them in jail, to make their lives more miserable, and get them out of our guilt-ridden sight, but Mel understood the difference between being flat broke and having $200 million. He'd experienced the difference in the matter of a moment when he found the mother lode. Most of us look at street people with disgust at why they don't get up off their butts and go find a job. Mel always treated them respectfully as human beings, and he always gave down and outers a little change, a dollar. He didn't look at it the way most people do. Instead of being irritated at the street people for not taking care of themselves, he understood how lucky he was to have a dollar to give them. He understood that the day he was broke, and he understood that the next day when he was worth two hundred million dollars."

Tony sat before me his arms stretched outward, his palms turned upward. With his head slightly tilted, and his eyes cast down in memory of an old friend, he said. "We can look at it two ways. Either we can be repulsed by the street people and pass them by, or we can realize how lucky we are that we have the dollar to give them. Mel understood that perspective. He knew that it's not the $200 million that matters in life." *It's the people.*

Two women stepped to our table, middle-aged women dressed in bright multi-colored flowered sundresses with spaghetti straps and easy walking side slits. Acting childlike as if they were secretly rendezvousing with a Hollywood star or their favorite Grammy winning singer, they asked with a slight hesitation, giggles, and starry eyes. "Are you Captain Tony?"

"Yes." He smiled humbly with no hint of irritation at the intrusion. Pointing up to them, his hand moving playfully from one to the other as his sly smile grew, drawing them in. "Which one of you did I have an affair with?"

More school-girl giggling erupted as they turned to each other accusingly, as if one owed the other a guilty confession. Finally, the shorter one with the playful eyes gave Tony a little full arm swing pat on the shoulder saying. "You're so bad."

"If you think that." Tony grinned and gave her a sly, charming wink. "You and I never had an affair?" With the ladies laughing like pubescent teenagers, Tony beamed. He had them. From now on they were all his to play with. "And that's a shame. You're beautiful, both of you. Beautiful ladies." As they waved his kind words away with their feigned embarrassment, Tony pointed to their chest. "Nice boobies, too." He raised his hands to his own chest, pressing upward as if lifting D-cups. Both ladies blushed with silliness, laughing even more, behind protecting hands involuntarily hiding their embarrassment.

I sat there completely quiet, knowing this was not my game to play. Quiet because I knew that if I'd said the same thing, a comment about an affair or their chests, I would have rightfully been slapped across the face with the right hand of indignation and a blood-boiling glare from a wholesome Midwestern tourist, a harassment suit to follow. The normal man could not say such things, should not say such things, but somehow, from the thin lips of the swashbuckling Captain Tony, women ogled over his one-dimensional compliments.

I watched as they talked on, gushing to Captain Tony about what a great honor it was to meet him, and him returning the compliment that no, it was his honor, adding.

"If you want to lose your husbands and come back, I'll show you what it's like to have a real Italian lover." Grinning broadly rubbing his goatee, he added with a serious smirk and a convincing wave of his hand. "I'll spoil you."

What could I do but watch this charming act of blatant womanizing. It was Tony, part of his mystique, part of his character and charm. A flaw or a jewel, you'd have to ask others, but as I watched the ladies slip away, watched them back away, stop and say another good-bye, watched as the shorter one threw him a kiss, I knew to these women a one-dimensional compliment from Captain Tony was a word of kindness long remembered.

Tony was smiling with great joy at his barefaced flirtation. "I was always very compassionate with lots of women." A grin broke, his white beard spreading broader.

"You mean passionate." I laughed.

"Compassionate. Passionate." The Captain waved his hand between us, a motion of tit-for-tat. "They both mean *easily aroused.*"

I had found it to be such a contradiction that a man who had 13 children by eight women and brazenly admitted that the desire for the soft touch of woman will get you in a lot of trouble was revered in Key West for the quality of his character. He had the perspective of the early 20th Century, the perspective of one who appreciated woman more for their sensuality and mothering skills than for the quality of their companionship and intellectual capabilities. Some might call it a flaw, but I chose to see it as a glimpse of history, the culture of our country before World War II, that event that changed our country when women went to work as men fought for freedom in Europe and the Pacific. Times had changed much during Captain Tony's life, but his view of women and family was still very much entrenched in 1935.

"Was that an issue when you ran for Mayor of Key West? Your passion, all the kids, the women?" I asked.

"They tried to make it an issue at the Mayor's debate." He explained. "In the Miami Herald they profiled the two candidates, Tom Sawyer and me. Tom happens to be a banker, thirty years younger than me, my wife's age. He's just a nice guy. Everybody would have been happy with him, and in so many ways, I believe he would have been a fine mayor. In the run-off it's him and me. I'd known him for years, known his mother. Good family. I really love this guy, I really do. He's a true Conch, a good person. We're all friends. The Miami Herald profiles him like the nice guy he is, but they call me everything but a pimp. I was never a pimp, though I'd liked to have had the benefits." Somehow, as he snickered to himself, I believed he must have had the benefits despite never owning the job title.

"In the Miami Herald on the front page it profiles Captain Tony Tarracino and Tom Sawyer. Tom Sawyer is a banker and a family man, respected in the community, and dedicated to Key West. They put me down as everything bad that has reflected on Key West's image. I was called a bootlegger, hustler, gambler, womanizer, liar, you name it. There was one little line that made my skin crawl. I'll never forget the moment I read that line, the hurt it caused. It said Captain Tony's opinion of women is they're all liars and cheaters. I was so upset. I'd never said that, would never disrespect women in such a way, never."

"So we get to the Mayor's debate here in Key West. The Mayor's debate! Forget the presidential debate. This is more important in the Conch Republic." Talking about the election, Tony's enthusiasm erupted like a true politician thriving on the competition with a Pied Piper ego seeking a band of followers. "City Hall is packed. The local television station is there. It's so crowded they're sitting on the floor. This is the big debate, Tom Sawyer and me."

Tom and me are together before the debate. I've known him for years, and I love Tom. He's a great guy, but this is the debate for mayor. We wish each other well, respectful of each other, but I know it's going to be political. It wasn't personal with us, but the two are difficult to separate. Just ask Bill Clinton. It's hard to separate personal and political.

The debate's going to start, so Tom and I flip the coin. I win the right to ask the first question. The moderator introduced us, and directed me to start. I said, "Tom, we've known each other for years. I have a lot of respect for you. I don't really care for bankers." I get the audience laughing with that. I laughed too because it's the truth. "But, you know Tom, I remember when you were a little kid, this high." I held my hand just above my knee. "You'd come over to the boat, to my fishing boat the Greyhound, and I'd give you some grunts, some grouper for your Mom. It was my way of helping out, giving away some fish. And a few years later, you delivered the newspaper to my house. You were my paperboy. Do you remember that?" Now even Tom is nodding. Everybody's listening, everybody. "Oh, you were so proud. You really were proud to be my paperboy." I paused for just a moment. "But Tom, my question to you is as a paperboy, why'd you miss the porch every time it rained?"

The place broke up, the whole City Hall. Everybody's laughing, holding their bellies as tears are running down their cheeks, even his own people. I really got him with that, went straight to the point. Everybody's there, and the entire room's laughing. That really messed him up. It was all in fun, but when people eased their laughing, it made a point.

Anyway, we go through the debate and answered all the questions. The moderator says, "We have ten more minutes. What I'd like to do is ask Mr. Sawyer and Mr. Tarracino if they'd answer questions from the audience." Right away a bell goes off in my head that says 'This is it.'

The question comes to me, and this woman I know raises her hand. She holds up the Miami Herald and says "Captain Tony? What kind of mayor are you going to be if your opinion of women is that they're 'liars and cheaters'?"

I stood straight up, tall and serious as I could be, and I said, "I honestly don't recall ever saying that, and if you know me, and people know me, they know I have a very high opinion of women." She starts to sit down, and I say, "Wait, please. Before you sit down, I want you to know I've had ten great women in my life. Ten great women. Women can break a man or make a man. And it was them women that made Captain Tony. They made me the person I am today. I learned so much from those ten wonderful women.

They taught me about compassion and kindness." She goes to sit down again, and I say, "I want you to know something else. You see, I'm being honest. I'm not hiding anything. I don't know how many women I've gone to bed with. There's been a lot, but that's secondary." The audience laughs at that too. "But there isn't a woman in my life I've gone to bed with that it wasn't a privilege to know them. A privilege to sleep with them, yes, but a greater privilege to know them."

The audience erupted. Everybody stood up clapping. They're cheering my honesty and me. That's what won the election for me, that night and that honesty about women. The newspaper was wrong, and I set the record straight.

"You see." Tony grinned broad and bold with that light twinkle in his clear eyes, his willowy body bouncing up and down energized on the booth seat. Flipping his hand back and forth restating 'tit-for-tat'. "Compassionate and passionate."

When we'd shaken hands and parted late on that sweltering afternoon, I could tell Tony was tired, relying heavily on his oxygen.

"Damn body just can't keep up with my mind." He had told me as he'd stepped away, then promised to meet me at the bar later. "I'll take a little nap, and be good as new. Let's meet back at the bar tonight."

The early evening Key West streets were flooded with humidity-drenched tourists including young girls on vacation having had their hair weaved tightly into rows and rows of ornamental braids. Complimented by their scantly embracing tops, they caused the full-bellied, middle-aged businessmen on escape from real life to have visions of Bo Derek dancing in their heads. It was Buffett's lost verse in true life, I thought, as I walked past Margaritaville.

Stopping in front of Captain Tony's Saloon, Tony's daughter Coral was parked along the curb as Tony set both feet squarely on the concrete and pushed evenly with both hands from the car extending to a steady balance. As he straightened, Tony waved without looking, seeming to possess this magical power to know I was near. Standing squarely on two feet supported by stilt-thin legs, he glanced into the dark cover of the bar, and turned back to Coral mouthing instructions on when to pick him up. Then with the fluid coordination of a vacationing teen, he danced a slight side step and hustled the few feet into the bar.

The acoustic guitar player grinned a greeting, excited to see the Captain, and announced his arrival causing all eyes to pivot looking for the legend. Tony's ego could not help it, erupting as they did. Grinning like a boy in a candy store, he stepped to the microphone, ego fully gushing.

"Welcome to Key West." Burst from the speakers, a powerful voice from a fragile body filled the air as he waved to the patrons surrounding the bar. "It's great to have you all here. You must all be millionaires, coming all this way for a vacation." *Share a word of kindness.*

Spots of laughter echoed throughout the saloon, mouths opened in a chuckle like the laughing skeleton that hung dancingly behind the bar. A pirate bandana covering the skull, surely there was a history to the grinning boney buccaneer who seemed to laugh along with the crowd.

Tony spoke into the microphone, his hand wrapped comfortably around it.

I had a friend that went on vacation last week. I wanted to go with him. He went to Las Vegas. I love Vegas. Gambling, women, lots of beautiful women. But I couldn't go, so I gave him a hundred bucks and asked him to invest it wisely. You never know. I might win big.

He got back the other day and I asked him, "How was Vegas?"

"Great." He told me. "Did some gambling, saw some shows, had a great time."

"Did you win anything?"

He shrugged, "Not really."

"What about my hundred bucks? How'd you do?"

"Oh," He said, "I did great with that."

I got all excited, wanting to know how much I'd won. "What'd you do with it?" I asked.

My friend smiled and said, "I got laid."

Laughter burst from the crowd of beer drinking tourists, as Tony's shoulders shook up and down with his own amusement. Like the bouncing doll on the dashboard, a huge grin filled his face. He was at his best in front of people, cheering them up with a joke and a laugh, creating a moment of special connections between the rough and rugged *Salt of Key West* who had worked all his life and the upper-middle class tourists wealthy enough to buy their island fun. For many of them, they envied his life because it'd always been his.

Pulling himself to the microphone once again, he signaled to the crowd and broke into the smooth coordination of a hero playing air guitar with a rock star gyration. With his leg lifted, his right hand strumming the air, he had the energy of Jerry Lee Lewis. The afternoon nap had served him well.

"I hope you have a great time here in Captain Tony's tonight." Tony waved his hand about the bar. "Don't forget these waitresses, your bartenders, and this fine singer. They're good people who want you all to have a great time, so help them out, think of them with a little extra." Tony held his hands up before him, rubbing two fingers against his thumb. "Besides, this place pays them peanuts. I know. So tip them well."

Again, laughter came from the many faces straining through the crowd to see the legendary Captain. With one final wave, he gave-up the microphone stepping around the bar shaking hands as he did. Shuffling quickly to reach his stool in the corner, I was at his side guiding him through the crowd like a large, protective bodyguard in a squatty school superintendent body.

As he slipped onto his seat, gliding gingerly on frail legs, he looked up with a nod. "Always have compassion for the waitresses and bartenders. You've got to promote them when you can, help them out. They work hard and put up with a lot. A little encouragement can go a long way." *It's the people.*

This evening, I didn't have my recorder out, hadn't brought my camera with me. I was just hanging out with my friend Tony. Whenever I got him a soda, my accompanying beer was complimentary. Damn, I thought, that's a pretty good deal.

Talk about escaping the fish bowl. I was having free beers in the oldest bar in Florida, hanging out with my buddy as women flocked to greet him, and hearing colorful adjectives fly aimlessly about without having to lift a correcting finger to a teenager whose mother was sure he'd never use such words. So I took advantage of the fun and freedom standing with a Corona in my hand while singing to myself *crusin' left of center, my mind just glides along.*

Tony kept me busy, as busy as he was. With every tourist who greeted him, he introduced me. "This is Brad," he'd say. "Brad's a great writer, very talented, and we're working on a book together."

In a matter of a few words, Tony transformed me into a minor celebrity, and I laughed with the tourists, shared his stories, told them of the Third Man, his gambling scam in New Jersey, and his flight from the mob. Lovely women and their tourist husbands listened to my stories, awestruck at the bravado of the fearless Captain Tony. We were holding court, Captain Tony and Brad Manard on this little island oasis in a dingy bar that screamed of a long history of good times.

Soon he had me signing autographs right next to his on tee shirts, ball caps, and koozies. People wanted autographs of both the legend and the writer putting his stories to print. So I had my fun. I'd never published anything, not even begun the book we were working on together, but Tony had people wanting my autograph. Obliging, I sign *BManard* in a swirl of artistic cursive never once putting "Dr." before it because I wasn't Dr. Manard here. Here there were different rules, most of them unwritten and not followed. Here there were fewer expectations, the few that were self-imposed by my own pre-disposed conscience. Here, I was Brad.

"To Otis." I announced, and several tourists joined me in a cheering, echoed toast. "To Otis." They had no idea why they were toasting Otis but, if the famous writer was, they damn well better toast him too.

Finishing the toast, I drew them back in.

"That's right." I leaned into the group, and our circle tightened. "So Tony looked around and his bodyguards were gone. Out the back door leaving him to face the heartless mob muscle all by his skinny self!" I blurted louder.

"So the gorilla's in Gleeman's bar each have Tony by the arms, his feet dangling, and they're carry him toward the ominous Hearse of a limousine."

It was three hours later when I walked with Tony to Coral's waiting car, he gave me a slight disapproving glare. "You going out on the town, looking for women."

Laughing at the silliness of his perspective, I held the car door for him. "I think I'll stick with Denise, Tony."

"Yeah," he answered. "If I were you, I would too. Pretty hot for a school superintendent's wife."

I smiled at the thought of my wife. "Yes, she is."

"You calling her tonight."

"Every night," I answered.

"Tell her I wish she was here," he grinned slyly. "So I could show her what a real man is like."

I laughed again as he slid into the passenger seat. "Believe me Tony, she already knows."

He smiled up at me. "I didn't know you were Italian." Chuckling as he said it, he reached for the door handle. "Give Denise my love, and tell her if she'd been here tonight, she'd have been the prettiest girl in the bar."

"I'll do that Tony."

Then, as if suddenly a realization had hit him, he froze. "Listen Brad. If you really want to know me, you should spend some time with my wife. I've been with Marty thirty years, and everybody calls me a legend. She doesn't get the credit she deserves. Thirty years with me? Maybe I'm the legend, but she's a saint. You should talk to her."

"I'd love to." I said as I closed the car door.

CHAPTER 4

After a hearty breakfast of a fluffy omelet sprinkled with healthy chunks of shrimp and scallops over melted cheese on the patio of Two Friends Restaurant where there's *No Greater Love than the Enduring Tender Love...of One Drunken Friend to Another*, I strolled idly along the length of the quiet morning Duval Street in search of the gift gallery where Marty worked.

I was going to visit a woman who had spent more time with the legend than anyone. She knew the stories, the tales of gun-running, wild nights in the smoky bar, illicit escapades with wanton women, stormy sea voyages, and third world Caribbean adventures. She had lived the tales, sailed with him and surely known the pain of loving a womanizing gambler with an eye for soft skin. This was a person I needed to know, a person I needed to understand if I were to truly appreciate the seedy side of Tony.

Curiosity had the best of me, envisioning this wild woman who had put up with such an ornery cuss for so many years. I pictured a pretty woman, maybe a touch tawdry with a seductive body always set off with an extra low top and a bursting cleavage revealing a butterfly tattoo fluttering from her breast. She would be small, tiny to match up nicely with the wiry legend. And she would be a free spirit, a tabletop dancing dynamo in leather with free flowing hair that would snap over her bare skin shoulders as she stomped her boots to the beat of a hard driving song. She would be tantalizing in the stare of her eyes and the way she held her cigarette.

Reach out to her, I thought. Find the jewel. Get her talking, telling tales like Tony did, open and honest renditions of their past. Hear her visions, maybe without the stretching of the tale. I reflected on what to expect from a woman who was 30 years his junior, from a woman who had knowingly married a self-proclaimed philanderer. In my mind I repeated my questions. What is it like to be the wife of a legendary womanizer? Better yet, what kind of woman would be the wife of a legendary womanizer? Who was this woman who sat at home nights while Tony performed his act at the bar, squeezing firm young women in a flirtatious hug and offering to tenderly autograph their sensuously soft skin?

The most important question kept jumping in between the others. The most important question became every other question. Why would a man of questionable character, a man with an admittedly questionable character that he wore on his chest like a badge of honor, be loved and revered as a Key West legend? Surely, as Marty answered this most challenging question, the jewel of her own character would be obvious, either a diamond or a flashy ruby.

When I found the art gallery, I stood in front staring, hesitating. Somehow I had expected something different, something a little bit licentious and seedy. There would be paintings of naked ladies or at least beach seductresses in barely visible bikinis translucent over cartoon breasts. Or maybe prints of the hard life of sailing ships and high seas with men pulling on the nets or fighting a giant blue marlin, jumping high above the breaking waves on a thin sport fishing line. Of course I expected the obligatory collection of Key West beer mugs or Harley shot glasses proclaiming biking and whiskey for a perfect day in a pirate town.

Instead it was a quaint little shop sprinkled with artwork in pastel shades of blue like the coral reef tropics. The front welcomed you in like the cottage by the sea should, with a white wooden walkway to the beach. A wicker chair with aqua cushions and sailboat accents welcomed you to lazy relaxation in the afternoon sun bake as a slight breeze cooled the air. It invited shoppers to sit down and draw in the framed paintings of the front yard you'd always dreamed of, a yard of fine, soft sand, gently breaking waves, and the sloping reach of a palm stretching outward toward the sea and sun to umbrella your own private spot of shade. The gallery sign read *Welcome Home*.

Still, I hesitated to go in, standing stiff facing the doorway of the unknown. I was a stranger stepping into her life, a prairielander walking into her aqua world, and I was concerned that I might be intruding, or was it my own fear of an impious woman bred on the hard side of life, ready to kick some tail.

As it turned out, it was one of those strange moments in life when you're concerned about intruding, afraid of what you don't know, but instead you're greeted with kind eyes and welcoming arms of appreciation. As I stepped into the gallery, her warm smile immediately told me I had found a new friend. That was what it was like with Tony's wife, Marty. No tattoos, no oversexed biker leathers, no hard edge from too many years in a bar. Instead I found with Marty a warm and kind welcome hug and gentle, motherly smile. She was the absolute contradiction of tawdry, and surely that was part of what had attracted Tony to her, part of what drew me to her.

Immediately I knew why Tony had fallen in love with her. Kind with a genuine soft smile, obvious intelligence, and a conservative appearance, I could have stood in the gallery and talked with Marty for hours. And the strange connections in life? A feature artist in her gallery was a Des Moines, Iowa, furniture artist. My wife, Denise, works in the Iowa Artisan Gallery in Iowa City that carries the same artist. More connections, the artist's daughter worked with Denise while attending the University of Iowa, and they had become close friends. It's a long way from Iowa City to Key West, just not as far as you might believe. Maybe Tony, our worlds aren't so far apart.

"You came with this project at the perfect time." Marty told me, standing my height, taller than Tony with a resilient body and gentle greenish-brown eyes. She had sweet freckles that showed a once youthful innocence now highlighting her optimistic smile. "The last year was hard on him with the pacemaker and then the oxygen. It took him a while to feel comfortable moving around Key West dragging oxygen along, but he's doing better now. He was so looking forward to your visit. He needed this project to motivate him. After 87 years and a life lived hard, it's difficult to find new things that excite him, but telling you his stories? He's really looked forward to this."

"So have I." I shared. "I feel honored that he's let me into his life."

"He likes you. He wouldn't be working with you if he didn't see something special in you." Marty leaned against the gallery counter, her arms folded comfortably in the same way mine were as her hips hitched slightly at that baby holding angle. "Tony's a man who can recognize the character in a person almost instantly. He's drawn to character." She smiled then, a smile soft, like a mother's appreciation for her child's innocence. "Is he teaching you a lot of things?"

In his personable way, Tony was a teacher. He already was pushing me to think about compassion, seeking the jewel, and to share a word of kindness. I was already refocusing on people. My eyes opening wider, I was seeing more clearly the things that had long been in my vision. Not so much learning as reminding me of the important things in life, helping me refocus.

Marty smiled gently with a twinkle in her eyes. "I'm sure you'll learn from him. His outlook on life, the way he's lived it. Well. He's a unique individual."

"You know?" I smiled at Marty, who rewarded me with a sweet, high cheek freckled grin right back. "A lot of people will read what I'll write about Tony, and they'll question his attitude toward women. With thirteen children, eight mothers, three wives, and many, many more affairs, some people will find it offensive. His morality is certain to be questioned. Even, I have had my concerns. Such a history creates questions about his character. You've lived it and know his life better than anybody." I glanced away, not wanting to offend. "When people frown and turn away at the thought of his immorality, how do I answer that?"

Marty glancing about the store dutifully with her lips pressed together in thought. We watched shoppers cruise about wearing golf shorts and polo shirts as they lazily examined the artwork.

When her sweet smile returned, Marty answered. "Tony has been with many women and fathered many children with many women, but I've been with him for thirty years." Grinning with a mixture of happiness and as-you-might-expect acceptance. "I've met most of the women he had children with, helped raise half of his children. I've seen that he cared deeply for all of the women in his life, and I know his unconditional love for his children. He truly is a caring father to all of his children." Then, with a slight hesitation in her words, she added. "And I know there was a difference between me and the other women."

Now I smiled. "Such as?"

Self-assured in the way she answered, there was confidence in her kind eyes and in the freckles that dotted her beauty. "Tony never changed. He was always the same, but I came along at a different time. When I met Tony, I worked in the bar and on his charter boat. I was 24, having freshly arrived in Key West, and he was 55 when we first started seeing each other and fell in love. That was the early 70s. The Vietnam War was coming to an end, and hippies were the rage. We'd just gone through the peace movement, the love child era. I was a bit of a rebel myself coming from a wealthy Republican family in Michigan. Much to their dismay, I'd run off to the warmth and unconventional lifestyle of Key West. Tony had been here for years, and had always been the same, but his free spirited attitude, his communal love for women, it fit well with the youthful attitude of the late 60s and early 70s. In a lot of ways, the world had finally caught up with him."

I liked the way she shared, the comforting calm of her insightfulness. In my own inappropriate judgment, I'd wondered what kind of woman would fall in love with a world-class womanizer, bar owner, rebel-in-his-own-right, foul-mouthed, old man cad about Key West. What I found was a very sensitive, caring, and dedicated wife. Her intellect went to a depth that allowed her to fully understand all that she had stepped into when she had became legally bound to the womanizing world of Captain Tony Tarracino.

"I was with Tony for ten years before we got married." Marty smiled helpfully as two men browsed about the store admiring the paintings, the tropical artwork of bright colors and glowing sunsets. "So right there was a difference between me and his other women. But the real difference is that when they were with him or married him, they expected Tony to change. They wanted to pull him in and control him and not let him be who Tony is. They expected complete faithfulness, even demanded that. While I can certainly understand that, I grew up in the midst of the changing values of the 60s and 70s or maybe just because of the person I am, I never had that disillusion. As I said, I came into his life when people were thinking differently about relationships."

Considering that for a moment, I thought of my own marriage and the importance of commitment, the value of trust. Marty seemed so much like me, so much like Denise, our values grounded in our backgrounds. She showed a down-to-earth Midwestern morality, traditionally conservative in her knee length skirt, simple sandals, and slight scoop-neck top, yet she was completely at ease in her marriage to a man who loved women more than anything else in life. Glancing to make sure the customers were out of earshot, I lowered my voice to a private level.

"Marty," I whispered. "I hope I don't offend you with this question, but what did you gain from the marriage?"

"Oh," with glowing eyes, her grin grew to that smile that makes you smile more too, "at first it was a lot of fun. I was young, and we traveled. We sailed around the Caribbean and went to Las Vegas a lot. Tony was big in Las Vegas. Everything was first class and complimentary. He was a celebrity welcomed for his high-rolling antics that were complimented by his flamboyant personality, and he loved gambling. Then, ten years into our relationship, I was 34 and Tony was 65, and we were in Vegas when I told him I was pregnant. Tony didn't hesitate. Within an hour we were getting married using his American Express card to pay the way."

There was no sadness, no disappointment in the way Marty told the story. Her words, her expression, her excitement were all genuine. It showed in her eyes, her expression, that she was very happy with her life and in love with her husband. To her, her life was like the artwork of her gallery, pretty in pastels with a touch of claret red sprinkled here and there.

"Josie was born seven months later. Then T.J. was born when I was 38. People thought I was a little old to be having a baby, but heck Tony was 69. T.J. was 50 years younger than Tony's oldest son, Louie." Marty was quiet for a moment, reflective of that time 17 years before. "Tony is very committed to his children. He's always there when they need him, and I had the opportunity to stay home and raise them. How lucky was I as a mother to have a husband who allowed me that privilege? I raised Josie and T.J. and helped raise his other children especially Alicia and 'Little' Toni."

"Five years ago," she continued, "and there's more to the story, but…" Marty let that hang with her eyes diverting, falling to her left upon the worn floor, the first hint of sadness I'd seen. "Anyway. Tony had a heart attack. That's when the reality hit me that I was Mrs. Tony Tarracino, and Tony Tarracino wouldn't be around forever, so who would I be when he's gone. My children would soon be off on their own. College is so important, and I was determined that Josie and T.J. would go to college. Through that, I realized that I needed to reconnect with myself. That's when I decided to go to work. I do this part-time." She glanced around the gallery waving her hand before the artwork. "During the school year I work as a teaching associate in the public school's pre-school. I love teaching the children. There's so much good we're able to do. Me going to work though, that was tough on Tony, to have a wife that worked. It wasn't part of the old fashioned culture he grew up in."

"He came from a different time." I repeated.

"Yes," Marty agreed, "and he's such a worrier. People who only know the legend wouldn't expect that of him, they don't see the compassion. They probably think he's just running around having babies, and then looking for the next conquest. What they don't realize is he worries terribly about what will happen to us when he's gone." Her eyes glanced away from mine then back again. "And he worries about the little things. This weekend, T.J. and I are going to Tallahassee to visit Josie. She just graduated from Florida State with honors. It's suppose to rain, and Tony is worried about us driving in the rain." She shook her head smiling, glancing downward in appreciation, admiration. "People don't realize how he worried when he was the mayor. He'd be awake nights pacing the floor. He wanted so much for the people of Key West to be happy. That was enough for him. Others wanted high-rise hotels, commercial developments, and big projects. Tony just wanted the people to be happy. That was his purpose. That's what he wants for me too. He just wants me to be happy."

I asked the obvious question. "Are you?"

"Oh yes." Her grin brightened with her teenage complexion. "Our lives have changed many times. First, it was the fun life and being the girlfriend of a celebrity, then we had a family and I changed from his party girl to his wife and a stay-at-home mother. Now, as he's older, we've settled in quite nicely. Tony has such a good heart, and he wants so much to still be of value to the world. Giving is what creates quality in his life, and he just won't give up that part of his life. He's always meeting people, looking to help people, give them some happiness in their lives or just make them laugh. I admire him greatly for that."

Leaning against the counter, Marty Tarracino did not visually fit with the legendary Captain Tony. She was thoughtful, a traditionalist in appearance, soft spoken with an extreme kindness, so much like the many elementary school teachers I knew, and she was 30 years his junior. A contradiction of her husband, she created a calming, easy feeling of relaxation and trust.

"We have that unique relationship that allows us to live our individual lives as we each would, sharing the quality of both," she confirmed.

"How so?"

"Well." Marty's smile drew me toward her in the warmth it exuded. "Take Fantasy Fest, the annual celebration in Key West. The island is packed with three times its population each year during the festival. When I first came to Key West that type of fun was an adventure, but it has become more risqué, more flamboyant. All the body painting as costumes, the nudity, thousands of people walking up and down the street with nothing but a layer of paint covering them, well, I just don't appreciate it the way some might. Tony on the other hand, he loves it and makes a lot of money during Fantasy Fest. So while he's downtown signing his autograph on body parts, T.J. and I are at the park volunteering with the children's activities. We're far removed from the rowdiness, but we're both very much a part of the community." With each word she spoke, it was clear that she was happy in her life, as unordinary as it might be to have lived it married to the *Salt of Key West*.

Marty grinned once more, shifting against the counter as she did, her arms at her side. "When Tony was sworn in as mayor, we were all there, the whole family including most of his children. T.J. was three, and I was holding him, and Alicia, Tony's daughter was holding her child who's the same age as T.J. We were all so proud, and it was such an important moment for Tony. He was in a suit and tie, and we all stood behind him, a family proud of their husband, father, and grandfather. Afterwards, a reporter told us we had the appearance of a typical young, happy family." Marty looked up to meet my eyes. "What he didn't understand is that's what we are."

"Explain the difference to me," I asked.

"The people who only know Tony as this *legend* only know about his adventures. Most notable to people is the womanizing part of the legend," she rolled her eyes upward. "They count his kids believing that a man with so many children and women couldn't care less about people. They might even think he's irresponsible. They think he's just this guy who beds a lot of women and moves on negligently." Comfort shown in her smile as Marty explained this to me. "But Tony is a very compassionate, caring person. That's what drives him. It's not the sex or the adventure. It's the connection with people. He didn't just have sex and make babies. He had relationships, and he loves his children deeply. They're all very close and important in his life. People and his family are his motivation."

As our conversation meandered on like a nice stroll in the park with a close friend, my appreciation for both Marty and Tony grew. Yes, they were a unique couple, but it was their uniqueness that made them special and brought them together. I liked Marty, liked her very much, and I felt the same luck that I had met her as I had felt in meeting her legendary husband. Marty was kind with a good heart, and she was a person of compassion. She shared an optimistic smile, an uplifting joy, and a sense of acceptance for the differences in her world. By the time our conversation ended, I knew that from this short visit the connection we made would last a lifetime.

That afternoon, I met Marty's husband for lunch at his favorite seafood restaurant, a spot hidden in the maze of back streets on Stock Island.

"This is a locals-only place," Tony explained to me. "None of the tourists come to this part of Stock Island, and even if they did, they wouldn't find this place."

We wondered into the restaurant with its 70's décor of spindle back chairs and yellow plastic booth dividers with a swirling spiral design. As we walked through to a one-step raised area with six tables overlooking the rest of the flash-back-in-time room, people stopped mid-bite watching us, either curious about Tony or the stranger with him.

We sat down at a small table against the wall covered with black and white photos, pictures of locals with fishing boats named for their lady loves, but mostly fishermen and their massive catches.

As I glanced at the photos, my eyes scanning the history, I laughed out loud turning back to the Captain.

"You planned this." I shook my finger toward his slender bearded face.

Looking confused, innocent, if it's possible for him to look chaste, I pointed from Tony to the picture hanging between us on the wall. It was a picture of a young, slightly built, muscular Captain Tony with the black hair of a true Italian. He stood before six hanging fish, all larger than he and weighing much more. It was an impressive image of a fisherman showing off an assortment of a day's massive catch.

"Hey," grinning innocently, his voice bursting with surprise, "it's me." Then he added, "That was a good day. Big fish, lots of them. Grouper. I was a big shot on the docks that day. Nobody back then brought in fish like that, maybe one or two, but not that many. Everybody wanted a photo."

"Captain Tony." The waitress appeared beside our table, her generic order pad in hand and a click top pen ready to write.

"How are you?" He reached out taking her hand, decorated with slightly chipped fingernail polish, adding. "Beautiful. As always." *Share a word of kindness.*

A slight blush, the color of her nails, rose in the cheeks of our waitress, a nice looking girl with a mid-thirties body invaded by a few pounds too many.

"You're too kind." She squeezed his wrinkled fingers with hers.

"When did you work for me?" He asked, his kind eyes watching her closely.

"You remember that?"

"Of course," the Captain still held her hand. "You worked at the bar one winter a few years ago."

"And I loved working for you." She leaned in, soft and gentle. "You look so good. How do you stay so healthy?"

Tony winked, "I exercise."

"You exercise?" Her eyes widened.

"At my age, I do a lot of walking. I go to a lot a funerals." He laughed to himself as she grinned at his silliness, pointing back at her. "I got you with that one, didn't I."

Giggling, she gave Tony a playful slap on the shoulder as he laughed right back.

They talked for a moment longer, and I listened at how they shared the pleasantries of friends too long a part from each other. Tony asked her questions to catch up on his Stock Island pals, and she told him about the regulars at this little restaurant hidden near the shrimpers' docks.

Pointing at the menu, Tony shook his head disturbed. "Look at that. Potato skins. They're selling potato skins like they're some delicacy. We're paying for potato skins. Do you know how many potatoes skins I peeled when I worked in the restaurant back in Elizabeth? I used to peel potatoes so we could throw away the outsides. Now they're an appetizer, a delicacy. People pay to eat what I used to throw away. The world keeps changing." He pointed at the price on the menu. "Can you believe we're paying that much for potato skins?"

"Do you want some?" The waitress teased.

"Hell no." Tony was firm, his face like a stubborn child. "They're just garbage dressed up like parsley."

The laughter was loud as the waitress held her pen to the tiny tablet once again, chuckling as she told us the special. After she wrote down our orders, I told Tony about my visit with Marty.

"She's a special lady," He said.

"Yes," I agreed.

"She's never gotten enough credit," Tony added, disappointment in his eyes. "To put up with me all these years and be the mother; the wife she is. People who know her know that she's got a heart of gold. They know what a good person she is. Those who don't know her, don't know me, they judge her from my reputation. It hasn't been fair to her. She's so much better than me."

"I never would have put you two together," I confessed.

"That's just how special she is," he told me. "Marty always tells me that I'm too forgiving. She says I'm always defending people, and I tell her it's easier that way," Tony's grin grew bright. "But Marty's much more forgiving than I am, otherwise why would she be with me after 30 years?"

"She's got a good heart," I agreed, "an impressively kind and intelligent woman."

"Brad," Tony answered, "I understand my fellow man, and I've always been able to make an excuse for him. But for Marty, to make excuses to continue to love me, to support me, and be by my side, that takes a woman who is forgiving beyond what I understand." Tony opened his hands waving them down over his chest. "So much of what's good about me is because of Marty. Beside *compassion* in the dictionary, they should have Marty's picture."

After meeting her, I knew he was right. She possessed a rare heart and, obviously, incredible tolerance.

As we waited for our food, like old friends getting together over lunch, we spent the time chit-chatting. Tony told me about the old Key West, the Key West of shrimpers and the Navy, reflecting back before my time to when he and Ernest Hemingway roamed the streets at all hours.

"That's all it was," he shared. "It was all sailors and shimpers; sailors out to sea for months, shimpers and Navy wives having affairs. It was a wild town," laughing at the image vivid in his mind.

Tony chuckled with his shoulders bouncing up and down like Snidely Whiplash. It was at times like this that you both loved him and wondered what the hell he'd been up to in his life. He seemed to care deeply about people with this one exception. His testosterone ran strong like hurricane-whipped winds out of control, and it seemed that with all of his good values, he had this animal-driven desire to bed women. How much he thought beyond the moment to the potential consequences, I don't know. He lived for the moment, which was one of his endearing qualities, but I wondered how much the men whose wife he'd slept with had found it endearing.

"After the Navy left, the gays moved in," Tony went on. "They bought up all of the old homes left by the Navy officers. Everything was dirt-cheap because the Navy pulled out all at once. The gays came to the town and bought homes for $3,000 that are worth a million now."

"Was that good for Key West?" I asked.

"The gays saved us," he answered. "They helped turn us from a Navy town to a tourists town. When I first bought the bar, it was a gay bar, but I didn't like that."

I fought the wrinkle in my forehead. "Didn't like the gays."

"No," he shook his head defiantly, "I didn't like that it was only for gays. I wanted it to be for everybody." Tony nodded with a slight shrug that clarified. "I wanted all of us, everybody in our world, to live together, work together, and drink at the bar together. Why should we have to have separate lives? This bar for gays, that one for blacks, another one for shrimpers? That's what I didn't like about Captain Tony's when I bought it. As a gay bar, it didn't invite all people in."

When our food arrived, we fell into the quietness of a good meal. Tony was right. This place had local flavor. It did nothing to attract tourists, and by its location and décor actually discouraged them, but the food was something special. What more local flavor could there be than eating a great seafood lunch in this small town restaurant with my friend, the resident island legend?

"This legend thing," I said between bites of fresh broiled grouper, my eyes flitting up toward his without staring. "It bothers me a bit Tony, that you are so revered when there's obviously, as there is obviously in all of us, flaws in character."

Tony held his generic silverware, one fork prong slightly bent, over his fried seafood, and stared for a moment at a chip on the side of the plate. It wasn't a hesitation of anger or frustration, but from his pensive stare downward, you could exact the thoughtfulness before answering. His hands, like his mind, held steady despite age, wear, and wrinkles.

"In my life," he spoke deliberately, "I've chosen to surround myself with," there was a long hesitation, thoughtful again, before he looked up. "Brad, you're a positive person. You look for the good in people, you seek the jewel. We have choices in life, choices on who we associate with. I've known many good men and many bastards. What's Jimmy say in *Changes? Son-of-a-bitches – Seen more than I can recall.* I've known too many too, but they've been short-lived in my life. When they've slipped in I've chosen to let them slip back out. And women," there was a twinkle in his blues, "I loved many wonderful women, heartfelt women who taught me compassion. It was my choice to surround myself with people who understood compassion; with good men like yourself."

He smiled now, the grin of a content and confident man professing from the knowledge of variety and history, bright eyes as alive today as they had been when he first hitchhiked his way to Key West.

"There are people in this world who judge and dismiss based on what little they know about someone; people that fail to look beyond the judgment to the jewel, people who fail to seek the treasure in others." Calming, he took a small bite, chewing slowly, satisfied with both the flavor and the words. "I think there's a bit of bastard in every man." His fork pointed my way bouncing three times to the rhythm of his words. "The good people in my life, the people I have chosen to surround myself with, have been able to look beyond the bastard, beyond their desire to judge and allowed themselves the time to discover the jewel."

"So," I watched him watching me, "are you a good man?"

Chuckling, his whole body seemed to shake with atrophied humor. "There're moments when I've been a bastard, done bad things, made mistakes, selfish moments when I've forgotten about loved ones causing them pain." His eyes shifted beyond mine with a hesitation of private memory. "The difference is there's more compassion in me than bastard. That," he responded, "that is what I have to be thankful for, and that is what good people have seen when they looked beyond the bastard. Looking beyond that, they found a man of compassion."

"I see," I pushed for more. "So you're a good man?"

"More good than bad, Brad." Pressing his lips together, confidently, he nodded with the slightest of movement. "More compassion than bastard, and," now the Captain Tony grin broke across his face, "as I've grown, learned more about people, learned more about myself, compassion has almost erased bastard." He chuckled ever so slightly. "Too bad I didn't know then what I know now. If I had, maybe, just maybe, I'd have had Marty in my life sooner and longer."

That night, I found myself by the pool in the secluded evening solitude behind my guesthouse. The humidity still hung thick in the air, but without the sun, the blazing heat was not penetrating your skin. It was a clear night, bright stars filling the southern sky. I scanned the sky knowing the Southern Cross was up there somewhere, probably down closer to the equator.

Sipping a cold Diet Coke, I plunged it back into the ice bucket on the wooden decking beside where I sat, and looked down at the computer in my lap. I laid my hands gently on the computer keyboard and began to type.

When you meet a man who people call a legend, how can you not help but learn. There is good and there is bad in all people. Good and bad at different levels and different perspectives leading to life's lessons. Tony Tarracino is not a perfect person, not by a long stretch of the word. Certainly a man of questionable morality, he is also a man of unquestioned qualities. Where is the balance, the strength of his character?

He's a gambler, and gamblers take chances and risks, risks that can hurt others. He's a womanizer, and when you're a womanizer, no doubt you will hurt the woman who loves you. The immorality of a womanizer's acts can destroy all of the good that surround them. Then again, Tony believes that women have made him a man of compassion, and thus, guided him to his most important life lesson.

And Tony is an honest person, but from that honesty can come bluntness that sometimes causes misunderstanding. Tony can leave the wrong impression leading to hurtful misunderstandings. Yet people love to live through his stories for through his stories come the quality of his legend.

Hesitating, I took another sip of my iced down cola, cool against Key West's warm, 80 degree night. With that inner smile, I looked down at my computer, typing once again.

Captain Tony is a man of time, a man of many thoughts, a man of daring adventures and wild women. He is a man who has lived on the edge. He is a father, a husband, and a man who changes people. Most of all, Captain Tony is a man of compassion and from that compassion comes the knowledge that within us all is a jewel, and you should always compliment the beauty of

the jewel within others. Tony's heart is deep but unable
to be full for there is always room in a heart guided by
compassion. It is with that compassion, he had begun to
take me on a soft journey into my own soul.

I stared at the computer rereading what I had just typed. They were uncomplicated words ringing true.

I began to type again, putting words and thoughts together, poetic words with a rhythmic chorus, words that flowed like the lessons of a talented teacher. Appreciating the rhythm of the phrasing, I stood from my poolside chair, and moved into my rented room to retrieve the guitar I was learning to play, another of my mid-life changes.

Carrying it back out into the moonlight, I tuned then pressed my fingers into an A minor chord strumming as I sang the words written on the computer screen.

> *I met him at a bar in a pirate town,*
> *living his life out by the sea.*
> *With his knowledge of time,*
> *he spoke his wisdom to me.*

CHAPTER 5

It was a unique breakfast served in the now familiar morning warmth. Tony had brought me to Key West's renowned *Blue Heaven* because he loved the atmosphere and character of its eccentric personality. I think he loved too the spirit of the people who had opened this eatery on a shoestring and a prayer in the middle of Bahama Village.

It was an old two-story building with sea blue shutters, sporadically chipping white paint, and stairs that had settled slightly a kilter. It was a building of history. The courtyard was walled off with fences, the dirt ground was pressed dry hard by the feet of constant customers, and tables were set on the barren earth. Chickens strutted about eating the dropped remains of seafood Benedict, fluffy pancakes made from scratch and soaked in real maple syrup, or leftovers from the rooster special, two eggs, grits, sausage, and Betty's banana bread. As I looked down, a red crowned rooster of sun-brightened russet feathers high stepped over my shoes, pecking a crumb of pancake from the ground.

Louie, Tony's oldest son at 67 had joined us this morning. A hearty man with this great big Italian laugh, I liked him instantly, his grin as infectious as his laughter. Louie had the look of Hemingway, a cross between *The Old Man and the Sea* and *The Salt of Key West*. With a full beard, cloud white, and a stocky body that looked pure East Coast mafia, his necklace was a silver piece of eight encased in gold, a remnant from the treasure recovered by the Fishers on the ocean floor where the Atocha had rested for 300 years.

Pointing to the middle of the courtyard, Louie explained, "This place has so much history. In years past they held boxing matches here, bare fisted brawls that Hemingway used to referee."

Glancing about the earth patio of the fenced in yard, I could almost see the ghost of Papa Hemingway standing intently mid-ring, bringing the raw knuckled boxers together as the crowd of pirate dreaming ruffians cheered the fist bloody men they had bet their week's wages on.

Louie could be the heavier son of Captain Tony or the winner of Key West's annual Hemingway look alike contest. Either fit him well. Having moved to Key West a few years before in semi-retirement from New Jersey, Louie was a man much like his father in the sense that money was made to be spent and life lived with optimism and a hearty laugh destined to carry him through to the next pay day.

"Titi," Tony switched subjects, waving toward where the center of the boxing ring must have been. "My mate on the Greyhound, Titi. Titi used to have his cock fights here."

Louie pointed up the skewed stairs to the second floor of the old building. "That was a bordello up there. There're still the little rooms along the far wall. Big enough for only a small bed, the rooms line up one after another." Louie grinned as if it might be a place he'd be enticed to visit. "They've still got those sliding peek holes on each door."

"I remember when they opened," Louie shared. "The restaurant, not the bordello. In the middle of the Bahama Village surrounded by the island's black community, everybody was afraid to come down here."

Tony agreed, "I used to send people from my bar. I'd say go to *Blue Heaven.* Don't be afraid. They're good people down there. Walk down and have a great breakfast. That's what I'd tell those hesitant to venture into the black community." *Seek the jewel.*

"But the owners, Richard who was a writer and Suanne the artist, would sit on the steps out front, nobody in the restaurant, their chin in their hands saying *What did we do?*" Louie shrugged, sorrow in his eyes for his friends' pain. "Back then, the white tourist wouldn't come into the black area of the island. Richard and Suanne'd put their hopes and dreams into this restaurant, but the tourists were too intimidated to come to Bahama Village."

I looked around at the atmosphere, and thought of what those tourists must not have realized they were missing. History and character surrounded me. Almond and Spanish lime trees, a water tower atop the Tiki bar showing a spirit of time tested fun, and in the back of the courtyard was the rooster cemetery, a tribute to the many great cluckers who'd graced the dirt floor shedding it of its dinner crumbs. The rooster cemetery, right near the outdoor pool table, was just over from the outdoor shower where the sign read *$2.00 to shower, $3.00 to watch.*

Louie picked up the menu, pointing to the historical summary on the back. "Slowly, they began to do some business. Then Richard lured his brother, Dan, down from North Carolina. His brother's a chef, and when Dan put his touches on the dinner menu, word began to spread." Tapping at a quote on the back of the menu it read, "Journalist Charles Kuralt said *Dan's scallop sauce would make cardboard taste good.*"

"This is where I gained the people's support as mayor." Tony pointed with his fork out toward the street. "Not their votes, but their belief that they had elected the right man to return Key West to the people."

"You ran for mayor five times?" I asked him. "Is that right?"

"1975, '85, '87, '89, and '91," he nodded knowingly in his thoughtful way, slipping back into the volume of his near-capacity mind. Tony did this often, slipping back into the quiet to search for the answer, but he always came back. I had learned to give him time to sit in silence, for he always finds the answer and brings it back to me. "I won in 1989 by 31 votes. I went out the night before and convinced all the hookers to vote for me. I got 29 hooker votes. It's the only election in America won on the hooker vote." Tony couldn't help but laugh at his own masterfully crafted tale. "Lost by 2 percent in 1991. Where were the hookers then? That was my own fault. Too much time spent on politics and not enough on women." His ornery grin came around once again as he sat slightly slouched, his eyes watching me from beneath the white bush of his coarse eyebrows. "I took it very seriously, being mayor, but I got so busy I forgot that the people elect you." He reached over with a slight tap to my arm. "Maybe a good lesson for a school superintendent."

Louie glanced from his father and back to me, a curious look in his blue eyes.

Tony just smiled.

"In '89 I begged people, don't vote for me. From my heart I told them the biggest favor you could do me is don't vote for me." Sitting straighter, his forehead frowned, "And I was serious, but then I added. Don't vote for me unless you believe in me. If you don't believe in me," I told them all this. "If you think I'm just a lot of bull, vote for the other guy. He's a nice guy, he really is. He means well. I think I'm a little smarter, but he's a great guy." Tony gave a dismissing wave of his wrinkled hand, his head tilted slightly to the right as if remembering that time years before, "I was so damn honest."

Guys are running for president, and they knock each other playing political assassins. I was running against my Key West friend Tom Sawyer. Presidential candidates attack each other, their lives, their love lives, everything but their mentality. When I ran for mayor I was honest. I didn't hide anything, and I told them to vote for Tom if they thought he'd be a better mayor. I was sincere about that. I wanted what was best for Key West. I just happened to think I was what was best.

Tony was leaning forward over the breakfast table, an intent glare, very sure, very concerned that I was listening. As he spoke his animation grew. His arms waved, his eyes lifted, his head nodded vigorously as if the more his body moved, the better he could make me understand. The energy that burst from him as he talked about his years as mayor was a contradiction to that of a man needing oxygen to feed his slight body. He sat before me with such enthusiasm and vigor, a joy in remembering his service to his utopia. Giving me that squinted look of single-mindedness that nearly hid his blue eyes by drawing the wrinkles together like the tight, rough bark on an old Iowa oak tree, he spoke from the heart.

When I was elected in 1989 it was a huge night in Key West. It was the biggest celebration. I think even people that hated me celebrated. When I was sworn in my family was there including Marty, most of my kids, and my grandkids. Even Mimi, my first wife and Louie's mother, and her husband Richard Hardy came down. She hated me, but Richard and I had been friends long before they married, and he came down for the celebration.

A broad grin broke across Louie's bright red cheeks.

"My mom." His smile grew even more with crimson rising over his face as if a laugh needed to escape. "My mom never called him Tony." Louie explained about Tony's first wife. "It was always *that son-of-a-bitch*. When she was dying, she was not coherent, lying in her hospital bed without acknowledging anyone. She hadn't been awake for so long, hadn't said a word for days. We knew the end was near. We're all sitting there, the family at her hospital bedside, and someone mentioned my father by name. They said Tony. Suddenly, out of her deep sleep my mom sits up, her fist in the air and yells *That son-of-a-bitch*. Then falls back down into her hospital bed and without another word returns to her own semi-conscious world."

I looked over at Tony and he grinned, a slight shrug as if to say welcome to my world. Then, without further explanation, he went on.

It was when I was being sworn in as mayor that I realized I was elected to be the father of 28,000 people. That was my job, my commitment, to be the father of 28,000 people. They were my responsibility. I had to provide for them and make their world a good place. I was a great mayor for the people because I cared so much about my 28,000 children and our Key West home.

The first week I was mayor, a black guy out of Miami was making a drug buy here at Key West in Bahama Village. The problem was he didn't know he was buying drugs from undercover police officers. When the cops went to search him, he shot one of our officers in the stomach, the other one in the leg. The cops shot back, but they had already been wounded. They were down. The rescue squad came, and they got them to the hospital as quick as they could. They called me at 3:00 in the morning, and I was at the hospital before they brought them in. But there was much more to the story than two shot policemen.

What happened is the black guy, the drug dealer, was running away from the cops he shot, and when they fired back, he got shot in the backside. Injured and trying to keep from being caught, he hid behind the weeds not too far away. When they got the police off to the hospital, somebody found him and yelled, "There's a guy lying in the grass over there."

Before they got the drug dealer to the hospital, he died. Word began to spread and anger built as the people of Bahama Village believed the rescue squad had taken care of whitie first and said to hell with the black guy. You know how the rumors must have flowed;

the rescue squad takes care of the white police officers, ignoring the black guy dying in the bushes. At the time they were giving aid to the officers, nobody knew the drug dealer was even in the bushes. They found him later, but the people began to believe that whitie was given aid and rushed to the hospital while they ignored the black guy. It was bad, very bad. The residents of Bahama Village were infuriated by the rumor and began to gather as an angry mob. Of course, as the mob grew, the rumors spread, and the rage was on the edge of erupting into physical violence. The mob was in such frenzy, they were ready to burn down Key West. It was a mess, a dangerous, explosive mess.

"When a child gets hurt, the father goes to them, and I was the father of all 28,000 people. The people of Bahama Village were just as much my children as the two injured police officers." Tony's eyes brightened with a satisfying depth of his love and determination to help all of the residents of the Conch Republic. "So I got in my car and headed down to Bahama Village."

I got down here, and the street is filled with people, angry people building toward violence. They were yelling and beating on the cars, infecting each other with their misinterpretation of the true events. The police had the area blocked off, and they begged me not to go in, but I told them a father goes to his children. They tried to stop me, but I was their mayor, so they stepped aside and let me go in.

Things were pushing toward violence, and you could see the fury in the eyes of every black person. I knew things were about to explode. Hell, the volcano was erupting, and I had to do something. I'm the only white guy around, so everybody notices when I'm standing on this car waving my arms so everybody can see me.

I got their attention, quieted the crowd with my hands, and began to speak. "I'm your Mayor Captain Tony, and I want justice just as much as you do." I said, "Look, we don't know what happened. We don't know whose fault it was, but I'll promise you something. If they did what you think they did, meaning the medical people, if they let that man die just to take care of the whities, Key West deserves all of your anger. If that's what really happened, I won't let an act like that go unpunished. I'll get to the bottom of this, we'll learn the truth, and then we'll do what is right."

Tony raised his aged hands charismatic as a third world leader, pausing slightly as he simulated the quieting of the black community, then brought them down slowly to show the calming effect. There was a confident determination in his stare, as the eyes of a man so small in stature penetrated my soul. It was the same stare, the same sure eyes that he had shared with his children, the souls of the Conch Republic, that night as mayor. They were trusting eyes, eyes to believe in.

"I put my life in their hands right there. I put my life in the hands of the black people of Key West because I believed in them. I'm only Mayor a week now, but we calmed it down. That stopped the violence, and instead of having a race riot, we began to bring the black and white communities together."

I had learned that an amazing range of people supported Tony in his quest to become Key West's mayor. Jimmy Buffett had served as his honorary campaign manager, using his name recognition to gather support. With the charisma that oozes the attitude of tropical adventure and a pirate's soul, Jimmy Buffett helped get Tony elected. But it wasn't just celebrities. Everybody in Key West knew Tony, an icon of the island for so many years. They knew the man they were voting for.

"Many people still believe in Tony and what he did as mayor." Louie held a bite of omelet on his fork, talking with a thick east coast accent, his white beard and open shirt showing a bold chest added authenticity. "Tony was a mayor who looked out for the people rather than how much money could go into the city coffers. At the time he was elected Mayor, Key West was changing with too much development in progress. A lot of people come here with the carefree attitude, but the people who stay and live here can't survive on attitude alone. They've still got to make enough to live. Tony recognized that." Louie slipped the omelet into his mouth, pointing as his father had with his fork. "People can't afford to be here in Key West, new arrivals or Conchs. That's all due to the development and the impact it has on the cost of property. Tony recognized that the typical island person can't survive with such costs. As mayor Tony fought development to try and control the cost and maintain paradise for the Conchs, the true people of Key West."

As we continued eating our scrumptious breakfast, equal to Charles Kuralt's description, the multi-colored chickens strutted about sharing in the delight, and Tony told me of his quest to be mayor.

I fought for the island, ran on a platform to stop developments. The developers loved cement. It was like their cocaine. They couldn't get enough cement. They wanted to put it everywhere, and they were taking the gulf away from us. The gulf is beautiful with its sunset, and I fought to stop the developments that were taking the gulf and beaches from us all the while making it too expensive to live here.

In City Council meetings a big shot developer would get up to talk, and he had three minutes. He talks five minutes. A little guy would get up and want to say something, and they cut him off saying his three minutes were up. I'd say, "Keep talking sir. Talk as long as you want. You have the same right to talk as anybody." I didn't care about the time limit for the little guy if the City Council members gave more time to the big shot developer and his addiction for more cement.

During one Council Meeting this Key West development lawyer Jim Hendricks comes to us, and I announce loudly, "And the next speaker is High Rise Jim Hendricks." The crowd starts laughing, cheering for me as Jim steps to the podium. I greeted Jim and said, "You know, I never listen to you, Jim." He says, "I know Tony. You turn your hearing aid off when I get up to speak."

That's the way it was, me for the little guy against the big guy developers. But I was an honest man. There were so many developments in progress. The offers I had, different developers seeking any way to get past me, but I never took any of them. I wouldn't allow them to corrupt me. I was a real mayor true to the people of Key West.

Hidden within that determination to keep Key West for the Conchs, the little people, I knew there was a desire to preserve the island as it had been at the time of Tony's arrival years before. When he'd come to live here it'd been like the Barbary Coast. It was the pirate in Tony, the free wheeling adventurer living on the edge that didn't care about big hotels, cruise ship docks dominating the shoreline, and rules made into laws that bind the untamed spirit. He wanted to maintain the past when people were a greater focus than concrete. Flashing back, he told me of the swashbuckling town.

Outside of Key West, I might get a bad rap for being a womanizer or a rough talking sailor, but years ago the whole town was like that. The town was very different than today. We were a Navy and shrimping town. The sailors on the Navy ships were out to sea for weeks at a time. The Navy wives got bored, the shrimpers came in from being at sea. A lot of people in town had little flings on the side. Shrimpers and Navy wives. It was pretty common.

It was a rugged town on the edge of America. There were many more bars on Duval Street than there are now, like the Old West of the Sea. Gambling was everywhere. You could go into the bar back room or upstairs, and it was just like a casino. I was still a character because that was the image I wanted to create, but I was a character that fit right in, a colorful pirate in a pirate town.

Skirting the law, that was the whole town's atmosphere. Shrimping, bars, gambling, and women; I just may have taken it one step further and had many, many women, and a lot of them had my children, but everybody just laughed. "Oh, there goes Tony, a new woman on his arm. What a character."

We were the Conch Republic, and we had an attitude of being separate from the United States. With the Navy and shrimpers, the Conch Republic was like a modern day port with a 1700's attitude.

When the Navy pulled out and the tourists started coming, one of the tourist attractions was the chance to see real ocean bearing fishermen. The fishermen used to come in from a day on the ocean and display their catch hanging the fish up on the docks. The tourists would come down to see the display of big fish. They were always so impressed with the size of the fish unlike the blue gills they caught in the lakes back home in Iowa.

Tony gave me a sly wink.

Tourists are so gullible. They don't understand the ocean, so one day, I'm coming in on the Greyhound, and see a dead goat floating in the water. Titi and I pull the goat on board, and when we hang our fish to display our catch for the day, in the middle is this dead goat. Sometimes we'd spray-paint the fish so they were all different, bright colors. We'd have the tourists amazed at the brilliant colors of the saltwater fish.

"That's part of his connection with the Key West people." Louie added. "The shrimpers and barkeeps, the small inn owners and penniless guitar players. It's like they all shared in the joke, treating the tourists to a little something special."

"My love for the little guy." Tony said, tapping his cup as he smiled kindly to the young waiter for a refill. "It goes back to 1935. It goes back to living poor, to watching my father struggle to provide for his family, to living in the projects with my own young family, Mimi and the kids. Louie," Tony nodded toward his son, "his sister Tonia and brother Richard. I grew up poor, lived in the projects when I first got married. I know what it's like not to be able to afford a decent place to live. So I fought the developers, and I fought the big guy to make sure the little guy was treated fairly."

"How successful were you?"

Tony shrugged slightly, that shrug of fighting City Hall even when you're running City Hall. "I slowed them down. Stalled some of them, but I was the mayor. My only power over the City Council was with a tie breaking vote, so when the votes were against me, I couldn't stop it. Go down to 0 Duval Street today and see what you see. Hotels, cruise ship docks. We've got one little tiny beach at the end of Simonton Street. It's about the size of a regular house lot. That's all that's left of our oceanfront. The rest is cement."

Looking down, you could tell this was a disappointment to the old man. It had not all gone the way of his vision. He had slowed them, stopped them for a time, but he had not been able to convince everyone of his hopes for the people of Key West. He still loved the little island of Conchs that lived on shrimp and the military influence, and he'd wanted to preserve that. The tourists' dollars had made much money for him, but it had come at a price. Tourism overran his little island, changed it, and had taken away much that he and the Conchs loved.

"I didn't win all the battles, but I gave the people back their self-respect. It wasn't monetary or anything like that. It was their self-respect. I loved being mayor, loved being a father to 28,000 citizens." He sat with his head down, staring at his empty plate, his son Louie, quietly, respectful beside him. Then suddenly, with a great big smile of joy, his head jerked up, and he pointed to me.

I'm in my office one day, the Mayor's Office, and this old woman calls me up. She says, "Captain Tony… oh, I mean Mayor, Mayor Tony." I answer very softly and kindly, "Yes, who's this." She says her name, and I ask where she lives. She says she lives on Elizabeth Street, Elizabeth near Eaton Street. I write this down, then I ask what I can help her with.

She says, "I have a very serious problem." I ask, "What is it?" She says, "They didn't take my garbage." I say, "What!" Like I'm shocked that such a thing might happen. She says, "That's right, it's true. They didn't take my garbage." I ask her, "Is it a lot of garbage?" "No." She says, "It's just two little bags, but I'm concerned that the cats are going to get them." You know about all those wild Key West cats, six toes and running everywhere. She's worried they'll get into her garbage.

So I asked for her house address, write it down, and tell her. "All right. You look out your window at 1:00 and see if the garbage is still there. If it's still there, there's going to be hell to pay." Delighted, she thanks me for helping her, couldn't stop thanking me. I've let her know that her concern is important to me.

I hung up the phone, went down to the street, got in my van, and I drove to Elizabeth Street and picked her garbage up. I get back to the office, and she calls me up. "Mayor Tony, my garbage is already gone. Thank you Mayor Tony, thank you so much. They came so quickly, and I didn't even hear the truck. Thank you for listening to me and being concerned about my garbage."

Tony pulled out his billfold to pay for the breakfast, and when I protested, he put his hand between us stopping me.

"My greatest accomplishment as mayor." He put a 30% tip on the table slipping it under his coffee cup then looked up at me, our eyes connecting. "I gave the people back their self-respect. Key West is filled with good, kind, and compassionate people. I let them know how important they really are. It's not the developers, it's not the big hotels, and it's not the big business money. It's the people that are important. I let them know they're important. That's all they needed to recapture their self-respect."

I nodded slightly, watching the satisfied smile of the man who had been named Key West's Mayor Emeritus. He tapped his finger next to the money, waving his hand over it to cut off any more protests I might have.

"Dr. School Superintendent," his eyes captured mine with their intense blue, "never forget, it's the people that are important." He waved his arms like a preacher on the pulpit proclaiming. "Fill you heart with compassion, seek the jewel in every soul, share a word of kindness, and remember, the people's what it's all about."

Absorbing the thought, I nodded my appreciation for the value of the lessons in leadership.

CHAPTER 6

I had spent the heat of the afternoon sweating by the pool, fiddling with my guitar and the Captain Tony tribute song I'd started the night before. With sweat beading my forehead, the guitar sticky in my arms, I matched chords to Tony's words from breakfast. *Fill you heart with compassion, seek the jewel in every soul, share a word of kindness, and remember; the people's what it's all about.* G to Em followed by a quick C – Am ending with a D. The music sounded like the man, intense yet uplifting.

By the time I headed back out, it was nearing the cooling hours of disappearing sun. Hanging at a deep angle over the ocean with sky blue on blue, the sun and the mercury still bubbled near sweltering having dipped a degree below 90. As I drifted lazily along Duval Street, the dampness of my body resisting the tropical heat began to build in my third tee-shirt of the day, the humidity baking through me like a sauna in the desert.

Wondering casually along the street drenched with shops, my mind drifted like a soft cloud in a blue sky with compassion being the bright sun. In front of the Key West Women's Society, a dispirited man with dirt caked feet and longing-for-shampoo dreadlocks sat on the sidewalk pounding out 60s songs on a five-string Willy Nelson guitar. His blank stare was at odds with a surprisingly pleasant and commanding voice. A few tourists, all with nicely trimmed hair and wearing rainbow colored clothes, those styles that have perfect creases pressed into their shorts, stood a cautious two-steps back from the homeless street performer. He was bold in his style strumming hard on the strings. His music was played on a guitar that, along with the homeless musician, lived trapped in the outside elements. I stopped for a moment watching and listening, the sound filling the air with an ardent melody.

In that instant, I consider how his life must have its benefits. Free of other's edifying expectations, he could play his music and sing his songs, always having curious onlookers but never showing a glimmer of awareness at the hypercritical populace passing by. His life demanded little.

I pulled some bills from my pocket, dropping them to float the last foot into his sweat-stained tattered hat, applauded my appreciation for his surprising depth of talent, and moved back into the flow of colorful pedestrians in the steady wave along Duval toward Greene Street.

One block south of Greene Street, acoustic music hung in the thick evening air floating from each of the many bars soothing the strain of mugging humidity. In Key West, affectionately called Key Wasted, there is a thing called the Duval Crawl, surviving your quest to drink a beer at every bar along the historical street that spans the mile wide island from the blue Atlantic to the aqua Gulf of Mexico. It's hard to get past this block long stretch of rowdy bars because they stock fun. Wild, enthusiastic, and often raunchy fun with gifted entertainers combining music, humor, and a devout tie with the crowd of revolving faces and bawdy belly laughs on vacation and seeking wild times. Thus, the belly cheers heighten the mystique of escaping to Key West.

Passing a bar next to a bar that was next to a bar, the energized sounds of a singer pounding strum upon strum beat out powerful chords with a fervent rendition of *American Pie*. I listened from the sidewalk, smiling to myself at the revamped chorus *and the three men I admire most, my father, his son, and Jimmy Buffett, sailed the last boat to Jamaica, the day Bob Marley died.*

Strolling on the half block to Captain Tony's Saloon, I discovered him sitting in his isolated corner with a short line of tourists who practiced foot-tapping patience as they waited to meet the legend. The bar manager, Randy, leaned on the humidity sticky tee shirt counter, half listening and half smirking. Randy knows my life. He knows traditionalist Iowa having left it behind years before escaping to warmer climates and wilder times. In many ways, I envied him, and I knew from our talks that he envied me as well. There's a sweet calm about Iowa that breeds goodness, kindness, and a heart-filled honesty. Sometimes wholesome can have its benefits.

As I stretched the one step up into the bar, Randy reached out with a handshake, firm and friendly.

"He's got'em going again." I pointed toward Tony where a flat-bellied girl was posing for a picture, her lips firmly locked onto Tony's as she lifted her shirt to show where he'd signed her tummy. "She should be treating him like a grandfather," I said.

"It's amazing." Randy shook his head with a cartoon fox smile. "I've watched him for years, and the older he gets the more he gets away with." Then he laughed, "He knows it too, 'cause he's always pushing it."

The young girl broke her lip lock and moved to kiss Tony tenderly on the check. There, I thought, there was the warmth that she would be showing a grandfather. The first kiss was for prosperity, for the picture, a souvenir of her moment with the Key West Casanova. She had kissed the Caribbean's legendary womanizer and had photographic proof. The second kiss had been for the charm, the warmth, and the kindness that exuded from him, the connection she felt with him. It was a kiss of affection for a good man with a great heart and a prized spirit.

Tony gave her a slight hug, a squeeze to her shoulder saying with all of the spirit and sincerity he could evoke, "If you ever want to have a baby, you just come see me."

Maybe 20 years old, she had a beach-built body and rich brown eyes. "You and my boyfriend," her hand rubbed seductively to his stubble cheek, "you're the only one's I'd sleep with."

Tony's grin broke wide as he waved a pointing hand toward her. "With me there'd be no sleeping."

How crude flirtations could be such a warm compliment, I was still to figure out, but the pretty, post-teen sweetheart just beamed. With sparkling eyes, bouncy hair, and a big, bright grin of delight, she leaned in and gave him one last tender kiss on his whiskered white cheek.

In that typical look of mocked shock, Tony's mouth opened, his blue eyes brightened, and he looked from me to the eye-catching temptress. She glowed buoyantly, her slight hips accentuating a chest emphasizing Victoria Secret created ripe round cantaloupes. The macaw-blue midriff top highlighted her shimmering brown hair that framed her tanned face and full, lively smile.

"You hear that Brad?" I didn't even realize he'd noticed me come in. "This beautiful young woman wants to sleep with me. That's how I want to go, making love to a beautiful young woman, someone 60 years my junior. Soft skin, firm curved body like hers," Tony grinned, still holding the fresh girl's manicured hand. "How old are you?"

Gripping Tony's hand in both of hers, she shared a hint of redness. "Twenty-two." She answered.

"Perfect," Tony exclaimed. "Meet me back here in two hours. I know a great little place. Quiet, hidden out of the way. Nobody will even know we're there. You'll love it."

Another round of laughter burst from the crowd surrounding the raunchy old man as beers lifted with a natural toast that seemingly broke out every time he spoke.

Stepping in, she gave a loving, gentle kiss, to the flirtatious Captain Tony. In his life, he was never left short of soft affection.

At the bar, I ordered a libation served in a giant Captain Tony cup, and the bartender waved away my dollar bills. Above him I could see the small trap door that led to the steamy attic room where Tony had lived for years. *Up the ladder.* It had been a moment of enticing anticipation for a woman when she went *up the ladder* with the prolific Captain Tony. Tony had lived up in the stifling second floor room for nearly two decades, lived above the bar without air conditioning, yet had no trouble leading women to the sweaty confines of his innumerable escapades.

I imagined a woman first peering above the trap door into the ventless confines where the air got even thicker. Seeing the small room of rumpled sheets and clothes thrown about, that was their grand entrance of an adventurous escape into the heat of passion. In the attic, the wench would find herself in the fertile arms of a dashing buccaneer, the wily captain of the sailing ship on the run. It didn't quite fit the true image of Tony who was short, skinny, and handsome in that Italian, fisherman way. Still, he was the captain of the ship, and the maidens loved their captain.

There was so much chronicled in this historic building, a past improved by tales of the philandering Captain. Behind the bar hanging like a dangling puppet ready for action was the pirate skeleton, scrawny like its namesake. I'd heard the rumor the skeleton had been dug up when they'd poured the concrete floor in the pool room; that it was a native Conch that was a remnant of Bone Island, or it was the last person hung, a young woman, hung from the hanging tree that actually grew, large and round, through the roof from the middle of the bar, tilting toward the Atlantic. Tony had laughed when I'd asked him about the pirate skeleton. "So many stories," he had grinned. Years ago he'd gotten the skull from a coroner friend of his. Hardly any of the bones were from the same person. They'd just kept adding to the skull until it was a full skeleton. Then they'd thrown on a pirate's bandana adding the sensation of a Disney buccaneer adventure ride.

The bar's ceiling was wallpapered with layers of time-tested business cards and bras of multiple sizes dangled from above, most with a name and date, a trophy commemorating an ill-gotten night in Captain Tony's. I looked up at the sheer aqua of a bra and thong panties that hung just beyond the hanging tree and off the end of the bar, delicacies that created a vision of sensuality. I wondered who had left this memorial surely commemorating one wild night in Tony's bar when life had taken a turn from the mundane to the moral slippage of exuberance and gaiety in Key West. To some sensuous beauty, it had been her badge of honor, a lasting memory of both her love for Tony and one fantastic night when she'd allowed her judgment to become unraveled by the island's freedom.

As the crowd broke, I was resting against the counter across from Randy when Tony stood from his four-legged stool greeting me with a firm, kind grip of my hand. Small talk went back and forth as I sipped my beverage, one arm leaning down upon the glass top counter. I was just hanging out in Captain Tony's. Curious about the history, I asked Tony a simple question, an innocent question.

I should have known that with Tony there is no such thing as simple and innocent.

"Tony." I asked, pointing at the ceiling with layer upon layer of business cards left to say *I was here and want to be a part*. "How did the business cards get started, putting business cards all over the ceiling and walls?"

Without breaking a beat, Tony danced into another of his life's tales. "I've worked hard all my life, lots of hours, determined to make my way in the world. Back then, I was working every minute I wasn't sleeping. Shrimping by day, running the bar by night, living up above the bar in a small, hot room. It was a brutal pace." As he spoke, he had the look of a man proud that he had made his own way. "Sometimes, I just needed to get away, so I'd go to Las Vegas at least one weekend a month. Sometimes I'd take my wife, sometimes my girlfriend. This time, the girl I was living with was up in New York visiting her family, and I just needed to get away, so I went to Sin City on my own."

Months before I'd been sitting at a bar in a casino in Vegas, just enjoying time alone when these two girls come up to me, gorgeous girls. Girlfriends from L.A., they had a style about them, rare beauty and a sensuality that I adored. Of course, they were working girls, prostitutes. Pretty common in Vegas. Some people might not like their profession, but to me it was simple. They were nice girls trying to make a good living with the talents they had.

So when I didn't bring anybody to Vegas with me, I'd call them. They'd come to the airport in my complimentary limousine and pick me up; all dolled up and making me look like a big shot. They'd stay with me, and I never paid them for their services, there was no business transaction. We never talked about it, but I knew what it was all about, so I'd give them money to have fun with. Remember, I'm a very gracious tipper. It was my way of thanking them for the fun we had together.

On this trip, I had one of those nights. It happens sometimes, not often, but sometimes. I had one of those nights when you can't lose. That night I was so hot if I was playing blackjack and got two queens, twenty, I'd split 'em and I take another two cards, both aces. Twenty-one twice. It was just one of those nights when I couldn't lose.

I can't lose, and I'm getting bombed on twenty year-old Scotch. Mary and Jane are watching out for me, know my luck's going one way while the Scotch is taking me another. Mary keeps saying "Come on Tony, it's time to cash in. Tony, let's cash in while you're way ahead." Knowing I treat them well, they've got a vested interest in my winnings, so they don't want the Scotch to take control and the money to slide the wrong way across the table. Besides, they liked me. How could they not when I tip like I do?

This is pissing off the pit boss. He wants to win the house money back, and this working girl's trying to talk me into leaving with all my winnings. They have opposite vested interests. This tough-guy pit boss said something to Mary, something offensive about her profession, and now I'm pissed off. I said, "Look sir, don't you question her. She's my friend, and you leave her alone." The manager of the floor comes over. We've known each other for years, and he says, "You having a problem, Tony?" I said, "Look." I didn't want the pit boss to lose his job, so I said. "Look, these ladies are with me." They knew who they were, knew they were working girls. "We're just having a good time here, and that's all

I want. Is everything okay?" I look at the pit boss, and he says, "Everything's fine sir."

I've been winning big all night. Looking at the table I'd say I'm up $70 to $80 thousand when Mary leans in again and whispers, "Tony, come on. You're way ahead. Let's call it a night. You don't need anymore aggravation, so why don't you cash in." Then she whispers a little suggestion in my ear.

I say to the pit boss, "Check me out," and I leave him a tip, a couple thousand dollars and tell him to take $10,000 out as a tip for the floor. You see people don't realize all these casino employees are getting minimum wage. That's all they get. They live on tips, and a good gambler is a great tipper. Even when I'm broke I'm a good tipper. It's my way of making sure wait people make a living. So I leave the tip, and tell the pit boss to put the rest in my account.

The next morning I wake up, me and these two playful beauties with their voluptuous, showgirl bodies. I'm trying to remember how much I'd won the night before, but my mind is foggy from Scotch and too little sleep. Now that I haven't been drinking, reason has reentered my mind, and I'm thinking about taking my winnings and going home, but I can't remember how much I'd won. I call the cage up to check on my account. They tell me that besides my marker of $50,000, I had $87,000 in my account. More than I had realized. It'd been one big night.

So I looked at the girls, all gorgeous and titillating in my bed. Nice girls, I loved these girls, cared for them and they cared for me. This is pure Captain Tony, the way I live it up with beautiful women and gambling riches, so I said, "How'd you girls like to go on a vacation, go back to Key West with me for a few days."

They're all excited, bouncing up and down, and they say, "Tony, we'd love it." I tell them I'm going to make our flight arrangements, and I gave them each $10,000 to go buy whatever they needed for the trip. That gets them even more excited.

So we're off to Key West. They bought little suitcases and some clothes though they both put most of the money in the bank, and I felt good about that. As we left Vegas, I told them, "No working in Key West. It's strictly vacation." It was all fun without the burden of money, and that was the way they liked life.

Anyway, we get to New Orleans to change planes, and we've got a three-hour layover. I'm trying to figure out what to do with three hours, and I see there's a flight leaving for the Bahamas. I get all excited and I say, "Girls, let's go to the Bahamas." Well, do you think they'd disagree? Hell no, so instead of flying into Miami, we fly to the Bahamas to do some more gambling. I'm still hot, and I win another $8,000. I can't believe it. I just couldn't lose. I'm a big shot at the tables, winning with these two gorgeous women, one on each side and getting double kisses for luck each time I roll. So we split the money three ways, and we're off to Key West.

By that night I'm walking Duval Street, these two stunning women on my arms, a ton of money in my pocket, and I'm cock of the walk. It was lifting my ego to be seen parading all over town with two magnificent beauties. People are pointing, saying, "There goes Tony again with more women. That bastard, he never lets up."

We had a great week, me and my two girls going up the ladder. At the end of the week when they were getting ready to leave, Mary says to me, "Tony we shouldn't even ask you this, you've been so good to us." I'm frowning, saying, "Go ahead, whatever you want." Mary says, "You know so many high rollers, big gamblers. Could we leave our business cards with you so when your friends are coming to Vegas you can recommend us?" Jane says, "We promise, if they mention your name, we'll be extra good to them."

Tony grinned slyly then, a smile of gratification. "I was like their coupon. Something a little extra, no additional charge, and they were so beautiful how in the hell could I say no?"

So that's how the cards got started. There used to be a pay phone over on the wall by the bar, and I told the girls, "Why don't you put your business cards on the wall above the phone." So Mary and Jane put their business cards on the wall above the phone. Then other people started putting their cards by the phone, then up on the walls and the ceiling to say they'd been to Captain Tony's Saloon.

"So that was the beginning of the business cards." Tony pointed around the bar.

I looked up at the tens of thousands of cards stapled layers of paper mache coating the bar covering the ceilings and walls. The fire codes must be loose in Key West, either that or Tony's business card wallpaper scheme was grandfathered in when the codes were adopted because the room was a tender box of dry, curled, rectangle cards from a world of business travelers who'd stopped by for a brew. Cards upon cards in layers thick of dried up kindling made the saloon look like an exploding flame waiting to happen.

The cards were so typical of Tony. Everything had a story, everything was a great adventure, a fantastic experience, and everything was connected with people. I couldn't see Tony with a woman without this great desire to know her, to learn about her, to go beyond the physical to the intimate. He liked to portray the playboy image, the man who always beds the woman, but it's more than that. He surely always got to the woman's mind first. They connect because he cares deeply about people. Two things he cares deeply about, people and sex, so his connection with women creates an intimacy, and bam, sex is happening before they know they've been consumed by his charm.

"Sounds like the girls made out pretty good with your $10,000." Call it that or not, he'd paid them pretty well.

"I was glad I could help." Then Captain leaned back on his stool studying me, his eyes boring into mine. "Remember Brad, they agreed to come with me before I gave them the money. It wasn't about money, and it wasn't about being hookers. It was about our connection, our relationship. People think of hookers as cheap women that you disrespect, but I think there's a little bit of hooker in many women just like there's some bastard in most man. Sex is somehow connected to almost everything, it drives men, it's a great motivator, and women use that." His stare was deadly serious. "A guy buys dinner, and he expects something. Don't you think women understand that?" Tony spoke with intensity as if explaining the first bite of the apple. "You think our worlds are miles apart, Iowa and Key West." His arms stretched skinny and long before me. "You ever make Denise a nice dinner, some special food, candles on the table, maybe a chocolate desert she really likes."

"Sure," I answered, "we have dates like that all of the time."

"Why?"

"Because I like doing nice things for her, making her feel special."

"Bull. It's because you like getting laid." Laughing, his finger pointed between my eyes. "Admit it."

"Well," I searched for a better answer, but knew he wouldn't accept my innocent thought of simply loving and caring for my wife.

"Don't try and fool me," Tony's finger continued its laser point at my forehead. "Do you end up in bed after those dinners?"

I looked down with a hint of embarrassment. Why, I'm not sure. "We have a healthy relationship."

"You make the meals with that in mind, don't you?" He didn't wait for an answer. "Don't you think she knows that's part of the deal?"

Like a preacher from the pulpit, his hands turned open before me.

"You see there's a little bit of that attitude in women. We men know it, and we like it. We just don't like to admit it. By not admitting it, it keeps us separated, pure from the world of Mary and Jane. But the truth is your world of special dinners and intimacy isn't so far away from my world and two very warm-hearted, beautiful, and seductive call girls. You make chocolate dessert. I give them

$10,000." His hands came back together to rest calmly in his lap. "The end result is the same. So," he put his hand to my shoulder, "if you don't judge my world quite so much, I won't make the same judgments about your world. Is that a deal?"

I stared straight at him, caught in a moment of speechlessness, unable to respond with clarity to his logic. Smiling, I surrendered to his reasoning, and nodded hoping the discussion would move on.

Squeezing a surprisingly firm grip of pressure into my shoulders, he finished. "Before you judge people, Brad, seek the jewel."

As Tony's head tilted slightly to the side, his eyes still bore in on me when three large, loud and playful women stepped through the saloon entryway.

"Captain Tony." One shouted, rushing forward arms spread wide like an eagle to embrace his skinny frame. Laughing as she did, I shook my head amazed once again while relieved at the rescue from our conversation.

As Tony hugged all three girls at once, I gave him a thumbs up, stepping around the corner of the tee shirt counter trying to erase the judgmental large-loud-woman ridiculous prejudice from my brain, trying to shake away the thoughts not based on knowledge.

Randy gave me one of those head nods, one of those 'whatdaya-think-about-that' nods. "Have you seen those *One Human Family* bumper stickers around Key West?" he asked.

"How can you miss them?" I'd seen them on cars, buildings, bicycles, those white stickers with the bold black printing proclaiming *"Official Philosophy of Key West, Florida – All People are Equal Members of One Human Family."*

"Hookers, homeless, gays, business people, musicians, tourists, jerks, deadbeats, lovers, politicians, and hard working bar managers," Randy shrugged his own understanding of the slogan. "Tony welcomes them all."

I repeated the words in my head. One human family. Then I reminded myself. Seek the jewel in every soul.

"This bar has so much history," Tony's hands waved like a magic wand. "Years ago this was the end of the island. The ocean was about a 100 feet that way." Pointing to the west. "Then they kept filling in and filling in. Developers," he shook his head with disgust. "Concrete junkies."

I pointed toward the tree in the middle of the bar. "So that was once a hanging tree?"

"Tennessee Williams had a lover," Tony jumped into what I thought was a different subject. "When he died, well, Tennessee had bought his lover these two monkeys. Lioness and ... Oh damn, I forget the other one's name. Anyway, with his lover gone, Tennessee didn't know what to do with the monkeys, so he convinced me to put a wire cage around the hanging tree. We put the monkeys in there and for three years they lived in the bar and climbed on that tree."

I pointed through the dim light of the dingy bar. "One of the bartenders told me that there was a lady buried on the other side of the bar, where the tombstone is in the cement, and she was the last person hung in the tree. He said she haunts the place."

Tony waved his hand at the silliness. "There're so many stories. People get them mixed up, confused, though they make for great lore." Tony took a slight sip from his ginger ale. "The hanging tree, the lady buried in the pool room, the tombstone, and the ghost. They're all different, except I think the ghost might be the last lady to dangle dead from the hanging tree."

This part of the bar used to be a patio, and that tree which is still alive was in the middle of the patio. The tree used to get little white caterpillars all over it. Things would fall off the tree and hit people. Plus there was the heat. You could only sit out here about four months out of the year.

This was one of those moments with Tony, one of those times where he starts into a story, and you find yourself intrigued, captured by his sharp memory, his life worlds apart from Iowa, and his knack for taking a great story, throwing in a little color, and making it even better.

I was going to make the bar bigger by enclosing the patio, and I'd made up my mind that the tree had to go. You can see it from outside, all green and tall towering above this bar in the middle of old town. I had guys come down from Miami to look at cutting it down. We were just going to get rid of it.

About a week before they were going to come in with the chainsaws, this old man stops by. He says, "Captain Tony, are you going to cut the tree down?" I tell him, "Yes, we are. The caterpillars are making a mess." He says, "Captain Tony, you can't cut that tree down." He must have been about my age now, 87. An old man with a lot of history, and this was about thirty years ago. He says, "You can't cut that tree down." When I asked why, he says, "That used to be the hanging tree." I love the old stories of the town, so I asked him to tell me about it.

His name was Mr. Roberts. He was an old man then, in his eighties who had lived much more of the history in Key West than anybody in town. He says, "When I was a boy, we used to come here on Sundays with a soda pop and sandwich, and we'd watch them hang people."

Tony looked up, his eyes alive. "After I heard that story, Brad. I couldn't cut the tree down. How do you cut down such a piece of history?" Flipping his hand with a wave of surety, the answer was so simple for Tony.

There're a lot of stories about the bar. Back in the 60s there was this big deal going on about old bottles. People were collecting them, selling them, antique old bottles. The bar was built on top of an old city dump, and the pool room used to have a dirt floor, so we started digging in there looking for old bottles. We found a bunch. You can still see them in the foundation where we dug down a couple of feet.

Anyway, we dug down a little ways, and we found this big flat piece of metal. We lifted it up, and it's covering an old well. Down at the bottom of the well is a body, a female who's been preserved at the bottom of the well for God knows how long. We had no idea how many years she'd been down there, no idea who she was. There was a story that the last woman hanged was having an affair with the mortician who ran the morgue that was in this building then. They said she was hanged to prevent her from telling of his indiscretions. Some people thought that was her at the bottom of the old well. I don't know. We tried to find out who she was, but never could, so we covered the well back up, and poured concrete onto the floor.

"There really is a person buried over there?"

Tony nodded with his matter-of-fact surety.

I walked around the bar, past the smiling pirate skeleton, between the acoustic guitar player and around the fireplace where Tony used to sit with Jimmy Buffett. I stepped two steps down into the pool room, and there on the concrete floor was a tombstone. *Elvira. Daughter of Joseph and Savannah Meads. Died December 2, 1822. Ag'd 19 years, 8 m.s. & 21 d.s.* Glancing up, in the rough foundation between the poured floor and the rock wall foundation were pieces of old bottles, colored bottles, green and brown, sides and bottoms sticking out from the edge.

Tony was smiling when I came back, knowing it had been exactly as he'd said.

"So," I questioned, "the woman buried in the well is not Elvira?"

Tony shook his head. "Everybody thinks it is." He gave a simple shrug as if it didn't matter. "After we found the body, my girlfriend Stacy went back to Virginia to visit friends. She found the discarded tombstone, and brought it back. We put it over the grave. No connection except it was nice to have a tombstone over the mummified body of the woman buried in the well."

"But you think she's the ghost?" The mystique intrigued me.

"Don't know?" Tony stated then he went on.

They've done cable television episodes on the Lady in the Blue Dress that haunts this place. Nobody knows exactly who she is, but many of us have seen her. Years ago, when my girlfriend Stacy was working with me here in the bar the Lady in the Blue Dress appeared. I was cashing out and Stacy was cleaning up late in the night after the bar closed, and the Lady in the Blue Dress walks right through the bar. We looked at each other wondering who the hell that was. The bar was closed and empty except for us, so where'd this blue dressed lady come from?

I ran outside to see where she went, and there was nobody there. She was right there walking through the bar and then disappeared the instant she stepped outside. Later the same thing happened again to Stacy. She's here alone in the bar, and the Lady in the Blue Dress walks through without saying a word. Scared Stacey to death. That's why she left me. She couldn't live above the bar, up the ladder, knowing this ghost in a blue dress was wandering around.

I looked over at Randy as he leaned against the tee-shirt counter, and he gave me a slight shrug as if that's just the way it is.

"Have you seen her?"

Randy duplicated his shrug. "I haven't but I've heard the stories, and I can tell you that some weird things have happened, unexplainable things unless you believe in the Lady in the Blue Dress."

There I was standing in the oldest bar in Florida set on top of a filled in city dump and named for a philandering sea captain. There was an historical tree towering out the roof that use to be the hanging tree, a buccaneer skeleton of discarded body parts laughing a pirate's grin, a woman mummified and buried in an abandoned well, and somewhere floating among us was a ghost dressed in a flowing blue gown; all in an ancient, rickety tilted building that surely held the spirits of many more who had been hanged and left captured between life and the hereafter. I wondered what Elvira would have thought about being thrust into the middle of this pirate's cove.

Tony greeted another couple, listening intently as the husband introduced himself telling of his admiration for the Captain. When he backed away, his lovely wife with a Stepford smile stepped forward decorated in department store creased designer clothes of white and red with perfect hair sprayed unyielding in place and shimmering red manicured nails glued on in simulated exactness. As she leaned toward Tony, I expected her to offer a make-up protecting air kiss, but instead of air separating them, the woman bowed to hold him warmly. Giving a gentle hug of genuine affection, she whispered intimately into Tony's hearing aide. They seemed to hold each other in a way that they'd known before until she stood, and with unspoken words in her eyes, they shared a lingering moment.

From behind them, the husband couldn't see the way they held hands gently, the way she squeezed his hand before letting go, or the slight tears forming in her eyes. When they separated, her head remained bowed, and she moved past her unsuspecting mate, never looking into his eyes.

Tony watched her slide easily away leading her husband to follow, as she silently left the saloon and disappeared down the tourists filled walkway.

"You never know," Tony said, his head shaking to revive the memory. "I recognized her right away. A few years ago she came in with a bunch of girl friends. Her friends wandered on, but she stayed and sat at the end of the bar. Right over there, where Jimmy and I sat that one night." He pointed to the corner closest to the stage. "Cried a lot that afternoon. That's what I remembered about her. How she cried through her make-up, black streams like rain in mud streaking down her face."

The softness in his voice was gentle like a caring father remembering the pain he'd helped his daughter through. It was not something sorted or inappropriate between them, as I had imagined. Instead it was something deeper, something of friendship, kindness, and compassion.

"She'd had an affair, and was afraid her husband would find out," Tony explained. "I spent a lot of time just listening and giving a little advice." Tony took a deep breath, releasing it slowly from his damaged lungs, his shoulders drooping slightly as he did. "You never know how you're going to impact people."

"What'd she say?"

"She said, *Thank you Tony. I took your advice and my marriage has been wonderful ever since. Thank you for saving my marriage.*"

"What was your advice?" I asked cautiously and curious.

Tony smiled, his grin compassionate and charming all at once. "Hell if I know." His shoulders lifted then fell in a lost memory. "I remember her face. I remember all the pretty girls, but I can't remember a damn thing I told her." His eyes brightened a bit moving past the memory of her sad moment in time. "If I had to guess, I'd guess I told her to go back and give her husband all the love she felt for him. Never tell him about the affair, I'm sure I must have told her that. People call that honesty, telling about an affair, that crap about not being able to live with themselves and the dishonesty in their relationship. Truth is, they know it will hurt the other person. It's the final act of inflicting pain on their spouse by somehow thinking it relieves them of their own guilt. Deep in their mind they know it only hurts the other person, and the relationship never really recovers from the honesty of their betrayal. I probably told her if she loved him to cry so much, she should show him that she loved him that much. Quit the affair, and make love to your husband in a way that shows him how much you love him. I probably told her something like that."

"Strange words," I said, "from such a philanderer."

Tony shrugged, "A philanderer who has been with the same woman for 30 years." Then, with a bit of sadness as his voice dropped, "Not that I haven't had my indiscretions."

When I was 82 I had a heart attack. After twenty-five years, I'd moved out of our home, away from Marty, and I was living with a 30-year-old. We were having sex, great sex when 'bam,' I had a heart attack. I remember lying in the hospital bed in Miami. My girlfriend was on one side of the bed, and my wife,

Marty, on the other side. I had to make a choice, my girlfriend or my wife. That was when I realized how important my marriage was. I had to go home. It took me until I was 82 to fully appreciate Marty and the commitment of a lasting relationship. I'm a very lucky man to have married her. A philanderer, yes, but a very lucky man. Like that woman that just left. If she was crying that much over her husband, she loved him and needed to be with him. I felt the same thing in that Miami hospital. I loved Marty, and I needed to be with her. That's when I finally realized I loved one woman and made a lasting commitment to Marty.

"Hey." Tony interrupted his own story, waving to a thirtyish man stepping into the bar. "Doc Mike."

The man reached in engulfing the Captain's hand with his own hefty grip. A tall, athletic man with robust dark hair, Doc Mike looked like somebody fresh off the beach version of *Northern Exposure*. He smiled with an unassuming grin as if he expected nothing but knew much more than he should.

"Tell him Mike," Tony pointed toward me. "Tell him I'm indestructible."

"He should have been dead two decades ago," Doc Mike's smile grew with his first-hand knowledge. "He's a contradiction of medical science. The cigarettes alone should have killed him not to mention a whole bunch of angry husbands."

Randy reached over the souvenir counter, shaking Mike's hand as he did. "Tell Brad the fishhook story." He pointed from Mike to me.

Mike gave me a nod as I felt the firm warmth of his handshake.

"Brad's a great writer, writing a book about me," Tony explained. "That fish hook story'd be great in the book. Tell him that one."

Mike laughed a bit, that chuckle of bringing a memory back to the present, then turned to me and started telling the story. "Tony got caught," he grinned.

"I had this girl who was hugging me, kissing me right here." Tony reached for his earlobe. "She's got this earring made from a fishhook. All of the sudden, the hook caught here."

Tony stuck his finger inside his lip and yanked like he'd just been hooked, his head tilted sideways dangling helpless from the imaginary fishing line.

"We couldn't get it out because of the barb." Tony wiggled like a fish fighting to be free, his body gyrating as his finger still played the hook yanking on his lip. "Her ear's nearly in my mouth and neither one of us could move. Everybody's gathered around trying to figure out how to unhook me, and somebody's saying call Mike. We need to call Doc Mike."

Mike, leaning on the counter, spoke as if it's an everyday part of his doctor life. "It's about one in the afternoon, and I get this call at the clinic. They want me to come down to Captain Tony's." He wrinkled his face like what the heck for? "I ask why, concerned that Tony might really have a medical emergency, thinking they should call the EMTs, and they tell me Tony has a fishhook in his face. No heart attack, nothing serious, just a fishhook in his mouth. So I have to come down and perform a little surgery right here in the bar. I do a little cut and snip to remove the fishhook and the lady attached to it from Tony's mouth."

Tony was bouncing up and down, wiggling like a fish just thrown back in the ocean, laughing at the story. "For a moment, I'd thought my fourth wife had caught me. Set the hook and wouldn't let go."

I watched Tony with that inner feeling of wonder, not so much from the story or the vision of Tony hooked to some lady that I'm sure was a quarter of his age, but of this man of 87 years. He was bursting with enthusiasm bouncing in spirited delight at the story. His energy, the energy motivated by his stories about people, electrified him causing his arms to become as animated as his hearty laugh. As the joy of life spread around him, Tony was in the center drawing us all in, the master storyteller. He loved his stories.

As the laughter slowly faded to that moment after the story when nobody talks but everybody communicates, a family of tourists gathered behind us. I could see in the eyes of the mother that hesitation, that moment of wanting to step forward but some unsurety stopped her, her hand resting on her young son's shoulder holding him in place.

"You want to meet Captain Tony?" I motioned her forward.

The woman shook her head in the same way I might. Wanting to, but not wanting to interrupt, not wanting to be a bother, and being content to be this close. I knew that when she left without meeting him, there would be the disappointment of being so close but never knowing, knowing what the moment might hold when she shook his hand, talked to him eye to eye, and shared one private moment with a legend.

"Tony." I stepped back to open the space between myself and the boy. "I think this young man would like to meet the legendary Captain Tony."

Tony's face jumped into excitement as his arms opened to welcome him, his goatee surrounding a happy smile with bright obliging blue eyes, big and round.

"Have I got something for you." Tony danced sideways back to his stool and pulled a paper from beneath his oxygen tank. Holding the picture up, it was a letter size copy of the 30" x 30" black and white print that graced the wall of the bar. Tony waved the boy and his mother to him. "Do you know who Jimmy Buffett is?"

The blond boy with bangs cut straight across his eyebrows, maybe nine years old, a third or fourth grader, stepped closer as Tony held the picture before him. With a slight nod he spoke shyly, "My Mom and Dad always listen to him in the car."

Again, Tony's surprise broke out all over his face, his bushy eyebrows lifting high on his forehead. As he grinned, he leaned forward holding the picture closer for the boy to see. "This is Jimmy Buffett," his hand moved slightly, "and this is Captain Tony. The picture was taken right here in this bar."

The young boy's eyes opened wide realizing he was seeing a famous singer.

"Can I give you this?" Tony asked now nearly eye to eye with the young towhead.

His mother's excitement brightened the glow in her eyes. "He'd like that very much." She spoke kindly to the Captain, obviously wanting it too.

Tony placed the picture on the counter. "What's your name young man?"

"Alex." He spoke at ease with the grandfatherly legend.

Tony pressed his marker to the picture writing above it *To Alex* – and below it he signed *Capt. Tony.*

"Now." Tony gently touched the small boy's chin, his eyes glancing up at his young mother. "I want you to do two things for me. Can you do that?"

With a slight rebound in his blond hair, Alex nodded childlike agreement.

"Good," Tony said, patting him gently on the shoulder as he handed him the treasured picture. "Two things." He leaned forward, his blue eyes only a foot from the boy's. "I want you to hang this picture someplace special in your room. Can you do that?"

Again the boy nodded, his eyes not leaving Tony's. Above him, his mother stepped forward to slightly touch and admire the photo. His father joined them now, offering a respectful nod of thanks to Tony.

Turning his eyes back to the boy, Tony said. "The other thing I want you to promise me." The boy was nodding, whatever the Captain wanted. "This is very important." Tony's voice turned softer, more intent. "Whatever you do in your life, I want you to promise me this one thing. Okay." He waited for the next nod as the boy's hair flowed up and down. "Whatever you do, no smoking. Okay. No smoking cause those cigarettes will kill you." He tapped the oxygen tub in his nose. "I smoked for sixty years, and now I have to breath this oxygen to live. Smoking did this to me, so please, no smoking ever. Do you understand?

"Yes," the young man answered clearly.

"What are you going to do?" Tony asked.

"Put this in a special place," he held up the autographed photo, "and don't smoke."

"Good." Tony spoke in a calm, kind voice while the boy's head bobbed. As he did, Alex's father reached his hand over his wife's shoulder.

"Thank you Captain Tony." He said with heartfelt sincerity.

I reached toward the camera in Alex's mother's hand. "Can I take your picture with Captain Tony?"

Tony stepped back to make room. "Please. Right here. The whole family."

I motioned for them to step in.

"Could we?" She asked, still not wanting to be a burden.

"Of course." Tony waved them forward, slightly hunched and shuffling to the side for them to join him. "Please," he waved again, "right here next to me."

When they all huddled around him, Alex down in front with his parents on each side, Tony squeezed a bit closer to Alex's mother whispering so only the adults could hear.

"After you get your husband back to your motel," his head tipped against the pretty young mother's, "you sneak out and come back here. I'll show you a good time."

I snapped the picture as Tony and Alex's parents all laughed with Alex standing in front, beaming a big boy grin, Captain Tony's hand resting on his shoulder.

An hour later the bar was shoulder-to-shoulder people as the late night drinking crowd began to arrive, yet the line to meet Tony had faded for a moment. As a Parrothead, my curiosity had been strong, but I had avoided the topic. My relationship with Tony was becoming so valuable that I didn't want him to think I was in anyway taking advantage of our growing friendship. Still, I'm sure he was expecting it. Jimmy Buffett and the song he'd written about his old friend had helped make Tony the legend he is today.

"So, Tony." I sensed the comfort of a trusted friendship. "The song by Jimmy Buffett, where did the title *Last Mango in Paris* come from?"

"You know, Brad. I'm not really sure." He went silent with that, as if searching the archives of his mind for that relic of history that might be a clue. "I'll tell you where I think it came from." His grin was deadly serious.

"Please." Intrigued, I pulled closer.

For the past few years I had been listening continually to Jimmy Buffett. He was my diversion from the mundane life of a school administrator into the fun of an expatriate's escape to the lower latitudes. His songs eased the stress and made me feel playful, adventurous. In my car, driving between schools, to meetings, or late in the evening away from a long day at work, Jimmy Buffett's music gave me a sense of calm, youth, and tropical adventures.

Tony edged toward me as we huddled, Captain Tony and I in a whispered moment alone in the jam-packed saloon.

"The mango has a very beautiful fruit." His voice scratched hard from so many years of smoking. "It's very beautiful, the mango fruit, and it has incredible blooms that are very beautiful flowers, colorful and bright flowers that are like a lei flower." Clearing his throat with a slight cough, a twinkle came to his eye as Tony imitated a long drag on his nicotine inhaler. "Jimmy knows me very well, very well," his voice lowered even more. "I like to believe that Jimmy knows me so well that in the song title the mango is representative of a beautiful woman."

Gagging on my drink, liquid spurted from my mouth, and I jumped backward as it ran over my chin like the overflow of a too full bucket. The unexpected image of the Captain and the song lyrics flashed in my mind with too much visual clarity, and I fought the surge from my nose, choking away the image.

Pointing at me, Tony's chest moved up and down in the hilarity of his own joke. "I got you good on that one." His laughter grew louder as his hand fell on my arm balancing himself against his own raunchy humor. "I got you good, Brad."

Our laughter settled in with both of us holding each other like long lost friends caught up in their greatest memory, unable to stop chuckling, to control the humor of the past. Tony moved closer as if whispering a shared secret. There was an intimacy in the way he spoke, a trust that I knew I would not violate.

Years later, I'm sitting at the bar, and I see Jimmy walking out front along the sidewalk on Greene Street. I called out to him 'Son come and have a seat.' Jimmy came in, and we sat right over there at the corner of the bar. We talked for hours, me and Jimmy. It was like a father and son getting together after so many years. There was so much to say, so much to talk about. We talked about the times he played in here, the people we knew, the friends we'd made, and our love for this island. Jimmy looked at me, and said 'Tony, you've been doing this for so long. You have money. Why do you keep working, coming to the bar, telling stories and sharing with everybody that will listen?' I looked at my friend, and I think my exact words were 'Because, Jimmy, there's still so many things to do.'

After a couple of hours, I realized the sun had fallen and it was darker, getting late. I told Jimmy I had to meet my wife. I knew she was waiting for me, and I had to go. Then I went to the restroom. When I came out, I walked straight out of the bar because I hadn't realized how late our conversation had made me. So like the day, I just disappeared. I can see Jimmy, after I left, wandering into the pool room and reading all the newspaper articles and accounts of my life on these dingy walls.

I now understood why I felt the warmth of emotions every time I heard Buffett sing Tony's song in concert. I realized that Capitan Tony had just shared with me something so intimate and so important in his life. He had shared with me his memory of one night with Jimmy Buffett. Not the famous Jimmy Buffett, not the legendary Jimmy Buffett, but Jimmy Buffett, his lifetime friend. Tony shared with me his memory of one night of conversation with the man he had been like a father to, an evening between two life-long friends that had become the inspiration for one of my very favorite Jimmy Buffett songs.

A while after that Jimmy stopped by and handed me a tape, told me to listen to it. We were busy, and I put it by the rest of the music and forgot about it. A few days later I was in New York on a speaking engagement, and I heard a song come over the limo radio. It was Jimmy's voice, and I heard the words 'I went down to Capitan Tony's.' I said to the limo driver 'What's that?' He thought I didn't like the music, rock n' roll modern stuff, so he switched stations. I was in a panic, yelling for him to find the song again, but he never did.

All the time I was in New York I wondered what that song was about, that Buffett song with the line 'I went down to Captain Tony's.' Days later when I got back here, I found the tape and put it on the bar stereo. There it was. Last Mango in Paris. It was about me and Jimmy and our conversation that night here in the saloon.

Tony stood as tall as his aged body would allow. There was a depth to his eyes, a deep blue of time and knowledge as he spoke with pride.

"I like to think," the old man said, "that song was Jimmy's thanks to me for helping him along the way."

As I listened, I knew that was the moment Tony and I became true friends. It was in the way he shared the story, the warmth of his smile, his clear blue eyes unhesitant to look straight into mine, and the caring touch of his hand to my forearm. It was the intimacy with which we spoke, one to another without regarding the rest of the world. I had found a friend, a friend that would not judge but accept, a friend who would not forget but remember, and a friend who expected nothing more of me than my friendship. In the trust and the teasing and the way we laughed together, I knew I had found a friend for life.

Yes, I was writing a book about a legendary man, but in that moment the book seemed irrelevant. Whatever I had committed, the time and money, if the book was never published, my time with Captain Tony was the most important part of the experience. We don't have many of those friends in our lives, and to have a man of compassion draw me into his life as a true friend was a treasure found. I could almost hear him saying *Brad, it's not about the book. It's about the people.* I was beginning to learn the lesson.

The Salt of Key West – Captain Tony

Captain Tony, wife Mae, and daughter Coral
showing off a day's catch in 1955.

Captain Tony as a charter boat captain with three
regular customers from Cleveland.

Captain Tony celebrates the Conch Republic independence
from the United States 1992.

Photo by Rob O'Neal

Record 12' tiger shark caught by Captain Tony with his daughters
Little Toni and Coral in 1964. Jaws were in the Smithsonian
Institute.

Capt. Tony as a pirate in the 2005 movie *CrossBones*.

Capt. Tony and a young Jimmy Buffett in 1987

At the Chart Room, Capt. Tony and Doug Rassler, lead
singer of the Cedar Island Band from Cedar Rapids, IA

Author Brad Manard, wife Denise, and Capt. Tony
at Capt. Tony's Saloon 2003

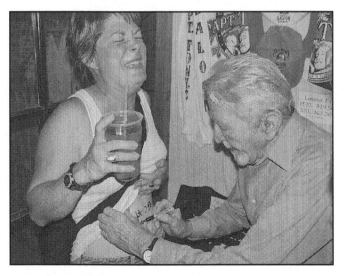

Amy Beenblossom of Iowa City, IA, has her belly autographed
by Captain Tony in Capt. Tony's Saloon 2004.

Captain Tony with Isle of Iowa Parrotheads Deanna Steggall,
Denise Manard, and Deb Rassler.

Illustrated by Diana Neville – Key West 1990

Captain Tony celebrates his 85th birthday.

Photo by Rob O'Neal

Captain Tony does "Fins" for his Isle of Iowa Parrothead
friends at MOTM in 2006.

Captain Tony, Jimmy Buffett, and Sunshine Smith
at the 20th Anniversary of the first Margaritaville
opening in Key West, FL 2005

Photos by Rob O'Neal

Captain Tony (90 years old), son Louie (70 years old), and son Tony Junior or TJ (20 years old) 2006.

Photo by Rob O'Neal

Captain Tony and wife, Marty, at Tony's 90th Birthday Party 2006

Photo by Rob O'Neal

CHAPTER 7

It was another sun-drenched morning in the sandy land of palms, so I had slipped into my comfort clothes, a white tank top adorned with an animated pirate parrot, cool khaki shorts, and suede leather flip-flops. I could easily be mistaken for a local strolling the deserted morning streets before the tourists began to emerge from a restful night in their lavish suites.

I had walked the several blocks down Duval Street in rhythm with the snap-snap of my flip-flops, nodding good morning greetings to the storeowners readying their wares for the daily invasion. The connection with Tony had created a renewed optimism that overpowered any pessimism that might slip into the mind from its well-hidden recesses. *It's the people* kept floating in the air about me, and I felt like everyone I passed was a friend-to-be.

Wandering lazily down Caroline Street, I enjoyed a tasty pecan pancake breakfast in the open air of Pepe's, Key West's oldest restaurant serving locals since 1909. Afterwards, as I strolled somewhat aimlessly, I thought of Buffett's *Changes* and the lost connections in my life. We should not let that happen with friends. *The people's what it's all about. Take time.* Echoed in my mind. *Take time for the people you love*. We all need a shared bottle of Caribbean rum, a beach drenching sunset, and time with friends. "Cheers."

I raised my imaginary rum tumbler to old friends and new ones to come.

At noon, I found myself strolling the wooden planks along the harbor of Key West Bight. The docks of Key West have become an expression of the island's changing times and transition. Once a fishing mecca of salty sailors and smelly shrimpers, the docks now reflect the combined economy of life and lifestyles. The shrimp boats still speckle the multitude of slips throughout the harbor, but intermixed among them are tall sailing ships with masts restored as statements of preserved history. There are military boats now used for commercial nostalgia tours, and small sailboats owned by those who live to have the wind at their back. Bleach white yachts of the rich and famous dwarf the one-man operated charter fishing boats. Catamaran sailing cruise boats designed to pack 40 tourists onto the deck for snorkeling or dolphin tours lined the boardwalk, and every so often there was a dinghy. After all, what would a small island harbor be without a dinghy?

Tony met me there, and we strolled the slatted walkway along the docks from the fine dining restaurants past Jimmy Buffett's well-disguised recording studio to the open and airy modern day pirate bar. We found ourselves sitting among local ruffians and early drinking tourists at a table slightly teeter-tottering on the rock floor, an arm's reach from the warm summer water at the Schooner Wharf.

A smoky-voiced man of dry humor was playing a worn acoustic guitar, singing about how much better life was drinking beer in a tourist's bar then living up north with his ex-wife and her greatest physical attributes. As he sang a sly smirk appeared below his long billed hat. The bartender sported a sweat stained tank top advertising the bar while our waitress had to be barely out of high school. She was surely living an adventure that must be distressing her protective parents, who were probably somewhere in the Midwest greatly regretting that one last family vacation they took to Key West.

"Used to be all shrimp boats out there." Tony waved his hand as if casting a line out across the harbor. "It was a hard life, shrimping, but a good life on the water. Pink gold they called the shrimp. You can only catch them at night down here. Shrimping at night for pink gold."

As the young waitress approached us, her face was pure silk and tan. She had long, straight blond hair with sun-kissed highlights pulled back into a tight ponytail. Her too small tank top and more than tight-fitted flared shorts were designed specifically for generous tips. Tony's eyes brightened, and I could already envision him leaving too many dollar bills on the tilty table. When she greeted us with a co-ed smile of bright teeth and shiny lip-gloss, Tony was quick to draw her attention.

"You're beautiful." Pointing to her as he turned my way, his eyes were round like blue marbles as if he were seeing rare exquisite beauty. "Isn't she beautiful? So beautiful." His mouth hung open astonished.

"Yes she is." I gave her a playful nod more reserved than the blatant flirtations of my philandering friend, and she grinned right back with innocent dimples decorating each cheek.

"Your boyfriend's a very lucky man." Tony patted her manicured hands where they rested on the edge of the table.

Blushing slightly, her eyes diverting downward. "I don't have a boyfriend."

Tony's face perked up with optimism, his smile ready for a great laugh. Leaning in he whispered loud enough for everybody to hear. "You want one?"

As her youthful blush grew only accentuating her beauty, she slipped one smooth hand from beneath his seasoned one, pointing at his ornery grin. "The bartender told me about you. You're Captain Tony aren't you?"

"Yes I am." He sat just a little straighter puffing his skinny chest full.

Waving him away, she held her own, a waitress already experienced with oversexed men released on vacation.

"I like *The Last Mango in Paris.*" she said with a sensuous flutter of her eyes. "Would you sign my tee-shirt?" Handing him her pen, she leaned forward for him to autograph her tank top just above her left breast. "My dad's a Buffett fan," she told him. "He'll get a kick out of this."

"Sign your tee shirt? Sweetheart," he said. I knew what was coming. I'd heard it so many times, and every time the woman smiles as if she'd just been given the greatest of compliments. Tony held the pen between them. "Honey, I'd marry you."

Then Tony reached up, his hand resting unoffensively just above her breast, and he wrote across the rim of her tank top *I love you. Captain Tony.*

"Thanks." She smiled all young, blond, and innocent, leaning forward to kiss him on the cheek causing Tony's grin to grow like a smiley-face balloon.

As she left with our drink orders, Tony admired the sway of her slight hips. "Beautiful. Nice girl. Key West is full of them. Striking young girls come to live their dream in the tropics. They have a vision of life in a bikini on a beach and end up spending all their time working in bars to pay the rent."

"Yes," I agreed, as there was no doubt. Looking off over the half-empty mid-day docks, I pointed outward, "Did you spend a lot of time here?"

"The docks? This place was my life." His hand lifted to his white goatee rubbing it knowingly. "This is where I learned about people, learned that people are what it's all about."

The cute waitress slipped between us, setting a soda before Tony, an iced tea with a healthy slice of lemon in front of me. We both thanked her, and her smile along with a mischievous wink thanked us back.

"First I was a cook on Bernie McCracken's shrimp boat. Then I learned to be a striker." Tony pointed out over the boardwalk. "That's how I got started. Then I became a shrimp boat captain and eventually a charter boat captain. But I worked hard. I always lived hard. I'd be on the boat at seven in the morning, back in at five, and I'd head down to the bar where I lived. I've told you that I lived in a little room above the bar. You had to climb up the ladder to a little trap door above the bar. I told you about that."

I nodded acknowledging the stories of the night before.

"The women used to love it, going up the ladder. Anyway, I'd be behind the bar by seven and work until two in the morning. Then I'd go up the ladder. I'd be back down at six cleaning the bar, hosing down the sidewalk, and then head to the Greyhound for a day on the ocean. It was a hard life I lived."

I was a shrimper, but I used to hang around the charter boats. Mae, my second wife, we'd just had Coral, and I were always looking for some extra money. One charter boat, the Greyhound, owned by Captain Clyde Montgomery, was a party boat that would load up with tourists and take them fishing. He was only getting five or ten people a day, and Captain Montgomery told me every customer I could get on the boat, he'd pay me a dollar.

Mae and I, we were typical New Jersey hustlers, fast and smooth talking, you know. So Mae would put on this little short shorts outfit with a push-up bra and a little captain's hat, and we'd hustle people onto the Greyhound, Captain Montgomery's boat. Me, the fast talker, and Mae, all gussied up, people were drawn to us. Pretty soon, we were getting all the customers and making an extra dollar off each one. It's a great deal for Mae and me, and a great deal for Captain Montgomery because he gets more customers, more profit, and he gets to keep the profits from the fish he sells after his customers catch them.

There was this one customer on the boat. His name was Vincent Neiman, Vincent and his wife. They were involved with a new frozen fish business in Doylestown, Pennsylvania, Mrs. Paul's Frozen Fish. On this day, he had a big grouper on. Montgomery was trying to tell him how to land it, and Vincent was fighting with everything he had, but he tied the breaker too tight and broke the line. Montgomery went crazy, called Vincent a "horse's ass," screaming at him about how stupid he was for not listening to him. Vincent didn't like that too much, so when we got back to the dock, he invited Mae and me out to dinner.

Vincent takes us out to a nice restaurant and says, "You know, I like you and Mae. You're nice people. The captain wants to sell the Greyhound. He wants $5,000 for the boat. Why don't you buy it?" I said, "Vincent, $5,000 might as well be five million to me. I don't have that kind of money." That's when Vincent told me what he wanted. "I need fresh fish for my frozen fish business."

He's thinking how this can benefit us both. He needs the fish, and I'd love to have my own boat, so after a long discussion, he convinces me to allow him to loan me the money to buy the Greyhound. It turns out to be a good deal for both of us. I'm shipping him fish in dry ice, and he's giving me a penny a pound for shrimp and fish. That's how I was eventually able to pay off my first boat.

"You see, Brad, good things come to good people." A slight glimmer came to the Captain's eye. "Montgomery didn't look for the jewel, he only criticized the person. In the end, the simple act of being nice to Vincent Neiman changed my whole life."

Mae and I loved the charter boat business, and we were good at it. Our charter business was growing. I would hustle and Mae'd smile and shake her hips. People'd come up, the men with their eyes on Mae, and I'd say, "Where are you from?" And they'd say something like, "Columbus, Ohio." I'd say, "What a great town. I'd love to talk to you about it, but I need to get a cigarette. Could you wait right here for just a moment?" Course the men wouldn't leave with Mae doing her thing, and I'd run down below deck where I had a little book that listed every city that had 125,000 people or more. It listed the mayor, what the businesses were, important information about the city. I'd come back up and say stuff I'd read in the book, stuff like, "Columbus, Ohio. You're mayor's Italian. He must be a great mayor, being Italian and all. And you've got a great university there. Are you an Ohio State fan?" After I'd talked them up, created a connection between us, they couldn't wait to get on my boat.

Tony looked out over the bight, that inlet of water surrounded by the docks, his finger tapping the table in a steady rhythm between us. "I had trouble back then. Key West wasn't a nice tourist town 50 years ago. Men were rough and tough. Sea goin' sons-a-bitches."

I looked in the direction his finger tapped toward. "What kind of trouble?"

"The charter captains had a good life then." He leaned backward picking up his soda and sipping slightly, a drop trickling into his beard. "They'd sit back and wait for the business to walk in. Weather not so great, they'd say come back in an hour and we'll see. The tourists always came back." Tony dabbed his beard with the cocktail napkin, and the drop disappeared. "Then this little WOP and his wife with that sweet little sailor's hat comes along and hustles all their business away."

I shrugged, leaning in. "You had to make a living too."

"Yeah, but I was an outsider." He shrugged back. "They did stuff, bad stuff."

"What stuff?"

"Brad." He looked at me like my father looks at me about to tell me the ways of the world. "It was different then. Nearly lawless." The Captain took a deep ocean air breath then allowed it to slowly ease from his soiled lungs. "They cut the lines on my boat, stuck ice picks in my car tires. One day I walked down on those docks to my boat, and they had smeared human waste all over it."

"No shit." I blurted.

Tony broke into a big, laughing grin, "Lot's of shit. All over my boat."

Belly laughs filled the air between us as we each reached for the other's arm, holding each other as our bodies shook in spasms of laughter. Choking through the deep voice cackling, I held his forearm tighter as Tony did the same, a firm grip on mine. The laughter lasted, not wanting to go away, good friends hooting uncontrollably like a night in a comedy club.

"So," the words surged from me despite so much breath lost on laughter. Slowly, reluctantly, I released his arm, regaining the oxygen flow to my lungs and brain. "I bet you were pretty angry."

Tony's gaiety quickly turned to a distraught nod. "Sad to say, I bought a gun. Didn't want to hurt anyone, but they were ruining my business. My boat smelled so bad. Human waste spread all over it. When I came back with the gun, the police chief happened to be on the docks. I'm thankful for that now. There was a lot of anger in me." Tony's eyes lifted to mine, his atrophied shoulders slightly rounded. "I wasn't looking for the jewel so well that day, not focusing on compassion."

I was so angry, I went down to the hardware store and bought a .38 and 50 shells. I walked back to the dock and near my boat there were five captains sitting there waiting for tourists to come to them. One of 'em says, "There goes that smart-mouthed WOP." The anger was just boiling in me, and I spun around, pulled out the .38, and I pointed it square into his face. I was furious, and if they'd have said one more word...I didn't want to kill anybody, but what they had done. I had to stop all of the sabotage, all of the damage they were doing to my boat, my business, and my family.

As I'm standing there with the gun pointed at this guy's face, I feel a barrel of a gun pressing against the back of my head, and somebody says, "Give me your gun, Captain." I don't move the gun, finger on the trigger as I ask, "Who wants it?" The voice behind me says, "Chief Perez." He's the Chief of Police, and I know I've got a problem. Reluctantly, I handed the gun back to him, and he asks, "Captain Tony, what's happening here?" I point toward the Greyhound, "Look what they did to my boat."

We went down on the dock, and the chief's looking at it. It stunk, so putrid, and it looked disgusting, the defecation smeared all over my boat, brown, disgusting smears. The chief looks at this, and he hands me back my gun and says loud enough for the other captains to hear, "You catch anybody doing anything like this again, you shoot them."

Tony's eyes drifted once again toward Key West Bight and over the docks that filled the pristine waterway. A slight breeze drifted in from the ocean shifting strands of his thick white hair from their slicked back position. While the dry humor of the guitar player's gravelly smooth singing voice filled the air, Tony grew quiet. When he looked up with his eyes drawing downward, a slight expression of understanding revealed itself as his head swayed side to side.

"That was wrong," he said to himself, "to forget compassion."

Then his head dropped, shaking again in disbelief as a hint of laughter slipped from his lips. This time when he looked up, his mouth opened as if astonished, and for a moment he just stared off toward the gulf.

"How'd I do all this shit?" He asked, struggling to believe it himself. "I didn't plan this, didn't plan to do all this. I was just a New Jersey hustler that got displaced in a land opposite of Jersey. Shrimping, boat captain, the bar, being mayor. I was just a gambler who loved women and had some skills in organizing people. I didn't plan this life, but I've lived it well. I've done some bad things in my life, done some good things. I hope the good have outweighed the bad."

"And why'd you let me into it?" I asked. Why was this educator from Iowa sharing this time, this moment, and this friendship with a morally questionable Caribbean legend? "Why'd you choose me to write this book?"

Tony grinned in that comforting way that makes you want to listen, his eyes drawing to mine. "I didn't choose you, Brad. You chose me. After all these years, you came to me honest and sincere. I trust you, like you, and I think you feel the same about me. This isn't about writing a book. This is about my life and your life. It's about friendship. The book is stuff. We're the people it's about."

As I watched him my mind flashed back to a year before when I'd first met Tony. I'd known little about this Captain Tony character. Jimmy Buffett had written *Last Mango in Paris* as a personal tribute to him, I knew there was a shady bar, and had heard Buffett mention Tony's election as mayor. That was it, but when I'd heard Buffett in concert singing *Last Mango*, it was like he was alone on the stage singing from the heart like a son singing to his father. There was something special in the way Buffett sang that song, as if he were not aware of the 35,000 people singing along. It was as if Jimmy was singing only for himself and for his aged friend from years before, back when they were ordinary Joes, not legends of the world.

As I sat silently observing the old man sitting across from me, I had the same feeling, that feeling of respect and appreciation, that feeling of wonder and amazement, but most of all that feeling that Tony was sharing an understanding, a knowledge of his life that helped bring clarity to mine. I felt an alliance that only comes with a truly caring person, a person of compassion that seeks to harness the good in others and bring it out to dominate their spirit. I was appreciating Jimmy's song, understanding why he sang it from the heart.

I reached over, a slight touch to Tony's warm and wrinkled hand. "It is all about the people, isn't it?"

He pressed his lips together nodding, his soft eyes never leaving mine.

"Thank you, Tony." My hand patted the top of his, and I felt the age and atrophy of time. The emotion caught me off guard. I press my hand warmly down over his with that worthy feeling that comes from caring and being cared for. "Tell me a good fishing story." I said. "I'd love to hear a good fishing story."

Tony flashed a happy grin back from his big-fish memory of years on the water.

"Back in the early 60s," he told me, "I had a little boat. Today, the Coast Guard would only let about six people on it, it was so small."

In them days with no rules, I used to take twenty, twenty-five people out fishing. We'd do our hustling on the dock, get the boat filled with people, and leave at ten o'clock. We'd charge five dollars for a six-hour fishing trip. We supplied the bait, sold Pepsi-Cola. It wasn't much of a boat, but we made a good living on it. It was the first Greyhound. The one Neiman bought me.

We had regular customers that came back to us because they liked the way we treated them. This day we had Cy, a welder from Pittsburg, John who owned a spaghetti factory in Brooklyn, another guy who was a school teacher from Chicago. Boyhood friends, they would meet every year in Key West and go fishing with us. They'd get on the stern of the boat where you can catch the big fish, and that was their spot. These were our regular customers, so we'd charge them three dollars instead of five, but we got to keep the fish and sell them.

We're all ready to go out. It's about five to ten and a guy pulls up with his wife. He calls out, "You got room for two more?" I tell him we're pretty full. He yells back, "I'm the Champion Bullhead Catcher from Jasper County, Iowa."

Tony's mouth fell open, and he swung his stunned expression to meet mine. "Is there a Jasper County, Iowa?"

"There sure is," I stared astonishment back. "It's the Newton area 30 miles east of Des Moines on I-80."

"I swear to God, that comes out of me after all these years." Tony opened his hands from his mouth outward. "Jasper County, Iowa. After all these years, I remember that. Are there bullheads there?" He held his hands about twelve inches a part.

"Of course," I flashed back to the many river fish meals I'd eaten with my parents at the bars along the Mississippi, "in Iowa we call bullheads fresh seafood."

That brought a laugh from Tony.

"Well this guy was the Champion Bullhead Catcher from Jasper County, Iowa."

So, I say, "Jasper County, Iowa?" He says, "Yes sir. I'm the Champion Bullhead Catcher from Jasper County, Iowa."

He looks like Khrushchev, a big, round, bald headed guy, gonna bring a lot of weight onto the boat, but I tell him, "Well, we can sure fit you on." He says, "I've heard if you don't fish off the stern, you can't catch the big ones. I want to fish off the stern, and my wife's going to come too, but she's not fishing." I said, "Bring her aboard, half fare." I like the guy. I think I've got a live wire here. I go up to the guys on the stern, my regular customers, and I convince them to make room for the Champion Bullhead Catcher of Jasper County, Iowa.

So we go out, and this guy has two tackle boxes full of fishing stuff that's no good on the ocean. Hell, we're just going fishing, but he thinks he needs all this stuff. Two tackle boxes. I guess it takes a lot of junk to be a champion bullhead catcher.

Now, you've got to remember that Key West is on a reef with about 35 feet of water until you get to the edge. At the edge of the reef it drops to about 125 feet. That's where the big fish are. It's like a highway it's so busy with fish. So you try to anchor your boat so the stern is right over where the big fish are.

We've got these good fishermen lined up on the stern with the Champion Bullhead Catcher of Jasper County, Iowa right in the middle. He opens one of the tackle boxes and pulls out a twelve-inch rubber bullfrog, but it had too many feet like a centipede. It's like this giant rubber frog with a hundred legs. He's getting it all ready, and I say, "Sir, I want to explain something to you. You're in the gulf stream right now. For bait we use mullets, shrimp, squid. That's what the fish recognize. They won't know what that is." I'm pointing at the rubber bullfrog with all the legs. He straightens up and looks at me saying, "I want you to know I'm the Champion Bullhead Catcher of Jasper County, Iowa." All the guys are looking over his shoulder at me making faces like 'this guy's crazy.' He says, "I paid. I can use what I want." I put my hands up backing away. He's the customer, so I say, "Use whatever you want, sir."

So these guys around him are catching fish. I mean it's great, the fishing in them days was just great. One guy has a nice sailfish on. Another guy is working his line. The Champion Bullhead Catcher puts his rubber bullfrog on, casts it out, and it lands "splat" floating on top of the water. I say, "Sir, this is the last time I'm going to bother you, but I have to tell you something. To catch fish you have to go down to the bottom. It's a hundred and twenty-five feet. You go all the way to the bottom and then you pull up about five feet. That's where you'll catch the big fish." Now, I'm trying to help this guy out. "I'm going to give you a weight, and I'm not going to charge you for it. You put that weight on and let that rubber bullfrog sink to the bottom, then raise it about five feet." As I say it I'm thinking, what the hell's he going to catch with a rubber bullfrog?

So we're all fishing, my regular customers and this character from Iowa. It's July, and it's hot, but we're catching fish all over the place. Grunts, groupers, little yellow-tails. Everybody's happy, and we're having a good time. His wife's sitting there all nice and quiet like a good Iowa farm girl waiting on her husband. This is the early 60s, and she's just being very patient. I felt so sorry for her, so quiet in her little dress looking so shy.

All of the sudden the Champion Bullhead Catcher of Jasper County, Iowa says, "I got a bite." I'm thinking 'damn it, he's caught the bottom, and he's got about 80 ton of soil hooked onto that rubber frog.' Then I notice the tip of the rod is flexing down. Tap, tap, tap, flexing down. I turn to my mate Titi, and I say,

"*Christ, he's got a bite.*" *Titi says, "He can't." I say, "Not with that rubber bullfrog, but look." We look, and his rod is still flexing up and down. Tap, tap, tap.*

I say, "Don't tighten your drag, don't tighten your drag." He says, "Don't tell me what to do. I'm the Champion Bullhead Catcher of Jasper County, Iowa." I say, "Okay, do what you want to do, but don't tighten your drag."

Five minutes go by and Titi says, "What do you think?" I say, "I don't know, but I think he's got something big on there." The water is so clear you can look down fifty feet, so I look down and there's this big black grouper. Must have been about fifty pounds. I say, "Titi, whatever we do, we can't lose this fish." We never use the double gaff, but I tell him to go for the front and I'll go for the back.

As it's getting closer to the boat, I start to give instructions. "Captain. Don't," he says, "don't tell me what to do." I step back shutting up. "Okay. Okay." After all, he's a champion bullhead catcher. What do they run? Six to ten pounds an a good day?

Finally, we hook on to this huge grouper, and pull him onto the deck. It's massive, a giant grouper, huge for catching on a line. All the fishermen, our regulars, are leaning back thinking 'I can't believe it. He caught that big fish with a damn rubber bullfrog.' Nobody can believe it. We're all looking down at this fifty-pound grouper wishing we'd caught it.

The Champion Bullhead Catcher is standing mouth open and all proud with his chest out, and he's looking down at this giant fish he's just caught. The rubber bullfrog is hanging half out of the grouper's mouth, his head mostly bitten off, one side's hanging limp, and all the legs are sticking out like tentacles.

I say, "Sir. I'll give you ten dollars for what's left of that bullfrog."

He's says, "No way. I've got a guarantee. I'm taking it back to the bait and tackle in Jasper County, and they'll replace it. After all, I'm the Champion Bullhead Catcher of Jasper County, Iowa."

There was an enthusiasm in the way he animated the fishing story, an enthusiasm borne from his love for the sea, the people he befriended while sailing on it, and the great adventures of trawling the massive ocean. As I watched Tony's slight body, appreciated his tales of fishing adventures, I remembered what his son Louie had told me.

"He was so tough, so strong. You should have seen him pull fish onto the boat. It'd take three of us to do the same job he could. He'd just hook onto these massive fish and yank them onto the deck all by himself."

Tony reminded me of that scrappy little kid in grade school. Smaller than everyone else, wiry, a smart mouth with an ornery smirk, and quick as lightening. In gym class he was always the best at the obstacle course, stronger, faster, more agile. He backed up his smart mouth with his physical capabilities, always shocking us with his athleticism. I'm sure Tony was like that. He was the little guy brimming with too much self-confidence, but he always backed up his blooming self-esteem with an unstoppable determination to succeed.

"So is that your best fishing story?" I asked, tipping my ice tea toward him.

Tony took a drink of his soda, his head disagreeing as he did.

"I got so many damn fish stories, that'd be a book by itself." He pointed off into the past. "In 1964 I caught what was believed to be the largest tiger shark ever caught on a line anywhere." He turned now, looking off to the west beyond the dock and over the ocean. "When we caught it, it was so big we couldn't weigh it. Had to rig a tow truck cable to pull it out of the ocean. It was something like twelve and a half foot long. When we cut it open, the liver weighed 86 pounds. We took out 56 babies. It was such a catch they put the jaws in the Smithsonian Institute in Washington. They were three foot in diameter. Now that's a great fish story."

We finished our drinks as I sucked on the remaining slice of lemon, and we each left a healthy tip, then Captain Tony and I strolled at an old man shuffle down the boardwalk, locals waving enthusiastically from their boats.

"Hey, Captain Tony, how you doing?" They'd call out, and Tony would lift his slight arm waving back with a happy grin to everyone who called his name. "Good, I'm good," he'd answer back. "I wish I was young like you, able to spend my entire day on the ocean."

Always a compliment. Young like you. Whatever he said, it was said to make you feel better. *Share a word of kindness.*

"You sure make people feel good, Tony."

His cockeyed smile curled upward. "What's that word in the dictionary I like?"

"Compassion?"

"Compassion," he echoed. "The thing I would like very much from this book, I think I'd like very much to help people understand what that simple word really means. If I can do that it'll make life much easier for those who truly understand."

He was shuffling along in his loosely fitting dark gray polyester slacks and worn black house slippers, his long sleeved shirt unbuttoned at the cuffs, and he looked like an old man, a very old man with the smile of a teenager. Out of pride, his oxygen was not wheeled behind him, but carried by his left hand in an unsuspecting brown paper sack. Grinning kindly to those he passed, he continued greeting each fisherman who called his name from dockside.

Tony slowed to a near stop, gazing out over the docks with a reflection in his memory of a time long ago. Then with a slight nod, the corner of his lips turned up to an inward smile, and he walked on.

"I've learned you can meet anyone, people you would never look at, and if you're trapped in a room together, let's say for a half hour, you'll find the jewel in that person." His face was soft and gentle, his eyes turned toward mine with the wrinkles of time surrounding the weight of full bags hanging below. "There's a jewel in every person. Sometimes we just have to seek it. Why is it so hard for us to understand that every person is a jewel?"

I was on my boat years ago. I was younger then, and there was this fellow from Michigan on board, kind of an older gentleman. We've got 20 customers on board, and I'm trying to keep them all happy, to make their day fun, and this guy is spoutin' off. Saying stuff like, "The baits no good. This boat's a beat-up piece of junk. It'll probably sink under us." His face is angry, like he doesn't know how to be happy. "The captain probably got drunk last night," he says. "The captain don't care. He's already got our money."

Looking up in all seriousness, Tony's face seemed to lengthen as his grin turned. "He was a hateful bastard, the things he said."

This was so bad for the people on the boat. We go out and start fishing, and this guy keeps complaining, saying stuff that isn't true about the boat, about me. It's upsetting everybody, and now the people are beginning to wonder why we're not catching any fish, starting to believe this fellow. Maybe the bait isn't any good, maybe the guy's right.

He's just a hateful man, so I got to the point where I'd wished I hadn't taken his money. I would have loved to say, "Look, I don't want you on my boat." But I couldn't say anything because he was married to a lovely woman who was on board too. She was such a nice woman, sitting back looking all sweet and kind, and you could tell she was embarrassed. He'd say something hateful, and she would cringe, leaning back and drawing her arms in close to herself, her eyes down to the floor as she turned away, trying to separate herself ever so slightly.

I'm trying to talk, to do anything to shut this guy up and entertain the people until we start catching fish. I say, "Man, the terns are coming in early this year." "Terns?" he asks. I point out toward the birds, "Every year they come to Tortugas. Lay their eggs." His eyes followed to where I'm pointing and a flock of terns are flying south. "Terns?" he repeats. I say pointing, "There they are, right there."

It turns out this hateful man was a bird lover, a bird lover. Who would have guessed this angry guy could love birds? So we start talking about birds. While everybody else is fishing, he and I are talking about birds. I'm telling him all I know about the birds in the area, pointing out the ones I recognize. He pulls out some binoculars, and he's watching the birds I'm pointing out to him. Unbelievable that while everybody else was having a great time fishing, we had this true connection talking about the birds.

"We went out again the next day." Tony talked on as we walked down past the turtle kraal, past where they used to harvest the sea turtles. "I'd gone to the library that night and checked out a book on birds, read up on those I recognized, the local birds." As he walked, Tony's hands moved quickly as if flipping the pages of a book, reading all he could. "He turned out to be such a lovable guy. If you could get him talking about birds, he was so kind and gentle, and his wife happily shared time with him on the boat. He loved birds. He became one of my best repeat customers, always quiet and peaceful out on the water with his binoculars watching the birds."

Tony put his finger to his lips, silent as he pointed down into the water. A pair of four-foot tarpons swam by with their silvery scales clearly visible in the slight green of the harbor water.

"You know," Tony pressed his thumb to his fingers, moving his hand up and down between us, "every person has that little something, and if you find it in them it's like opening a treasure chest."

I watched the calmness settle into his eyes, and knew this was part of the legend. The deeds and daring adventures might evoke legendary vision, but the way Tony looked for the jewel in others, that is what gave him legendary status. Nobody becomes a legend if people don't care about you, because a legend is not so much in the events as in the tale of the deeds. The legend is the quality of the character behind the deeds, and this character knew that it's all about the people. That's why compassion is the most important word, that's why we should always look for the jewel that is the treasure in others, and that is why we should share a word of kindness to lift up another's world. In doing those simple things, we could fill the world with legends.

That evening, I went down to 0 Duval Street to stand on the docks and watch the sun slowly slip from the sky as it melted into the ocean. On the way, I stopped in the parking area where the Conch Train does its rendezvous. I'd read where Jimmy Buffett had written *Tin Cup Chalice* while riding the Conch Train. It's a ballad of his decision to make Key West his home. Stimulated by just being there, I felt like writing a song myself.

The evening sunset was spectacular colors of pink and gold as I stood among lovers holding each other close along the deck railing and at the edge of Mallory Square. I had a great time strolling along, stopping as one lover began to take a picture of another, and offering to take a picture of them both. I was a picture taking fool as I moved along in a tank top tee as the sun bubbled to the warm blue waters.

It was well past ten o'clock when I found myself back on Duval Street, surrounded by the flowing crowd and standing just outside of Rick's. Music that made your feet move came from a big, sweating man with dancing eyes up on the small stage playing his guitar and singing like nobody could love their job more. He played hard and laughed, dancing to his own music all the while. I began to sway just a bit, swaying both to the music and the amplification of fun-filled bodies dancing in bouncing unison.

As I swayed, a woman tropical in her slight dress and slender legs stood from her chair and began dancing, her hips moving rhythmically before me. I grinned as I remembered her from Captain Tony's Saloon.

She winked, calling above the music. "Hey writer man."

I laughed at the new nickname, yet caught myself scanning the crowd, self-conscious at my own natural movements of hip swaying freedom. Then again, I was on vacation and the music was moving me despite my deeply ingrained resistance.

I grinned with a little laugh at my own lack of self-confidence, reminding myself that in Key West I was just another Otis absent of my own image of self-importance. With that thought clear in my mind, I danced right back with the smooth moves of a 70's American Bandstand icon out to win the annual dance contest. I was dancing with the spirit of Key West and it's people, the spirit of my youth, and the untamed spirit of Captain Tony Tarracino. I was dancing.

Waving me to her table, I joined her and her husband, their group of friends on the sly from their own lives in middle America. It was a sing-along fest of late night driven confidence that somehow brought from deep in our memories every word to every chorus of every classic rock n' roll song the singer could sing. It was high fives and laughter, back slapping encouragement and enthusiastic moves on a crowded dance floor. It was a world apart from my life in Iowa, and we had a darn fun night sharing and singing together in the land of legends.

CHAPTER 8

Tony Tarracino is a legend, and much of his legend is based on philandering escapades that would cause the minds of monogamous individuals to flee from the dreaded horny plague. Still, it's hard to believe that a man of compassion would not have a rare depth in his feeling toward the children he had fathered. That was the question of the day, the answer that I sought to the values of Tony Tarracino. I had told him, both he and Marty, that my one concern with writing of his life was the blinder vision of many toward the morally questionable antics of a man lacking personal willpower over the soft touch and sweet smell of a sensuous woman. I was concerned that once people heard he had a baker's dozen with nearly as many women, they'd close the book and send it toward the disposal for deviant behavior without seeking further to understand the symmetry of quality within his character.

I have also seen hints that Tony is a protective person, protective of his children and family. When I first arrived to begin this project, Tony had been cautious when I suggested meeting his children, particularly T.J., the youngest. A 17 year-old looking forward to his senior year in high school, I thought as an educator I'd connect easily with T.J., but Tony had hesitated. Up until now, Tony had kept his home life private from me, so I was surprised when I pushed to talk about this atypical side of his life that he and Marty invited me to their home.

Marty had chauffeured Tony to pick me up, and I was happy to see her again. Soft-spoken and quietly upbeat, Marty had that optimistic outlook of a distinctive soul who has chosen a different road. The Tony Tarracino Freeway was a conglomeration of curves, hills, and fast straight-a-ways with speedy passing zones and very few stop signs. This morning, Marty was radiant with the spirit of one who had found a wonderfully adventurous road to follow. I had grown to appreciate the thoughtfulness of her words, caring she showed for Tony, and wisdom from which her insights were drawn.

As we drove up to their home, I listened to Tony complain pointing at the newer homes near his own. "Can you believe the cost of these houses? All wooden tinderboxes, built cheap with low-grade material. Can you believe what we have to pay for these? It's robbery." They were the words of many men his age. *You know, they just don't build 'em like they used to.*

Watching Marty's reaction, she calmly nodded having heard it all before. Patience radiated in her warm smile, the face of one who knew the other so well. Thirty years with a man who regularly autographs other women's chests can go a long way in teaching patience.

T.J.'s black lab met us at the door with a howl and that winding, spastic dance of the terrible twos that young labs do so well.

"Quit, you pain-in-the-ass," Tony shooed the dog away, protecting me from body lunges of excitement as he waved his arms. Then, as the dog settled, Tony turned soft. "He loves to sleep with me when I'm on the couch, but he's a pain in the ass." He gave a snarled look as the oversized pup nuzzled up against his wiry leg.

"I'm glad we could visit like this," I said, looking around the living room. "You know, you're revered in so many ways, and some people find your life, your family and children, well, fascinating might not be the right word."

"Would depraved work?" He asked as he shuffled slowly, nudging the dog with his knee into the living room.

"That's one word that comes to mind. Deviant, philandering, uncommitted, even perverted are other words I sometimes hear." Smiling to myself, I glanced to see Marty as she stepped into the kitchen. She didn't blink. "When I mention that you have thirteen children by eight different women, people give me a look. It's a look that's hard to describe, Tony. They want to laugh and yet wonder what the heck you were doing? People don't know whether to laugh or be offended."

He didn't answer as if that was an answer in itself.

The Captain sat on his own couch with a blanket and a pillow resting neatly near his arm, a blanket designed for keeping an old man warm even in the heat of the Keys. With the smile of the cat-bird, he shook his head.

"They shouldn't judge me on the numbers. They should judge me on my relationship with my children. It wasn't about numbers. That would be deviant, to have children for the numbers. It'd be a pervert who'd father children without a deep love for them or a commitment to care and support them. Relationships are what make a family, and my children are my family."

When you don't know Tony personally, and you hear of his many children and his legend as a captain, you picture children scattered around in many ports, most not connected with their father because his image is of a pirate too busy sailing off to bed another bar wench. I was seeking to understand how much of that vision was truth and how much was the fanciful interpretations of those who either had judgmental eyes or wondering envy.

I sat down across from him in an older chair, the cushion slightly worn from years of sitting in the same position. "The numbers, 13 kids, that is a curiosity."

"Brad, you know I'm all about people." Turning to find the comfort spot in his couch. "All of the women I've know in my life, I've loved some and I've learned from them all. My life's greater because of them. They made me a better person. Plus," he gave me a sly wink, crafty eyes smiling bright from an old man who had lived well, "I love the touch of a woman's skin, I love the touch, the feel; soft like creamy liquid to touch. They're so beautiful, women, and their smell. Remember my teacher. I'll always remember her smell." Then his grin lifted the white goatee surrounding it. "Besides, there's nothing like good sex now and then. Don't you agree?"

I didn't answer as if that was an answer in itself.

"So, let me tell you about my children." Pride seemed to slip from the depth of his eyes. "Maybe if you know my family a little better, maybe then you can cross out words like *deviant*."

"Fair enough." I didn't believe he was a deviant. Deviants don't care, don't have compassion. Tony was an ornery, horny old toad with his own perspective of the importance of life, an importance motivated by a great sex drive. As he says *All you need in life is a tremendous sex drive and a great ego. Brains don't mean shit.* Sex is a great motivator for men, and on the sexual motivation spectrum, Tony tops the high end. He's proud of that, so I let him talk.

Mimi and I, well, I already told you that story. Mimi and I were married and living in New Jersey. We had three children. Louie, the oldest, who you've met. He lives down here in Key West. He's 67 now. Tonia, she's married and living in New Jersey. Very successful, she and her husband. They got money. And Richard, who was the youngest. He's still in New Jersey. Then I told you about how I went to Seattle, and it was all crazy. It was bad for me, and bad for my family. There was a child.

The word 'child' hung in the air unanswered, and from his inward expression, I knew it would remain unanswered.

Mimi had a tough time too when I was in Seattle, things were different in her life while I was gone.

He waved his hand in the air, sweeping away his thoughts, the past, and the difficulties. As he did, Marty came in from the kitchen and joined him on the couch. Sitting down patting Tony's thigh, she wore a plaid skirt of blues and greens and a wrinkle-free blue blouse. Crossing her legs, she placed her hands in her lap looking very much like the pre-school teaching associate she was. Kind, quiet, patient, and gentle, she showed nothing of the bar wench floozy you would expect to be cuddling with a renegade sea captain. They looked much more like father and daughter, generations apart but very much together, posing for a holiday photo.

"Mimi hated Tony." She announced, laughing at the humor, her eyes sparkling just a bit as she repressed her chuckle. The laughter was not at the hatred, but at the memory of how Mimi must have acted toward Tony. Even on her deathbed, Louie had shared, she'd found the strength to sit up and announce that Tony was a son-of-a-bitch. The stories, the anger, the comments, they all must have been of that venomous time but now seeming a bit funny. The wife who was 30 years his junior had seen things from a distance while being very close.

After I'd returned from Seattle and Mimi and I broke up, I met Meta. She worked in a factory where I was supervising her. A beautiful girl, beautiful Puerto Rican girl. Dark skin, dark eyes, very exotic. She used to tell me in her broken English, "Tony, I die for you." When she said it with her accent, it was so romantic. The way she said it, "Tony, I die for you." Beautiful girl, beautiful words said in a way that made you believe them. We had a baby named Lorenzo, a little boy that was Italian and Puerto Rican. Beautiful. Strong, dark, and Italian.

But that was the time when I was all messed up, messed up from Seattle and the divorce from Mimi. My life was shit except for Meta. Things were going bad for me, and I just couldn't bring her into it, so I broke-up with her. A few weeks later, I'm walking down the street, and I see Meta with another guy. I stopped and looked into a store window trying to avoid them, hoping they wouldn't see me, but Meta stops. She says, "Tony, I want you to meet ..." whatever his name was. I don't remember. Anyway, she introduces us, and says in her beautiful accent. "I die for him, Tony. I die for him." Can you believe that?

Marty's frown wrinkled her forehead as she turned to him like a mother to a wayward son. Tony wrinkled his forehead back at her like the son who was determined to tell his story.

After that, Meta decided to go back to Puerto Rico, and she asked me to promise her something. She asked me to promise never to bother her or Lorenzo again. She begged me, "Promise you'll never see Lorenzo again." I was all messed up at the time, and I don't know why. I wished I hadn't, but I made the promise. At the time, it seemed right. It's the one thing I regret in my life, that I made that promise. I know Lorenzo could probably never understand that, but it was what his mother wanted.

Marty's head moved up and down, a slow but sure agreement. She raised her eyebrows, her lips pierced together like my fourth grade teacher's. "He called here a couple of years ago, Lorenzo did. Tony wouldn't talk to him. I tried to convince him, got so angry that he wouldn't, but Tony wouldn't come to the telephone."

I was shocked to hear that, to hear that Lorenzo, the long separated son had sought Tony out, found him, yet this man of compassion would not connect with his son. As I watched him, Captain Tony, the rough and rugged buccaneer, sat small, thin and quiet beside his wife. He was not withdrawn, not incapable, but silent and introverted in the guilt of his story.

"It's my only regret in life. I should have talked to Lorenzo, but I'd promised his mother. I had promised her. Can people understand that?"

"That's a hard one, Tony." I stared at his downcast eyes.

As I watched him, I knew there was regret. It's the first moment in the time we'd spent together that I saw him to be meek. It was the meekness of his own guilt, his own sorrow. As Captain Tony sat within the frailty of his oxygen fed body, his hands silently in his lap, I saw his sadness. It was in the quiet and the way you could not see the brightness of his eyes. He diverted those eyes, not wanting to make contact, diverted them away from Marty, ashamed to face her anger.

It was like that for a time, the quiet of guilt, personal disappointment at his decision not to go to the phone, not to reconnect with his son, the disappointment of keeping a promise that should have been long forgotten. Tony sat silently avoiding our eyes.

After a time, his head lifted once again, and he nodded slowly as if he had come to grips with his decision, moved through the guilt, and was ready to go on.

That's about the time I left New Jersey, ran from the mob and ended up in Key West. I don't think I was a very good man then.

That's before I was 'Fucking up first class.' Back then, I was just plain 'fucking up.'

So I'm in Key West, and a girl I know from New Jersey comes down. That was Mae, my second wife. With Mae, I got my life back on track. We worked hard together, Mae and me. We hustled on the charter boats, bought the Greyhound, and really developed our own business. As we did, we had two children. Good job, working hard, a little house here on the island, and a nice family. I was settled in to the American dream.

Coral was our first daughter.

"Coral." Tony pointed up at me, his shame having faded. "You know Coral. She bartends on Duval Street, a great bartender. A tourist comes in one year on vacation and orders a gin and tonic. The next year he's back, he goes into the bar, and sits down on the bar stool." Tony grinned with pride, that deep look in his eyes that this was no exaggeration. "And she puts a gin and tonic down in front of him. Coral's that good. Sharp mind, and she knows people. Like me, she's a great people person which makes a great bartender."

My other child with Mae, that was "Little" Toni. And then I had Alicia with Shirley. Both girls live here in town. We spend a lot of time together, holidays and other events. Just like a regular family. Alicia's husband runs an air conditioning business. Good business to have in Key West. Anyway, Mae and I were doing fine with our family until she went crazy. I don't know what went wrong. Something in her head made her crazy. She got violent. Did crazy stuff, damaged property, said things, and she was out of control. It was ruining our business and our family. We had to get her some help, put her in an institution. It was after that when she and I divorced. I had to divorce her to save the business and my income to support our children.

When you hear stories of the Captain, part of the legend is his 13 children and all the women. But when he sits before you, when he's staring you in the eyes telling his story of family and children; well, this is not legend, this is not lore, this is family. It is the intimate, brutal truth of love, relationships, and events that turn on the emotions of family.

Some trust, some quiet understanding had developed between us for Captain Tony to open his home to me, but this was the perfect place to hear about family. This home was not of the legend. It wasn't a room above the bar or a bunk below deck or some Las Vegas hotel room or a house with fifteen bathrooms. This was a home on a nice street in a town where there were neighbors and friends. In this home there was family all around. His loving wife and companion was sitting beside him, his son was upstairs in his room probably on the computer, and, of course, the dog kept sneaking back in between us for one more scratch behind his ear.

When he spoke of his children it was with caring pride. These were the days that contrasted the legend. These were the days when a friend would walk down the street to knock on their door and ask if T.J. was around. Marty would greet the friend with warmth and kindness, calling up the stairs for their son who would bound down them to meet his buddy. All the while, the legendary Captain

Tony would be lying on the couch, the family lab at his side, while watching the Yankees win another game. Ward Cleaver would have been fooled. He'd have seen a family, not a legend.

After Mae, I was with Shirley for a while and besides Alicia, we had a son, Anthony. He was two years old when he climbed a fence. He slipped away, got over the fence, and drowned. There're some things you never forget. I'll never forget that pain.

There was a long silence between us. I didn't know what I was to be thinking, but I was feeling his pain, watching him stare silently down at the floor. Marty too, sat respectfully beside him waiting for his inner time of quiet, resolute in his own need for a moment in the past. Looking up, our stares met, and he nodded a sharp little nod with the blinking of his eyes, then went on.

One summer I was driving back to New Jersey to see my older kids. It's a long way to New Jersey with one long highway right up the coast. As I'm driving, I pass this pretty lady in a car. Soon, I see her at a gas station. Then that night she's at the same motel I am. The next day I drive on, drive all day until it's late, and I check into the motel. This same pretty lady is there, so I invite her to go with me to dinner. We talk, she's good company and really good-looking; hair, nice body, legs, a real looker. I do what I do, telling stories, get her laughing. Before you know it, we're in the motel in bed together. Her name was Ruby and the baby's name was Jo-Jo.

Back in Key West I was dating a young waitress named Shirley.

I looked up from my pad where I was trying to write this all down, trying to keep all the women straight, line up the right kids with the right mothers. "Alicia and Anthony's mother?"

Tony shook his head no. "Another Shirley. My second Shirley."

She was young and from a very religious family in Ohio. Anyway, she became pregnant, and when her family found out, they made her move back to Ohio. I went up to get her, to bring her back to Key West and be a family, but they wouldn't let her go. She told me to go back to Key West, to go back and forget her.

I finally met that child a few years ago.

"A man called." Marty said. "I listened to him on the phone, and he said he was doing a television show on adopted children finding their parents. He wanted to interview Tony."

"I told her to hang up." Tony waved irritated toward the phone as he must have that day.

Marty smiled in her gentle way. "But I told Tony," her voice more defined, "there's something about this guy. I think you should talk to him."

"So," Tony went on, "we set up a meeting at Pepe's, a great old restaurant here in town." He shrugged slightly, his shoulders sagging a bit more as he let the breath escape from his tired lungs. "Turns out it was my boy, Shirley's and my boy. His name's Keith Famie. You may know of him. He's a chef, owns restaurants, and publishes cookbooks. He has a television show called *Keith Famie's Adventures*. It's a cooking and travel show. He was also on the second

Survivors. You know, that T.V. reality show where they drop you on an island, and you see who the last survivor is." I nodded my recognition. "That's how I met Keith, Shirley's and my son."

After Shirley sent me back from Ohio, that's when I met Marty. Marty was working in the bar and later I hired her on the charter boat. We were together for ten years, been married for twenty. Josie was our first child. She just graduated from Florida State. She made the Dean's List. I thought 'My God, what's she done? She must be in real trouble to be on the Dean's List.' I'd never been to college, never had another child go to college, so I thought the Dean's List was a bad thing.

T.J. is our youngest. He's seventeen, fifty years younger than Louie. He plays on the golf team at the high school, a thinking man's game.

I wrote T.J. in my notes, glancing over them as I did. "That's only twelve." I counted again.

"That's correct." Tony said, and he went unexpectedly quiet.

I penned through my notes realizing what I'd missed, twelve plus a baby in Seattle. I glanced from him to Marty as she gave me a slight shake of her head. Her eyes told me to let it go, and as I looked back to Tony, his distant, disconnected stare told me he planned on saying nothing more. With that, Marty leaned forward, speaking slowly but taking me away from the question of the thirteenth child.

"To understand our family, I think it's important to know about Keith." She held her hands folded on top of her legs. "When Keith came into our lives, we had a family reunion of sorts. All of the kids came together. From Louie to T.J. Jo-Jo came down to join us. It was a wonderful gathering of family."

Tony agreed. "My kids all get along great together. They had a great time meeting Keith, and everybody hit it off. They all got one thing from me. Compassion. There was no jealousy or distrust or anger. They opened their hearts to each other. Jo-Jo and Alicia even discovered that their mothers were pregnant at the same time, and they got this great laugh over that." There was deep pride in his face, the way his eyes brightened and his grin grew as he spoke warmly of his children. "My kids are very forgiving and very accepting; key things to having true compassion. I like to believe they got that from me."

"Our family is very traditional," Marty added, then laughed at what she had just said. "Well, traditional in the sense that Tony was the bread winner, and I was a stay-at-home mother. The family has remained close and all of the kids are friends."

"You see," Tony said, "it's not about the numbers. It's about the people, the family and the way we connect. People have this image that I just have kids scattered all over the place, and went on with my life leaving a trail of babies. I've taken responsibility for my family, and I'm very lucky to have all the children I have. I've been blessed."

I looked him square in the eye, knowing he believed all he said. "What about Lorenzo?"

With a distant stare of a man lost sailing on the ocean, he looked beyond me then withdrew slightly into himself.

"My one true regret." The words came slowly, hesitant. "My one regret in life is that I promised his mother never to see him again."

"Tony," I said, "That was over 50 years ago."

"Yes, but I promised."

"There's a difference now." I sensed this need, this need for permission to free a man determined to keep his word to a woman decades ago even with his own inner pain. "When you made that promise, Lorenzo was a little boy. He's a grown man now, a man capable of making his own decisions. When he called you, he had made the decision that he wanted to meet you."

Marty edged forward to look at her husband. "He's right." Her words were soft yet sure.

"What would you say if you met him?" I pressed him.

Slowly, his head lifted to look to me. The bags of skin hanging full below his tired eyes were clearly evident. "I'd tell him I'm sorry. I'd ask him to please understand that I had promised his mother. Then," his strength seemed to return as if he was now enjoying the conversation with Lorenzo. "I'd ask him to tell me about his life, to help me know what I'd missed."

We sat quietly for a time. Tony moving his thoughts inward, Marty watching him for signs of what only a wife of so many years might recognize, and me, hoping that maybe, just maybe Lorenzo would call one more time, and this time, Tony would answer the phone.

Tony stood slowly, pushing against the arm of the couch for balance, and shuffled across the room to a table piled with papers, notes, and memorabilia, where he picked-up an envelope. Returning to me, he handed me a plain paper folder.

From the manila folder, I pulled a type written page. The heading read *June 3, 1998, 2nd Block, Favorite Piece.* Second block, classes scheduled in four blocks, I thought, something written in high school. Hand written beside it was *Father's Day. Dad, As always, Josie.* A school journaling assignment, something from English class that Josie had written years earlier. I began to read the words.

> *I was upstairs doing my weekend homework, when my phone rang. Too lazy to strain her voice, my mother was calling to tell me dinner was ready. I hurried downstairs and plopped down in my chair.*
>
> *I noticed my Dad's place at the table wasn't set, and I was wondering where he was. No sooner had I had that thought and he came down the stairs in a pair of tuxedo pants and a white dress shirt. He went to the mirror and began combing back his wet hair. He slicked it back and then made sure he had a clean shave around his gray beard. It was Fantasy Fest Parade night, and my Dad was to be on a float playing the one and only Capt. Tony. As he fastened the cufflinks on his shirt he panically yelled, "Where's my tie?"*

"Right here." I said, waving it in the air.

My mother helped him put on the tie, and he smoothly slipped into his jacket. He added some Old Spice cologne, he has to smell good for the women, then looked in the mirror one last time, and replied more to himself than to us, "Your old man doesn't look bad." I secretly rolled my eyes. This was Capt. Tony the hustler and womanizer. He placed his top hat on his head and with a twinkle in his eye, walked out the door.

The next morning I came downstairs to get breakfast. And as always there was my Dad. A cup of coffee and the Key West Citizen sat in front of him on the table. A cigarette was secured between his lips and the Weather Channel was on the T.V. He had been transformed over night. Capt. Tony was now the skinny old man in pin-striped pajamas that I saw every morning. His hair never combed and his main concern being what the lotto numbers from the night before were.

"Good morning daughter." He said in his annoying New York accent, nagging at me because I was getting up at noon.

"Good morning." I yelled because he keeps his hearing aids off until he's done reading the paper.

I never really look at my Dad as a famous figure in Key West. He's just my Dad. Every now and then I get a glimpse of Capt. Tony, and it amazes me how well he plays the part.

On the drive back to my guesthouse, Tony continued to talk, random stories about different things that must somehow connect to his enthusiasm from sharing about family and his children.

"I've never used drugs in my life." Tony announced. "I was too busy enjoying life to screw it up, but I have been affected by drugs, one of my children, a grandchild. They're a bad thing, drugs. Several years ago, I was up in Orlando in the office of Peter Barton, a very dear friend of mine. Back in the 70s Peter produced the movie *Cuba Crossing* about my trip for the government to Cuba right after Castro announced he was communist. Stuart Whitman played me in the movie."

"That was a wild time for Tony, making the movie and getting connected to Hollywood," Marty shared.

"Wild times, parties in Vegas," Tony agreed. "I was big back then, really big because of Cuba, the gun-running, and secret trips for the government."

These stories just went on from children to gambling to being mayor, and now a simple statement about gun-running for the government. A life lived on the edge, balancing a life of daring adventures that would bring an average man down, teetering on the verge of bringing the legend down, but they never had. He'd always managed that slight degree of balance necessary to avoid a fall into the fiery depths. All in a day's work for Captain Tony.

"Anyway, this guy comes into Peter's office and asked me if I'll do an anti-drug commercial. I was in my suit and tie, so I said sure. We did it right there on the spot."

"You didn't write it out first." I asked this knowing that Tony speaks his mind, and any producer should want the comments scripted before something profane came blurting out from his unrestrained thoughts.

"No," the Captain answered, "it was from the heart, one shot. I looked right into the camera, and it went something like this."

You know, your son or your daughter is graduating from high school, and they're going to the prom. Jeez, do you remember when they were born? You went out and bought cigars. All of your friends came over and you had a shower. Such a beautiful baby, and you loved them so much, loved them unconditionally.

Here they are today, about to graduate and ready to go to the prom. You look at your daughter in her evening gown, so grown up, so beautiful. Your son is in a rented tuxedo. You had to borrow the shoes because, well, financially things happen, but you've always provided for them. You've always given them a home, food, clothing, and you've always tried to be the best father, the best mother you could be. You're looking at them so proud.

But I don't want to talk to you parents. I want to talk to you in the evening gown, you in the tuxedo your parents rented for you. You two up there on the stairs waiting to come down and have your pictures taken before the prom.

You know, this is your mother and father down here in the living room. It was a challenge for them to get this all together, the money, the clothes, everything so you can have the best evening of your life. They're ready to take pictures, pictures of their handsome son, their beautiful daughter. They love you so much, man do they love you. You're everything to them. You're their whole life. You're the reason they live.

You look down at them, look down at your mother, your father. Remember when you broke your arm? Remember how they were there, how you cried and they held you and wanted to take your pain away. You've been their whole life. Since you were a baby they've been there for you wanting to protect you, to make you safe, and to help you be happy.

Tonight, for them I'm asking you to stay away from drugs. I personally am not connected to you two, but for those two people; they're your parents who've loved you and cared for you. They're the ones that will suffer. They're going to worry, and if you get caught up into drugs, they're going to cry. They're going to take mortgages on their house to help you. They're going to give up everything in their lives so you can get off drugs. They're the ones who will suffer.

So you might have a great high. You might feel good and think, man this is it, but before you do it, remember those two people down there in the living room waiting to take your prom picture. They love you with all of their hearts, and your high could be the worst thing that has happened to them in their lives. So before you get high, think about how much they love you. Think about how much they want to protect you from the evil of drugs.

Tony lifted his hand, his arms up in both strength and the disappointment that such a message was even necessary. "It was from the heart. I didn't want any other parents to have to live through it, and I wanted kids to understand that."

Days before when I'd arrived in Key West, there was this subtle sense of relief hidden unspoken in my mind that I had escaped my traditional life and was stepping in the adventurous world of Captain Tony. Now, having just left his home, having heard about his family, his children, I didn't feel the distance between our lives. Yes, his life had been much more daring than mine, but his family and children meant as much to him as mine did to me. Sometimes on T.V. we see an adventure-seeking Captain Tony character running off carefree and living a seafaring life of intrigue. We don't see them come home to their family to be with their children and people important in their lives. Yet today, Captain Tony had welcomed me into his home.

In the past few days, I had learned many things about Tony, some good and some not so good. Lorenzo was a painful mistake, not letting him back into his life, and the thirteenth child would remain an unspoken and private matter. Yet, he had a great emotional attachment to his children, an attachment of compassion in his caring and desire for goodness in their lives. I had seen the respect for Tony in Louie and in Coral, I had read it in Josie's thoughts of who her father truly was to her, and I had seen it in Marty's affection for Tony. This was not the story of a man who had pirated his way through life bedding wenches and leaving an unwanted trail of babies from port to port.

The stories of his family had shown carelessness in how some of his children had come into the world, but once in his life, he loved them dearly. Women had come and gone in his life, many without the respect of commitment, yet Marty sat beside him as a dedicated and loving wife, and now, at 87 years old, within his respect for her was commitment. This was a man who loved family, yet had struggled to come to grips with the simple appreciation of what a family is. That is until at 82 with his heart struggling to pump, he had looked up from his hospital bed and made a choice. He had to come to grips with his own mortality. That is when he had finally made his commitment to Marty.

As I said my goodbye to Marty and Tony, and we made our plans to meet later in the evening, I had a strong sense of family. I had never been far from my family, holding Denise and our son Wayne, my parents, brother and sisters dear to my heart, but I had always balanced my compassion with the tasks of the day. There was always something that must be accomplished, some duty, some task, and that always seemed to be a balancing act against time with family. Maybe, I thought, such a balance was not what I should be striving for. Maybe I should be tilting sharply toward compassion, toward family, and always reminding myself *It's the people.*

In this soft journey of my soul, that is a lesson Tony was helping me to understand.

CHAPTER 9

In a reflective mood, I rented one of those $5 a day Key West bicycles. Wicked-Witch-of-the-West like, it had big-horn-steer handlebars, a bent up basket on the front, a black, rusty frame, and a noisy chain that threatened instability as it clacked along on fat, white-wall tires over the brick and asphalt streets.

I hit Highway A1A in front of the stone pillars of City Hall and rode lazily along on the street dividing Old Town and Bahama Village until I reached the Southern Most Point. Stopping to watch tourists take pictures, blue waves of the ocean pounded the large red and yellow dome verifying that very spot as the United States' Southern Most Point. As a couple handed the camera back and forth to each other, two pictures, one for each with the kids, I stepped to them offering to take a family portrait. I'd gotten pretty good at this, I explained. They grinned happily as I framed them, mother, father, son and daughter all in their new flowered shirts against the last tip of American land at the end of the United States.

A few blocks later, I found myself laughing. I'd heard of this place, but today I happened upon it accidentally. It was a yellow trimmed house at the end of the block with its backyard jetting out over the ocean. *Louie's Backyard.* While inside the house was *Louie's* upscale restaurant of more formal dress and amazing chef-decorated entrées, the deck was actually *Louie's Backyard*. For me, this place had a special meaning brought from the words of one of Jimmy Buffett's songs written years ago when he lived a block away. It is an experience Parrotheads cannot pass by. I locked my bike to the rack in the sand on the edge of a tiny spot of beach and meandered around to the backside.

Ordering a Diet Coke, I sat on the railing edged out over the ocean and watched sailboats drifting away smaller in the horizon. I had heard a story about this place, about something that had happened months ago. During my October visit, I had gone to a singer's and songwriter's open mic that was poolside at the Casa Marina Hotel. Playing were many of the Buffettish musicians that, like me, migrated to Key West in search of some semblance of his magic. One such musician was playing. John Frinzi, a talented and quite personable acoustic guitar player shared a simple story.

"I was at Louie's Backyard last night hanging out with a couple of friends. There was just a small group of us on the deck." John had pointed down the beach toward Louie's. *"At about 10:00 I was ready to head back to my motel, but first, I slipped to the restroom. I went back to say goodbye to the new friends I'd made that evening, and then was heading out."*

He had paused strumming chords on his guitar then looked back to the audience. "When I stepped back out onto the deck, Jimmy Buffett was sitting there playing his guitar," he looked to the crowd, eyes amazed and mouth agape. *" Jimmy Buffett,"* he repeated. *"The man, the legend. I sat down next to him, and for two hours Jimmy played songs about good friends. For two hours he sang about friends to friends. Old songs, unique songs, songs that defined Buffett's life."*

John then shared that Jimmy had slipped onto the island unnoticed to honor the memory of a lost buddy, to attend the wake of his good friend. Jimmy knew people and focused on people, and he'd come back to his old haunt on this deck feeling the breaking waves of the ocean where he shared his jewel, his gift of music with those he'd just come to know.

As I sat where Jimmy might have sat that evening, I felt good that he had been able to leave the limelight, slip away from the overbearing rush of fans, hide from the notoriety of who he was, and connect with new friends over songs sung by the sea as he said his own private farewell to one lost friend.

Peddling on past the Casa Marina to the long stretch of beaches lining the eastern shore of the island, I stopped for a quiet moment at the memorial for the many Key West residents who had been lost to the AIDS epidemic. I thought of the pain that a community so allied with the gay population must have felt. So many friends lost too early in their lives. As I read the memorial, a lone man stood silently by me. Then, without words, he easily drifted out onto the pier moving in a slow meandering weave from side to side that spoke of his thoughts and the loss he surely had experienced.

At Higgs Beach, under a line of concrete canopies sitting on concrete benches at concrete picnic tables was a small convention of homeless people. Around them were their life's possessions. There were shopping carts filled with valuable items lost or left along the way by those more fortunate. There were a couple of beat-up bicycles with baskets packed much the same way as the shopping carts. Nothing looked clean and nobody looked healthy, yet there was some laughter and a few smiles.

I thought of Mel Fisher and Tony Tarracino, and I remembered a story my son Wayne had told me when he was in high school. The school band had taken a trip to New York City, and Wayne had seen his first homeless person. *I gave him ten dollars,* Wayne had told me. I remembered thinking of how naïve Wayne was to have given money to an able bodied man who chose not to support himself. It had not occurred to me that maybe Wayne gave the man money because he could. I had not understood his young wisdom or the depth of his understanding of compassion.

I parked my bike, and wandered over to those tattered and weary people sitting at the end of the concrete table.

"Good morning." I smiled awkwardly as they stared at me with that strange look of distrust. Tired eyes gazed over untrimmed eyebrows unaware of the stench permeating the air around them. In an awkward attempt to connect, I said, "Hi. My name's Brad. I'm working on a book with Captain Tony. Do any of you know him?"

Most of them knew of him, a couple claimed to know him personally, and I was surprised at the insight, the humor, the kindness, and the knowledge of these few men and one woman that I shared the sun baked concrete table with. I sat for a half an hour listening to the homeless people share their thoughts about Captain Tony, the island, the changes, and the tourists. We laughed a little, cast our eyes downward some, and then one bluntly asked me why I had approached them.

"Honestly?" I asked a bit afraid to answer.

They all nodded.

"Because I was afraid to," the truth belched from me. "Because for so long I've judged homeless people, and I felt it was time to quit judging and find out the truth." I tried to grin, diverting my eyes from theirs. "Because my friend Captain Tony made me realize that it's more important to know people than to judge them. I've been mistaken in the past, in my judgments, and I didn't want to continue making the same mistake."

The young woman with dark hair hanging unevenly down over her face, a spider web tattoo on her neck and an ear cluttered with piercings brushed the uncut bangs from her eyes. "Your friend Captain Tony is a smart man."

We talked some more before that moment came when awkwardness began to set in, and I knew I had invaded their lives long enough.

I pressed my lips together, thinking of Mel Fisher and asked. "Would I offend you? I don't mean to, but I'd like to give you a couple of dollars, something for lunch maybe?"

A skinny, terribly skinny man in a pirate's bandana reached his dirt-stained hand outward and answered. "Hell no. We'll take your fuckin' money."

That brought a round of laughter from a range of smiles sharing a variety of teeth.

"Okay," I took some bills from my pocket, "Then here's some fuckin' money."

That brought more laughter, laughter of a personal connection as they each took the paper bills I pressed into their welcoming hands. They were good handshakes, handshakes like you get from high school students at graduation. Some were terribly timid while others were aggressively strong. Some came with a smile, while others showed only an unsure glance at the floor. But they were warm, more warm than when I arrived, and they came with thank yous and hearty grins. Before waving goodbye and peddling onward along the coast, I reminded myself of how important this moment had been.

Two hours later, as the sun hit its blistering late-afternoon peak, I watched the shadows of two gigantic cruise ships towering over the yacht-sized gambling boat as I waited for Tony. I'd chosen to wait in the comfortable inside of the ticket office with its constant air conditioning, where I introduced myself to Marilyn Ibanez. She had already handed me our complimentary tickets, and I leaned lazily on her counter where the forced cool air blew down over my shoulders.

"So you're writing a book with Tony," she offered small talk. "You know, I've known him since I came to the island 50 years ago."

"Well then," I answered, leaning both elbows on the counter to face her. "Let me ask you a question. Tony's got so many stories. Is it all talk or has he truly lived like a legend?"

Marilyn smiled a grandmotherly smile of innocent truth, knowing the reality of the world she had grown up in. A pleasant looking woman with the slight roundness of age, Marilyn had puffed up sandy blond hair and full lips with a soft pink lipstick like my mother's.

"I came to the island as an eighteen-year-old, with my family. My father was military. Tony was already a celebrity here, a person known on the small island for his fun-loving and unique qualities." As she spoke, Marilyn shared calmness in talking of her friend. "I know this for a fact. When Tony tells a story, you think this can't be true because his stories are so amazing. But I lived it with him. I watched him for 50 years. When he talks about being hired to secretly sail to Cuba and drop men off who attempted to assassinate Castro, it's true, and he did get arrested the moment he stepped off his boat onto the dock here in Key West. Stuff like that made him a hero, a legend in Key West. You see Tony wasn't elected mayor by the developers or the tourists. He was elected by the Conchs, the island residents, those people who knew his past, knew Tony, knew the history of the island, and shared his love for its people. He's as true a Conch as an East Coast Italian can be."

"He certainly loves the island. No," I correct myself. "He loves the people who live on this island, and it's clear that they love him." Hesitating, I watched her eyes, and saw the surety in their softness. "I come from the Midwest," I shared. "In my world, Tony's behavior, well, it's concerning. The way he's lived, his reckless sexual behavior, the way he talks to women. I've listened to Tony say some pretty colorful things to ladies these last few days. Colorful, and if anyone else said it, offensive, yet when Tony talks to women the way he does, they seem to enjoy it." I watched as Marilyn's eyebrows lifted unconcerned. "Have you ever seen him offend anyone?"

Marilyn, with her oval face reminding me of a kindly Iowa farm wife, flipped her hand with a dismissing wave.

"He has a great sense of humor, he's a great character, and the older he gets the more he can get away with, the more the women love him. Tony's special talent is he reads people, so he knows how far he can push things. I've seen him say things to women that might offend certain people, but he knows very quickly what one person will accept and another won't. He seldom misjudges people's openness to his outlandish comments." Her eyes squinted slightly emphasizing her seriousness set off with the framing of her light hair and pretty smile. "Then he gives off that impish little gleam in his eye, and you know it's all pure devilment. Yet even at his most outrageous, I've never seen anybody take offense at him. They laugh right along with him because he charms them with his compliments. They may be shocked for a second, but then they realize it's all in fun. People love him. Sometimes he sings and he tells jokes, but mostly it's just his impromptu charm. People really eat it up."

A sparkle came to her eyes as a trifling laugh escaped with her own little look of mischievousness.

"He came into my office one night, when my cousin was down from Pennsylvania. She's a lawyer with the port transit authority. Serious business." Just for an instant, a frown brought wrinkles to her forehead. "Anyway, Tony walked in, and I introduce my cousin to him as the Mayor of Key West. She shook his hand in her best business posture, nodding with a firm grip, eye-to-eye, and feeling honored to meet this local political leader. That's when Tony pulled out a pair of his souvenir women's panties, you know the ones with his likeness on the front that reads *Captain Tony was here.*" Laughing at the memory, Marilyn's head shook at such shenanigans. "Tony doesn't hesitate. He puts the underwear on my cousin's head, and while she's standing there with these panties over her head, he autographs them right against her forehead. By the time he was done, she was laughing and thinking this was the craziest thing she'd ever experienced. No offense, no anger, just a formal lawyer charmed by a fun-loving old man. Then they began talking, and he captured her with his warm smile and wit. She took that silly underwear back to Pennsylvania as her greatest Key West souvenir, her most treasured vacation memento."

The expression on Marilyn's face shared a sense of appreciation. "All through the years people knew him, knew him as a fun loving character. When he ran the bar he was very much a businessman with that rakish side to his character. Everybody respected him, and he helped an awful lot of people. He's paid for funerals for homeless people, what we used to call bums, who happened to come into the bar now and then. They didn't have a family, so he paid to have them buried. I know he's paid people's hospital bills; loaned them money. He's done it all very quietly without any fanfare. Tony's been a benefactor to about everybody he's ever met, whether it was giving his sense of humor, his wisdom, or actual dollars. This is one of the most genuine people you will ever meet, and his entire family has that quality, all of his kids. They're just true. True good people."

Marilyn pointed out the window where Tony was slowly shuffling along the sidewalk toward us, his son Louie walking a slow pace at his side. They were swaying along, saying hello to passers-by as they did, Louie carrying Tony's oxygen. Side by side they defined two generations of tough Italians. The same strong, handsome Roman features including dominate noses with full heads of white hair, white beards, and charismatic blue eyes. Tony was the ancient father with a slender frame despite his love of pasta. His son Louie was the healthy, full-bodied muscle-man with a solid round chest who has transitioned to the island with his casually dressed khaki shorts and a silk flowered shirt.

"He's meant so much to this touch of land," Marilyn said, pointing toward her favorite mayor. "One year, Tony ran for King of Fantasy Fest. He was partnered with Lady

Victoria who in reality is a six-foot-seven drag queen. We all worked together on a casino boat here. Tony was the host, the greeter using his charm and notoriety to attract gamblers. Somewhere in the conversations at the casino we decided Tony had the potential to really draw in some money at Fantasy Fest. It was a good fund-raiser as all proceeds went to help with the AIDS epidemic. We'd lost so many citizens here on the island to that terrible disease. So Tony and Lady Victoria decided to run for Fantasy Fest King and Queen."

"One night, Tony and the towering drag queen Lady Victoria paraded down Duval Street on their campaign for King and Queen. They went into Sloppy Joe's with this gimmick to raise funds. Lady Victoria drew everyone's attention, then they promoted Tony. *Donations to meet the Captain, to kiss the legendary womanizer, Key West's man of great adventure.* The women were lined up out the door offering things like a $100 to sit in Captain Tony's lap. $50 if they could give him a hug. It was amazing. They raised about $5,000 for AIDS that night, people paying just to meet and greet Captain Tony."

As I had listened to Marilyn, her straight-forward, matter-of-fact honesty is what struck me. It was like hearing of a foreign time in a foreign place, yet for Marilyn, she was just telling of her life and memories of Captain Tony.

"Hey Brad," Tony waved as he stepped into the air conditioning.

"Tony," I walked to them, patting his shoulder as I reached out my hand for Louie's, "how you guys doing?"

228228

228228228

2282288228822822822822822822822822822822822882282282282882282282228882282288228282282288822882282282282228888228882282282282822882282882282282282288228822882882282282282282282282282282282288828282282228828282882282282282282228228888888888888888882282228228228228228288228228

 2282882282288822882288228 22222228888888888888888228828 22882288888228288282288222828882288228828

"Great." Tony announced. "I'm going gambling. Who knows? Tonight could be my night. Like Mel believed. *Today's the day.*"

We left Marilyn for the complimentary golf cart that was waiting to chauffeur Tony to the boat. Tony rode and Louie and I strolled along behind at golf course pace. Our conversation was much like our other talks had been. Louie was upbeat with a great willingness to laugh that hardy Italian bellow of optimism. He welcomed your friendship like it was an honor to be walking beside you, sharing that genuine quality so clearly passed down through the generations.

Boarding the casino boat, it was the first time I'd had the feeling of stepping back into Tony's 1935 world. He introduced me to the casino manager who greeted me with a giant beefy hand that covered mine like a boxing glove. Giving me that direct business grin, he welcomed me onto the boat in a way that made me want to turn and run for dear life. He was definitely not a Conch, but truly an East Coast Italian by way of Sicilian mob. He was a large man, healthy with a full chest and solid waist all highlighted by a black spandex shirt stretched tight over his deltoids and biceps. His hair was intense greasy black, slicked straight back with thick-combed lines from his strong forehead to the back of his nearly non-existent neck.

The difference between him and most Italians was he had piercing blue eyes. Not compassionate blue like Tony's, but piercing blue that gave you the willies both by their strength and the way they penetrated deep into your imagined fears. His eyes reminded me of that movie with the white wolf and the chilling white blue eyes. When the wolf snarled it scared the devil out of you as if hidden behind those eyes was some greater power with his fangs about to completely undo you. The casino manager didn't even have to snarl. He just smiled and my innocent Iowa background made me want to run for fear from this dark alley I had just stepped into.

Behind the manager was a smaller, more brick like version of himself with a flat nose and a dense sidekick look. The floor boss looked like he'd be a natural at holding a long, steel crow bar designed to whack kneecaps. Brawny cheeks and long, droopy eyes, he stood quietly by while rolling his shoulders front to back as a burning cigarette dangled from the left corner of his thick-lipped mouth. The manager and floor boss were most likely descendents of Gleeman's Bar, gorillas with arms to match. I watched them believing I was a victim of my own stereotyping, my mind brainwashed from too many episodes of *The Sopranos*. Whatever tricks my mind was playing, they were damned effective.

"Please," he invited us, "feel free to eat before we head out. We've got a wonderful buffet tonight. Lasagna with toasted garlic bread. All your Italian favorites, Tony."

Tony gave him an enthusiastic hooray swing of his clinched hand. "We will. We will eat. You're always such a great host." *Share a word of kindness.* Turning back to me, his grin grew. "Brad here is writing a book about me, writing about my philosophy. He's a talented writer, very talented."

The casino manager's smile was genuine, genuine and frightening as those blue eyes penetrated my psyche and the willies slid down from my throat and bottoming out with queasiness as it ping-ponged around in my stomach.

"It's great to have you on board." He nodded, a two-fingered salute extending from his ape-like forehead. "Why don't you find a table and help yourself to complimentary cocktails at the bar. We'll be underway soon."

We nodded our understanding, as we moved none too soon, past the big Italian welcoming committee and into the floating casino cabin.

"Tony," the word squealed of high pitch feminine.

I looked up to see a voluptuous true blond bartender waving her long slender fingers with full glistening red nails extending by an inch. I must say that seeing her caused me to hesitate just an instant. She was tall, a few inches taller than me. A stunningly beautiful blond with an enticing smile and bright, happy crystal eyes, she greeted Tony like a glittering star in an x-rated movie with a soft kindness that made you want to curl up in her arms in anticipation. And when she held you there were two wonderfully large and naturally soft pillows bursting from her blouse for your head to lay comfortable while listening to the thump-thump of her heart.

Stepping from around the bar, she swayed all tall, curves, and luscious lips to greet Tony. Her legs were long, slender, and shapely extending from narrow, trim hips, and her waist was nearly nothing. She strode one foot directly before the other toward us as if we were the beauty pageant judges. Reaching out, her long, manicured fingers of bright red wrapped around Tony's face, and she gave him a loving, warm kiss on his wrinkly puckered lips.

Tony again went through the introductions giving me much more writing credit than I had earned, but this beauty before me accepted his words in a way that she passed on her own adoring compliments to me. Taking it all in from her seductive compliments and sensuality, I found myself enamored.

"Tell Brad, what was the first thing I ever said to you." Tony squeezed his thin arm around her slender waist pulling her hips closer to his side.

Her long eyelashes batted innocently as if drawing you from the pages of a famous rabbit magazine. "Tony wants me to have his last baby."

"You'd love it." Tony reached up putting his other arm around her. "It'd be a night to remember, a night you'd never forget."

"How could I ever forget a night with you, Tony." Then she gave him another soft, full kiss directly on his weathered lips.

Louie leaned in close to me, speaking softly as she stood before us offering to take our drink orders. "She's the manager's girlfriend," adding in a whisper, "since she was a teenager."

I glanced back at the gorilla, the tough guy who had greeted us with offers of lasagna. This character acting they seemed to be doing was just too real. One big blue-eyed Italian mob boss, a voluptuous beauty queen right out of the Playboy mansion, a pit boss that looked like a hit man, and they were all running a floating gambling joint. I was nervous because we were about to set sail and the ocean was beginning to look more and more eerily like that dark, damp alley I was afraid to walk down.

We ate our wonderful Italian buffet with unlimited complimentary cocktails served by the voluptuous bartender babe whose body should have come with a warning sign.

Between bites, Tony gave me a wink. "Here's a little trick, Brad. I learned it in Vegas." He pointed as the boss's girlfriend working her way toward us. "I was sitting in a fancy place in Vegas, one of those restaurants where the waiters have European accents and everything is glittering gold. This very formal waiter asked me if I cared for any wine. I nodded that I did, but what the hell do I know about wine? So I looked up at him and said, *Sir, you look like a gentleman who would know his wines. What would you recommend?* You know what I was doing? I was searching for the jewel while sharing a word of kindness. Two things came out of that." The old man leaned in as the busty bartender jiggled toward us. "Better service and a great wine. "

As our blond bartender leaned forward, coyly dipping her cleavage between us, she asked. "Tony Honey, can I get you boys another round?"

Several answers swirled through my head when, from across the room the Italian wolf with penetrating blue eyes grinned at me with his fang like teeth, and the willies jumped back up into my throat.

"Brad," Tony said, "have you tried many liqueurs?"

I took his lead. "A few but not many."

Once again reaching around her slender waist, Tony grinned into her colossal cleavage and then into her eyes. "I bet you have a great taste for the best, the finest of liqueurs. What would you recommend for Brad?"

"Oh," she said giggling and jiggling between us, as liqueurs danced in her mind. "Brad, do you like almonds?"

I wondered if Tony too could smell the fragrance. Surely he did. "Why yes." Keeping my eyes on hers.

"Then I'd recommend one of my favorites. Amaretto. But it has to be Disaronno. Only the best."

"Only the best," Tony repeated. "Bring Brad a sip of Amaretto, only the best."

"Straight up," she said.

I knew now to accept her suggestion.

"Of course," I nodded seduced by her charm.

Her hand brushed slightly over my forearm as her eyes fluttered playful with mine. "You'll love it." Her breath was warm with her approval.

Immediately, the willies did a little race around my throat.

Sipping Amaretto with the Captain and his son, Tony's eyes got big. "Did you feel that?"

"Feel what?"

"We just untied from the dock." The *Salt of Key West* was looking at me. I sat for a moment trying to feel it, to feel anything different until finally I felt the slightest of motions. Years on the ocean had taught him to feel what my land loving legs couldn't detect.

Like Popeye, he swung his fist with enthusiasm. "Six miles out, and I'll be at the blackjack table. Jackpot!" Announcing it made him even happier.

"Speaking of jackpots," the aroma of Amaretto drifted from where I held the sugary liquid just below my chin. "I'm reading *Fatal Treasure,* the book I got at Mel Fisher's Museum. It says that you may have found the mother lode years before Mel did."

Louie was nodding as the gold set piece of eight swung slightly from around his neck.

"I did find that silver." Captain Tony's shrug was as if he'd just won 50 bucks at a nickel slot machine. That's just the way life was for Tony. Yes, he may once have found a 200 million dollar treasure lying on the bottom of the ocean. He may once have found the richest treasure ever discovered on the ocean floor. But, like any free wheeling gambler, he'd lost it as quickly as he'd found it.

We were out doing some diving off of my boat, me and two other guys back in the late 60s. We dove down to the ocean's bottom and found a strange formation of mullets and barnacles with a few visible silver bars. Because we weren't prepared for it, weren't looking for sunken treasure, we just brought up one bar. Seventy, eighty pounds each, we didn't have the equipment we needed to bring up more than that, so we marked the spot with an old buoy we had and headed back for Key West.

Went back to find the marker, and we searched for days. It's a big, empty ocean of unmarked water out there, and we never could find that buoy again. Probably broke lose in bad weather. It was junk anyway, the buoy, not the silver, but it was all we had at the time. So we never found it again. One silver bar was all we had of the Atocha treasure until Mel found two-hundred million dollars years later.

"Jeez Tony," shaking my head, "you could have been a multi-millionaire."

Smiling, he looked over his plate of lasagna. "Would all of that money have made my life any richer?"

"Besides," Louie laughed full-chested, "he'd have gambled it all away."

"Gambling and women," Tony was chuckling at himself, "I'd have lost it all on gambling and women."

"Gambling's played a big part in your life."

Tony turned to me with quiet sensitivity in his eyes. "Let me tell you…"

It's strange how things have happened in my life, the connections with people. Some of the greatest connections in my life came through gambling, and my compassion was touched by a gambling trip to Haiti.

There was this guy who I grew up with in Elizabeth, an old friend of mine. I'm on one of my Vegas trips having a good time playing craps, and I run into my long-lost friend Mike, a boyhood friend with connections; grew up with the mob in Elizabeth. He says, "Hey Tony, I'm running a little casino in Haiti. Why don't you come down and do some gambling, everything comped, hotel room, meals, booze are all free. For old time's sake, you know, the good old days, I'd love to have you come down to my casino in Haiti." So I started going to Haiti to gamble and have a good time in my friend Mike's casino.

I went there to gamble, but it changed my life. You can't have compassion, feel compassion, and not be impacted by Haiti. Unless you've been to Haiti and been to the Iron Market, you won't understand how it impacted me, how I felt that ache of compassion for the people and the children. Watching the Haitians, their lives, the poverty was brutal, children without anything, no food. You can't imagine how horrible their lives were, how they lived without.

At that time Haiti was run by the elected president, Papa Doc Duvalier. A little later, in '64 Papa Doc declared himself 'President for Life' becoming the official dictator of Haiti. Even before that things were a mess. He ran the country like a tyrant, a greatly feared and brutal monster. He was abusing the people, forcing the children to live in such poverty. Sickness and abuse were everywhere. Papa Doc was a selfish and evil ruler. Because of that, because of my understanding of living in poverty, I began to connect with the people of Haiti.

One day we were walking down a little Haitian side street and heard children singing "River, the great big beautiful river." The singing was so beautiful, like the voices of angels. We followed the voices through a gate and into a little commons area of an old churchyard. The dirt floor had been swept, the courtyard was of pure white walls, and a soothing fountain welcomed you in. It was a small orphanage with all these young girls singing so beautifully.

They were all dressed in white and singing from their hearts, such innocence in the face of great poverty. It was beautiful.

We stood for a time listening, listening to the angelic voices of all these young girls dressed in purity, surrounded by white, and singing beautiful music. These were poor children, orphans that didn't know anything in their lives but dirt floors, too little food to eat, and the poverty of a country ruled by a dictator who lived like a king. Yet they were of innocence, their bright, smiling eyes. They didn't know they were poor or living in a country of abuse. They didn't yet have the fear in their eyes that so dominated the adults of Haiti. They were the goodness of the Caribbean.

We couldn't help but became involved in the orphanage. How can you look into the innocent deep brown eyes of these young girls, beautiful children who have nothing but the care given to them by the church, and not have compassion spill from your heart? We became sponsors to the orphans, and every time we went to Haiti, we took them boxes full of things. We'd stuff the boxes with anything the girls might need. Clothes, food, toothpaste, hairbrushes, anything they might need. We traveled a lot to Haiti to gamble, but we also traveled there to help the orphans and deliver what we could to keep those innocent smiles on their beautiful faces.

"You never know how you might affect people; how you might help them," he said. "You never know when or how you're going to go, so you've got to live life for the day and not miss the opportunities it presents. That's how a gambler lives. I live for today, that way I never have regrets."

"No regrets?" I asked.

Tony looked away as the boat began to churn out into the ocean. "Only Lorenzo. That's my only regret."

With that, he stood and pulled a ten-dollar bill out of his pocket. Leading us through the cabin, Tony stopped at the bar, placed the bill before the sensuous bar maiden, and winked. "A little something for you." He waved to her as he moved to the grand winding stairway leading down to the casino.

As we did, she sang back, "Tony, I love you."

A knowing grin broke across Tony's wrinkled cheeks.

Following him down the curving staircase, I staggered against the swaying ship as Tony walked with complete balance. When I grabbed the step railing to hold myself steady, Tony skipped down the middle of the staircase like an athlete in perfect coordination. Sea legs, I thought. He still has them, and I never will.

In the casino, Louie and I watched as Tony did his meet-and-greet, everybody wanting to shake his hand.

"What kind of a father was he?" I asked.

Louie shrugged. "We lived in New Jersey, and he was in Key West. He was great to have as a dad. We'd come down and visit, go out on the boat. When we were of legal age, he'd let us come to the bar. A great dad." Louie smiled watching his 87-year-old father find his seat at a blackjack table where his pretty dealer gave him a wink. "As a father? Well, he let my mother raise us, except when we really needed him. He was there when we really needed him, otherwise, he was a dad."

With that Louie was off to his own blackjack table, and I was standing in a gambling casino hesitant to risk my precious money. I stepped over to a slot machine and quickly fed it $20. After a few clanks of the quarters to the metal, my $20 had been eaten. I felt my gut churning with the loss of my hard earned dollars, gambling not in my nature.

My penny-pinching limit lost, I sat down on a stool and looked over Tony's shoulder. He was as happy as could be, him, a card dealer, and people giving and taking money. It was the way he lived. Everything was for the moment, and money was not any different than anything else. You work hard, play hard, and have a great big fun time along the way.

For a time I leaned against the wall watching action at the craps table. I tried to figure the game out, having watched it before but never quite getting the drift of when seven and eleven is a good thing. Seven and eleven, I watched a guy with an EMT hat roll the dice. A collective squeal exploded from around the table, and heads from the other tables turned to look. The EMT guy danced a little jig as the dealer pushed a tower of chips toward him.

To a novice gambler, he made it look so easy.

An hour later, I was sitting in the cabin sipping on a beer watching the moon reflect off the ocean.

"Not much of a gambler?" Tony said as he sat down next to me.

"Maybe I worry too much about money."

"You know what I think?" His voice was breathy, free of the oxygen he'd left at his spot beside the blackjack table.

"You gonna tell me?" I teased my friend.

"Of course."

"Go for it."

We sat side by side on the stools in front of the slot machines, the night calm on slightly waving seas.

"I think you spend too much time trying to figure out what the right thing to do is, and not enough time doing it."

I nodded agreement. Not the first time I'd heard I was too analytical. "Explain that to me, Tony."

"I think you do many good things in your life. What you do with children tells me you're a person of compassion. I've seen the jewel in you. You have a great heart, Brad, and I've seen you with other people. You know how to make them feel valued. But you came down here searching for something." Tony sat slightly slouched in a natural old-guy way as I leaned back against a slot machine, my eyes rolling to the ceiling. "Brad, my advice to you is quit spending so much time trying to figure out what the right thing is and just start doing it."

With that, Captain Tony stood and walked across the cabin. Shuffling along, he stopped to tell two older women, one with a cigarette hanging limply from between her lips, a joke about a parrot, a monkey, and a goat in a bar. He left them laughing and moved smoothly down the steps disappearing once again into the casino below.

Standing on the bow of the boat, the stars filled the night sky. I looked up vowing that one day I'd have somebody point out that darn Southern Cross to me. I knew it was up there sparkling in the night as a guide to sailors, but heck if I could find it.

Thinking about the conversation I'd had with Denise the day before, I pulled out my cell phone, checking the time. Eleven o'clock. I looked out over the water, the phone still in my hand. Ten o'clock back home. By the moonlight I could see enough reception to connect, so I punched in Wayne and Lindsay's telephone number.

"Hello." My step-son's voice rang back to me.

"Hey." I answered, filling my tone with enthusiasm. "How you doing?"

"Good." His voice rose hearing mine. "How's Key West?"

"Well, Wayne. You can only take so much sunshine, palm trees, beaches, and acoustic music."

With his wonderful laugh filling the air between Key West and Omaha, he said. "I'm glad you could do this project. I know what the chance to write means to you."

"Thanks, Son." The boat was turning now, turning to head back in from international waters over the coral reef that separated us from the island. "Hey, your mom told me you're trying to buy a house."

"Trying." He hesitated, a slight drop in his tone.

"It's the right time to do that." I surprised him. "Interest rates are low. Financially, it makes good sense."

"That's what we're thinking," he said. "But…"

I cut him off, knowing from the past harshness of my intense expectations of him that he would need my reassurance. "Wayne, you're a good person with a great heart, and I know that heart is going to guide you well. Money, well sometimes it gets in the way of the journey." I took a deep, warm breath of salty night air while I knew the air was likely seeping from him like the squeal of a leaking balloon. "You're mom told me you're a little short on the down payment balance." I smiled at the comfort of *doing* instead of *analyzing*. "Tomorrow morning, I'm going to mail you a check to cover the difference."

There was a long silence between us, nothing being said until Wayne's voice came back softer than before. "Thanks Brad. I'll pay you back."

"No," I explained, "it's not a loan, it's a gift. I want you and Lindsay to have it." I listened to his silence for just a moment then said. "So, tell me about this house."

CHAPTER 10

When the sun peaked angles of light through the waves of the leaded glass window in the century old guesthouse, I laid with my head floating on a full feather pillow thinking for just a time about where I was and who I am. Throughout my life I have been confident, strived to do good things, and lived a good life. For the most part, I believe I've been successful living on the good side of the centerline, yet for some reason on this morning I felt more right with myself than I had in a long time.

Somehow the perspective had shifted just enough to the side of better. Now that I'd made the decision to send Wayne the check, I felt a surprising sense of clarity. In one simple and absolutely correct act, I had *filled my heart with compassion, sought the jewel that is Wayne's soul, and shared a word of kindness.* Thanks, Tony.

Smiling, I bounced up, brushed my teeth, splashed water over my hair that was punk rocking in every which direction, and sat down at the computer to write. I wrote from the early sun to well past noon, putting down the words of the good Captain until it was time to actually go meet him. Then I slipped into my flaps, put on the new coconut bracelet I'd bought at a kiosk from an exotic temptress of sun touched skin named Nikki, and as I headed

out the guesthouse door, grabbed a complimentary apple
for lunch.

We were meeting at Rick's on Duval Street right
around the corner from Captain Tony's Saloon. One of the
biggest, most diverse, and creative bars in Key West, Tony
wanted to meet there because he loved sitting on the second
floor balcony stretching out over Duval Street. He loved to
watch the people from the white, wooden overlook, and
gaze off toward 0 Duval where the street met the blue gulf
and sailing ships passed by in the breeze. From the balcony,
it was as if he was looking down upon his own kingdom
where he was the beloved ruler of Utopia.

When Marty dropped Tony off she was worried about
the stairs, the tall wooden stairway that we had to climb to
reach the balcony. Age, charcoal lungs, and a late night of
gambling all contributed to her concern. Tony waved her
off with his persistent determination to be independent, an
old man still confident in his once youthful strength.

"No problem," the wiry thin Tony announced, upbeat
with optimism and ready to conquer this wooden mountain.
"Brad, you carry my air, and I'll pull myself up."

Marty's lips pressed nervously together, the smile of a
wife who knew that fighting old grit wasn't a battle worth
the argument. She and I exchanged looks, hers asking for
my reassurance, mine giving it.

"Okay Tony. Be careful," Marty whispered softly, her
eyes frightened like a first day kindergarten mother.

Tony flipped his hand dismissively backwards as he marched headstrong toward Rick's stairs. "You worry too much."

Again, Marty gave one final glance my way, her anxious eyes met mine with a smile, and I reassured her. "I'll be right behind him."

Pull himself up is exactly what Tony did. Time had shriveled him to a lean 120 pounds, and that was a generous estimate, but he'd overcome the atrophy of strength with that prideful determination to live self-sufficiently. That included climbing the stairs to look down over his kingdom of 28,000 children.

Tony reached out in front of him for the white railing, all his weight tipping backwards as his sinewy thin arms pulled. One hand over another, like an able-bodied shipmate pulling the bulky wet rope from the dock onto the deck, he began his ascent. His weight leaned backward for leverage, and he pulled and pulled, the slight remains of musculature in his arms doing most of the work as he lifted his body, one pull after another, toward the second floor.

Stepping close behind, I held his oxygen tank in one hand, my other hand in place with those old gymnastics coach's instincts ready to steady his balance if needed.

We sat at the table in the solid chairs along the railing, Tony staring toward Tortugas, and me watching eastward in the direction of the Bahamas.

"Tony," I asked as he settled in to view the busy afternoon foot traffic, "at the saloon, in one of the newspaper clippings on the wall, it described you as a gun-runner."

His fingers lifted from the table then dropped flat back into place, and I hesitated realizing he was sucking hard on his oxygen. His other hand was to his mouth pressing the tube tight into his nose, and his face was pale, his eyes tired, the bags below them sagging heavily against his cheeks as he drew in life-lifting breaths from the tank. His wheezing gasps for more oxygen seemed to ease as the tube refilled his lungs pumping vitality back into his body.

"Damn lot of stairs," I said softly as I stood and waved to the waitress ordering a Coke for Tony, Diet Coke for me. While he breathed, I stalled without looking, giving him recovery time, fiddling to readjust the recording equipment, busying myself doing whatever I could to make an old man not feel like an old man. Finally, he sat straight up in his chair, and his color seemed to turn rosy once again. I picked up my writing pad, glancing down at its slight blue lines with this confused look, and asked, "What was I saying?"

Tony's chin lifted, his voice cleared with a slight cough. "Cuba." He took another long draw on the oxygen tube.

"Of course," I sat back down across from him, "there's an article on the bar wall about the movie *Cuba Crossing.* Tell me about that, about gun-running."

"*Cuba Crossing* was Peter Barton's movie about my surveillance trip for the government to Camarioca, Cuba. Stewart Whitman played me. It had a lot of the stars from the late 60's in it. Robert Vaughn, you know, Napoleon Solo in *The Man from U.N.C.L.E.* Woody Strode played my mate Titi. Michael Gazzo was in it. He played Frankie in the *Godfather* movies. Ed Blessington played the Cuban Commander in the movie. I had a great time when we made that movie. Those Hollywood folks, they know how to party. They loved Vegas almost as much as I did. Work on the movie all week, fly to Vegas for the weekend, and back at work on Monday. Damn good there was flight time to sleep."

Then his eyes cast downward, away from my curious smile. As Tony's head dropped, his eyes staring unmoving, and I waited for his thoughts to gather. After several moments, his head slowly lifted into a solemn glare.

"The movie was fun, but gun-running, that was serious business. You don't do things like I did unless you care deeply for the people. That's all that matters. I've taught you that haven't I Brad?" Tony pointed at the street where a thousand strangers filled the sidewalk. "They're all that matters."

It seemed strange, somewhat distant, to be sitting on this balcony deck in the middle of paradise talking about gun-running to Cuba, yet the Caribbean was filled with a history of power-driven, gun-aggressive conflicts. Glancing outward, just purchased banana plantation hats flowing along the streets oblivious to such violent history. The professionals and families wore them on vacation escaping the great dilemmas of their lives. Gun-running, well, that was outside of the reality of their cul de sac neighborhoods with just maturing trees and strict covenants. To tourists the Caribbean didn't mean third-world poverty. To them it meant glass clear blue waters, fine-grained sand beaches that tickled the feet, and concrete resorts with painted stucco walls surrounding their protected tropical isolation. They didn't notice that all the maids spoke Spanish.

"I got involved with both Cuba and Haiti," Captain Tony explained. "It was a different time then, the way we thought, the way we fought, and how the third world operated. Communication was different, slower, and we didn't watch wars on CNN. To help you understand, let me tell you about Haiti first. I think you need to understand Haiti and that will help you understand Cuba." Tony pulled his nicotine inhaler from his pocket, fiddling with it like a musical director. "We're all Caribbean islands, you know. Key West, Cuba, and Haiti. I'd fallen in love with Haiti. We used to go down there on the boat to gamble, down to Haiti. It's strange how things have happened in my life, the connections with people."

As I've told you, my connection with Haiti started through a boyhood friend from New Jersey and gambling in his casino. I went there to gamble, but it changed my life. You can't have compassion, feel compassion, and not be impacted by Haiti and the poverty subjected upon the good citizens by the satanic dictator Papa Doc Duvalier. The heartless cruelty and brutal abuse he forced upon his people was unspeakable.

When I first began to go down there, I'd go to this little bar run by a guy who'd been a commandant in the African Core. I'd be there with my friends drinking rum and coke, you know, several of us around the table in the open-air bar. There was the commander, a few Haitian friends, a couple of gambling buddies, and Captain Tony. We'd be having a good time in the bar, just me and my American and Haitian friends all drinking together. I loved Haiti, and as I spent time in the bar getting to know the people word spread about my reputation as a good captain. People began to know who Captain Tony was.

One day, I'm back in Key West fishing, working, running the bar, and somebody called me from New York. Said he'd heard about me from a friend, and asked if I'd be interested in helping some people, people that were depressed and living in terrible poverty. Then he mentioned Haiti. He touched my heart when he mentioned Haiti. That's when I started to listen.

Though I cared about the people, I knew this was a Third World revolutionary mess, and I didn't want to get involved. Whatever was going on, I knew it was dangerous, but the caller kept pushing. He said, "I want to bring a friend to meet you. A man named Colonel Leon. Don't say no to me. You talk to Colonel Leon, and then make a decision." Then it gets a little covert. They say, "We'll be there Sunday, but could we come sometime when there aren't people around, like five o'clock in the morning?" It's secret stuff, and they're all sneaking around like government spies. That worried me, but I kept thinking about the children and my friends in Haiti, so I agreed to meet this person, this Colonel Leon.

We made an appointment that he'd meet me at my boat at five o'clock Sunday morning. I got there at 4:30 and had a couple of cups of coffee to wake me up. At five o'clock, a limo and two other cars pull up. Surrounded by bodyguards, out comes this guy, this Colonel Leon, and he strides down the dock to the bow of *the Greyhound. Well educated, immaculately dressed, he's a good-looking man. Very distinguished with that diplomatic charisma. We shook hands and introduced ourselves. He came on board, and I asked that all the others, his bodyguards who were hulks like Gleeman's gorillas – only Haitian, I asked that they stay on the dock. While his bodyguards waited visibly on the dock outside, the two of us talked for an hour.*

As I listened to Tony, I couldn't help but have this vision of Humphrey Bogart on the bow of the African Queen. Full head of thick hair, stubble face with that rugged, unshaven look, and a hand rolled cigarette dangling from the corner of his mouth as he talked tough guy talk. Like the African Queen, the Greyhound must have been a weathered boat, one that had fought the seas and continued to win. And its captain, Captain Tony, well, he was as tough as they came with a presence that was a combination of cinematic charisma, bold confidence, and hustling womanizer. Katherine Hephburn would have loved him.

So Colonel Leon and I talked alone for an hour. At the end of that brief time he'd impacted me so, I'd have died for him. I'd have died for Colonel Leon. He was real, compassionate, true to his heart. I know a bullshitter, and he wasn't one. In the little time I'd spent with him, he reminded me of Jesus Christ, of a savior. So dedicated, so in love with his people in Haiti, and determined to lead the people out from under the tyrannical rule of Papa Doc. I could not say no to this man, not to Colonel Leon, and not to the people of Haiti that I knew he and I loved so much. Colonel Leon needed a boat and a captain to navigate, so that's how I got involved, when I began to prepare to help Colonel Leon in his effort to overthrow Papa Doc Duvalier and bring a better life to the children of Haiti.

Tony was leaning forward, his enthusiasm returned as his lungs filled with oxygen. This was his life he was talking about, his compassion, and he was passionate about it. Through the stories came the stare, that distant stare of knowing where you've been and why. It was a stare of belief, of confidence, boring intently into me as he spoke.

Those loyal to Colonel Leon were working out of a little warehouse in Miami across from the old Tropical Park Race Track. I soon learned that the people involved in this whole operation were commercial mercenaries, most of them white Americans that were getting paid for their work. These are the people that Colonel Leon had hired to over-throw Papa Doc. This concerned me because they didn't have a commitment to freeing the people of Haiti. They didn't know Haiti or its people. Their commitment was to the money.

In preparation for an invasion, Colonel Leon was stock-piling machine guns, hand grenades, and other live ammunition. You name it, he had it. They were building up quite an arsenal and were doing live ammunition practice in the Everglades. It was dangerous, working in the middle of the Florida swamp doing all the planning and preparing for an armed assault invasion of Haiti. While they trained, I prepared for my part of the operation. My job was to get them to the island under the cover of darkness.

During all of this, I began to realize there was something funny going on. I'd watch these mercenaries and the way they worked. Something wasn't right. We'd get a shipment of 20 machine guns, and there'd only be five left. We're getting all of this equipment for the invasion, and these mercenaries are stealing half of it.

We got ten cases of dynamite one day, and I signed for it. The next day there's only two cases left. The mercenaries are stealing it and selling what they took.

I was in a spot. I didn't know what to do, but I knew it wasn't right. About that time a very tragic thing happened. Colonel Leon steps out of a cab in New York, and they blew his head off. Papa Doc's men I suppose. They caught him on the streets of New York in a bloody ambush and killed him. He's gone, dead, been assassinated. With the loss of our leader, our whole invasion plan completely collapsed. The man I admired so much, the man I had made this commitment to, was dead. I didn't know what to do.

Everything was a mess, so I've got a friend with the FBI, and I call him. I told him what was happening with the ammunition. He started checking, and found out what I suspected was actually happening. The mercenaries were stealing most of Colonel Leon's weapons and selling them on the black market. That put the FBI after these mercenaries. It turned into a hell of a mess. Then the mercenaries find out I'm the guy that turned them in, and suddenly I've found myself in a whole new world of hurt.

Tony hesitated, lifting his eyes with that gleam, that smile of cockiness that sometimes shifts easily on his face like a gambler with four aces. "I've told you about the breaks in my life. This was a big break. It was a break that kept me alive."

One day Margaret Forestman, the editor of the Key West Citizen, is drinking at the Last Stand Bar in Homestead just north of the Keys not far from Miami. These tough guys, some of the mercenaries, are in the bar drinking and talking amongst themselves. She's not trying to listen, but the reporter in her peaks her curiosity, and she overhears them. They're talking about Captain Tony, so she listens closer. She hears them planning to come to Key West saying how they're going to "Kill the son-of-a-bitch." Me, they're going to kill me. They're talking about killing Captain Tony.

So, the editor calls the Monroe County Sheriff's Department, and reports what she's heard. The Sheriff's deputies do their job, and set up a roadblock watching for the mercenary's car, and they catch them on the Seven Mile Bridge. They're halfway down the Keys on their way to kill me when they're caught. I don't know any of this is going on. I'm back in Key West doing what I do. Fishing, charter boat captain, and running the bar. Then these mercenaries are arrested on Seven Mile Bridge and my life is saved without me even knowing it.

Tony gets one of his great big swaggering grins, his know-it-all smirk lifting more on the right side of his face like Bogart's cockiness.

"The breaks in my life," he said, shaking his head in amazement. "People in the United States don't appreciate what they have." With a serious tone, he pressed his lips tightly against each other. "This generation, your son and my young son, T.J., they've never known poverty. They take it all for granted. I hope they never know poverty, but if they do, I'm not sure they'll be prepared to handle it. Haiti. That was all about poverty."

With that, he looked beyond me down to the main street of Key West.

As I think back now, it's hard to describe why I got involved with Captain Leon and Haiti. Unless you've seen the poverty, it's hard to understand why I got involved. I'd learned to love the people of Haiti, and I wanted to help Colonel Leon lead Haiti out of poverty. I was hoping he could do that, and I wanted to be a part of it. I wanted to help. We were just never able to accomplish it. When Colonel Leon was assassinated everything collapsed, and Papa Doc stayed in power as the oppressive dictator of Haiti.

In complete silence, we shared each other's eyes. These days his eyes are blue, they're clear with confidence, but they're tired from so much effort, so much worry for so many people. He's a man looking back on a different time, a different way, and he knows that he has always been a fighter, a fighter for the little guy, the underdog, the innocent, and the children.

"A few years later." His eyes glancing away then back again as a stare of survival spread across his face. "Remember I told you about hearing the Haitian children singing from the church courtyard? The singing was so captivating, like the voices of angels." The Captain stared off toward the gulf, his look self-satisfied. "When Marty and I helped them, in a way I was finishing my commitment to Colonel Leon, my commitment to help the children of Haiti."

In a moment of memory, the seriousness of his stare caught mine.

"You know Marty now. Marty has such a wonderful heart. She is so much of the goodness that is in me. I go to gamble, and she leads me down a street to find where children are singing like angels. She knows how to get to my heart because she lives from her heart." Tony's face turned a touch ashen. "I wouldn't do anything to put her in danger."

On one gambling trip, they let everybody off the plane but me, me and Marty. Armed military stormed on board, pushing us into our seats, demanding that we sit silently. As we do, they do an extensive search everywhere, and our clothes are thrown all over the plane. They're turning everything inside out searching for whatever, I don't know. I don't know if they know who I am or what my past involvement was, but they were treating us like enemies of the country. Men with machine guns were standing over us, shouting obscenities in Creole, and ripping through our belongings as they searched.

Papa Doc, he was an inhuman man capable of anything. We were scared as if with the twitch of an angry finger, our lives could end at any moment. For once, I kept my mouth shut because if I hadn't, Marty would have killed me. It was frightening, and I had no clue how it would end until they finally stopped searching, finding nothing of whatever they were looking for. When they eventually let us off the plane, Marty and I headed for the casino trying to find someplace safe to put it all behind us and allow our nerves to settle.

Later on that same trip we're at the cockfights. Now remember, this is Haiti and this is a different time. Cockfights were a part of the culture, so we went to them whenever we were in Haiti. But this time Papa Doc Junior, the kid, is there. His real name is Jean-Claude Duvalier, and he'd become the dictator after his father's death. Junior was taught by his father how to be mean. He was ruthless, more murderous and vicious than his father. So after the plane incident we're in this dirt floor hut watching cockfights, surrounded by Junior and his armed men, and I'm praying he doesn't know who I am.

Junior has two .45s strapped to his side. That's the way it was. Armed dictator at the cockfights, and he says to me, 'Who do you like?' I tell him I like the red one, the red cock. He says, 'Okay, $500.' So I bet $500 on the red rooster. The red one wins, and Papa Doc Junior turns to me and says, 'You had the black one.'

This pisses me off, him lying and trying to steal my money. There's honor in gambling, and this was not part of the code. My nature is to challenge him, to take him on and demand that he honor his word. I'm readying for a fight with my fist clinched and my shoulder tight, I'm puffing up to argue the bet and let him know he can't steal my money, then I feel Marty's hand on my forearm, pulling me away.

He's foaming at the mouth like an idiot rabid dog. His eyes are full of anger, scary anger like from one of those movies they make these days, and Marty says to me, 'Give him the money and forget it.' She's begging me. 'Give it up, Tony. Our lives are worth more than $500.' I turned to Baby Doc and said, 'What'd you say?' He's looking all mean and foamy at the mouth, crazy in the eyes. He puts his hands on his guns and says, 'You had the black one.'

I reach in my pocket, pull out $500, and give it to him. That's when I knew they didn't know who I was. Had they known about my involvement with Colonel Leon, I'd have been as dead as that black rooster."

"You understand that Cuba was much like Haiti, a brutal dictator was over-thrown by Castro, then Castro turns into a dictator. Those were strange times, but because I had a reputation as a good captain, they came to me with these jobs."

I'd watched Tony, watched his intensity when he told the stories, watched his eyes when he described the conditions of the islands and talked of the children. There was not doubt, no regret that he had lived as he had.

"In their own secretive way, the United States government used me to help them just like Colonel Leon had wanted to." He spoke now in a calm, nonchalant manner. "Our government came to me during the Cuban Revolution and again after Castro declared that he was Communist. They needed a strong sea captain to help them without Cuba knowing our government was involved."

I pushed forward, my elbows pressing downward into my knees. This was where the legend had evolved. Without the gun-running, he was just a famous womanizing bar owner with local flavor. "So you did these things to help the people? The Haitians, the Cubans?"

"The Haitians especially. I helped with Cuba for three reasons." His eyes shimmered as he stared at me. Sitting back in his chair, Tony's beard was thick white like a story-telling sea captain's should be. He sat distinguished, straight backed and tall in his personal belief for the good he'd tried to do.

"I did it first because there were people, children of great poverty living in Haiti and Cuba who needed our help. These were civil wars I'm talking about, wars against dictators that caused their own people to live in severe poverty while the son-of-a-bitches lived wealthy on all the money they stole from the poor. It was like Iraq and Saddam Hussein, but it was a different time in our history. Second, with Cuba I did it for my country because it was my government that was asking me to do these things. We were in the middle of the Cold War, and communism was the great threat to our freedom. I felt it was my patriotic duty, so when my country called, I answered," he nodded reassurance, "And third," his smile twisted just a bit as his eyes glanced up to meet mine, "I did it for the money." There was the grin of a political capitalist. "Hey, 10,000 bucks is 10,000 bucks. Early 60s that was a lot of money. That's what I got for each trip to Cuba." Then he pointed his long finger toward me laughing at the honesty. "It's the gambler in me, but I gambled with a purpose. $10,000? That's an added incentive to help."

Tony's hand went still as he held the empty inhaler.

There's a jewel in every person, but sometimes it hard to find. I believe in people, and I believe in their right to live a simple, innocent life with food and shelter. All they want is a home, a family with some kids, and food on the table. It's not much that most people want. Why not try and help them have that? Shouldn't the people of Haiti and Cuba have these simple things? Shouldn't they be freed from a dictator who keeps his power by keeping them fighting for their family's survival.

"The work I did for the government was real top secret." Then Captain Tony shrugged away his own importance. "Like they hired this little, insignificant guy from Key West to do all the dirty work. I was too small to even be noticed or be missed if I was noticed. I was a skilled sea captain who was easily expendable."

Cuba was a mess. A revolution against a dictator the United States wanted removed. One day we helped Castro's revolt, and it's supposed to be good for the United States. The next day, Castro's turned on us, and Cuba's a Communist regime. It was a shocking betrayal to our country, and it was big here in Key West. So close to Cuba, and there are so many Cubans living here. It was like the revolution was part of our culture too. We were the island in between Cuba and the United States, culturally and physically.

He looked down onto Duval Street. "You should have seen Key West back then, before the military pulled out. The Navy dominated the island. Everywhere you looked, men in uniform. It was like a wave of marshmallows walking down the street, all of the white hats bobbing up and down." His hand reached out in front of him, gently rolling like ocean waves.

In the middle of the night, long after the bars had closed and the streets had emptied, somebody'd deliver the guns. Crates of guns and ammunition dropped off in the dead of night. That's when they'd drop off whatever it was I was to deliver to Cuba in support of Castro's revolution. I'd hide it under the stage in the bar until I was ready to take it over.

It's 90 miles to Cuba, a good day's trip. When I was making the delivery, my girlfriend Stacy would stay here to run the bar. Sometime while I was gone, a guy would come in and hand her a small package. $10,000 wrapped up in a paper package. That's how they'd pay me for each trip. I never met *anybody personally. I'd get back, go up the ladder, and there'd be $10,000 laying on the bed in my steamy little room above the bar.*

I made several trips for our government, running guns, ammunition, hand grenades, or whatever Castro's revolution needed to overthrow Batista who'd ruled the island with an iron fist for 25 years. It was a grassroots revolution by the people to free them from this dictator that the United States had endorsed for so long. Now, it was clear that a new government, a new leader was needed, but our country had supported Batista for so many years, the government had to work behind the scenes, quietly turning to people like me for help.

I was intrigued by the mystery of this governmental secrecy and international trickery. It was all secret espionage spy stuff, and I wondered if he ever had a pen that could shoot bullets or a jet-powered car that could transform into a submarine swimming stealthily into foreign waters. To me this spy stuff was all T.V. show hype. That was as close as my world came to 007. I wondered which movie Tony would star in next, a romance, comedy, or maybe the next conspiracy theory? I was beginning to understand the legend better. He was a salty James Bond, much more a Sean Connery than a Roger Moore, running guns, over throwing governments, and kissing the girl. And the truth is, it wasn't a movie.

"There was this big store in Tampa called Maas Brothers," Tony turned his hand over offering his palms upward in explanation. "There was this guy that was a photographer, photographed nude women. He was my contact man. Anytime they were trying to set something up, he'd call me from Maas Brothers. That's how they got in touch with me."

Leaning back in his chair, the Captain turned his hand 180 degrees over. "I did a lot for our government. When they asked, I was ready."

They called again after Castro had taken power. He proclaimed himself the leader, and aligned his government with Russia's Communist philosophy when three factions of political power in Cuba joined to become United Party of Cuban Socialist Revolution and rule the island. This was a devastating blow to the United States who viewed Communism as the Great Red Threat. We tried to stop it, supporting the invasion of the Bay of Pigs, but when that didn't work, we had to find some way of ridding our neighbors from Communist influence.

Camarioca, Cuba, that was one of the great trips. It was 1964, and Cuba was 90 miles off the coast of the United States where Communism had invaded our part of the world. By then we were in a real political conflict and at times war seemed as if it would break out any day. There were angry statements going back and forth, America to Cuba, Castro to Kennedy. Cuba becoming Communist, it was like a knife in the back to the United States, and there was much resentment, even hatred for Castro's alliance with Russia.

Castro got fed up with all of the rhetoric from the United States, so over the radio he told America, if you want your Cuban family members, you want your Cuban friends; you come and get them. If they don't want to be here, we don't want them. You want them, then we'll bring them to you at Camarioca.

So I get one of my calls. "Did you hear what Castro said?"
Then the voice told me, "Tony, we can't trust him. We need you
to go to Camarioca. We need to find out if Castro is telling the
truth."

"This was big back then. You remember the Cuban
Missile Crisis. The Communist were in our backyard, and
the United States was on the brink of nuclear war. The
Great Red Threat was controlling Cuba, and my country
was asking me to help." He fell back against his chair, the
stare penetrated deeply into mine. "This was as if we'd
known 9/11 was coming. This is what we were preparing
for. People were building fallout shelters in the ground of
their backyards, America was preparing for a nuclear attack,
and Cuba was providing the Communists access from which
the attack would be initiated."

I asked the man on the phone, "What's the deal?" "Well,"
the voice said, "we need to find out if Castro's telling the truth,
but you're also going to take reporters over. We need to get the full
story. You drop the reporters off, but you're not going to bring them
back. We need them in Cuba. Your job is to drop them off and
verify what Castro has said about Camarioco. We need to know if
he's being truthful about releasing Cuban family members to their
relatives in the United States."

I know this's pretty risky. Tension is high, our whole country
had a nervous twitch, and then the voice tells me, "We'll pay
$10,000." Well, that makes me think. I'm a gambler and
$10,000 is a pretty chunk of change, so I say, "This is dangerous
stuff. What if I lose the boat? It's my livelihood." The guy tells me,

"If you lose your boat, we'll guarantee that we'll compensate you for the value of the boat, but we need you to leave in 24 hours."

24 hours! That's fast. I'm getting worried about this, going into Communist Cuba in 24 hours. I'm putting my livelihood, my life and my family's future on the line for my country, and they want me to drop everything, and sail off into the heart of Communism. I don't really want to do it. It's too risky, so I stall telling him, "I've got to get a radio man, a mechanic. I just can't leave that quickly. Twenty-four hours does not give me time to put things together, to plan well." So the guy says, "Okay, $20,000, and we guarantee your boat. But you've got to leave within 24 hours."

Tony's eyes lit up like a slot machine smiling a row of cherries. "Well, you know, $20,000. That's a lot of trips to Vegas. I can have a hell of a lot of fun with $20,000." He rolled his nicotine inhaler between his finger and thumb, back and forth, back and forth. "In my mind I'm balancing my country's request, my ability to help America and the people of Cuba, and $20,000 against the risk. It was important." His eyes came back to mine. "My country needed me. I'm thinking *why the hell wouldn't I help my country*, so that's what I tell the guy on the phone."

I send out the word, and the crew is coming together, checking in to find out our plans. I had an alcoholic mechanic, a little Spanish girl to interpret, a Cuban radioman named John, and my crazy mate Titi. At the time, on the side I'm sleeping with a lady named Maggie. You know, Margaret Forestman, the editor of the Key West Citizen, and I tell her not to let this leak out. It's all got to be kept quiet, top secret. I told her this, and I told my crew the same thing. Nobody can know.

So the next night we gather at the dock, load the boat with supplies, and wait for the reporters. When they arrive, it's the toughest group of reporters you've ever seen. Military like, square jaws and stern looking, they could have been New Jersey mob gorillas as easily as reporters. Big bags they're carrying, but I don't see any notebooks, no pens to write with. Questions rise up in my mind, but that's not my job. I'm not to question, but to transport the reporters. So I shove the questions aside.

Well into the night, we head out in the light of a full moon. There's a 30 knot wind from the east, and a storm's beginning to creep in, but we've got our orders, so we push on into the growing winds. As we're sailing south the winds continue to build, blowing stronger, and driving the waves bigger. The storm begins to challenge the Greyhound forcing it to do what it was not designed to, conquer the rage of a massive open ocean storm.

The wind's against the gulf stream making the battle tougher for the Greyhound. The winds have grown until we've got 15 to 20 foot seas, a wall of water with each wave. The waves are crashing in over us, and it becomes nearly impassable, treacherous conditions. We were fighting nature with these deadly waves and powerful winds, and we know that if nature wants to win, she will. We shouldn't even be out on the water. I'm thinking this is nuts, my boat and our lives, there's too much at risk, but the reporters encourage me to keep going. They're insistent that I get them to Cuba, so I lower my head to the sea, and we push on. Our government is counting on us to get this done. We've got a mission, and a little seawater shouldn't get in the way.

My crew is working for their lives trying to keep us going as water is crashing over the sides. I've got these reporters on board who're fightin' the belly wrenching, gut churning ocean's fury. They say they're national press, major magazine reporters, but these guys didn't even know how to work their cameras. They aren't reporters. But I've got to get them to Cuba. That's my mission, and I'm fighting the worst seas I've ever sailed to accomplish this.

About half way over, Titi kicks me, and I look up to see the biggest wave I've ever seen. It's like walking down a New York City street and looking up at a skyscraper. A massive rogue wave is bearing down upon us. I tried to take it at an angle, but I was too late, and the power of the ocean hit the boat like a steaming locomotive, a wall of water covering with the wet blanket of a heavy waterfall; cold, crushing, and concealing like the lid of a casket. We feel the boat twisting, hear the snap, and know that the keel is gone, a victim of the storm.

The keel is the backbone of the boat. It keeps us stable. With the keel broken, the huge waves are beating us up, bouncing us around like a toy in a whirlpool. Now the boat's swaying without its stability, and the stern is moving up and down like a buoy in a hurricane. The Greyhound has turned from sturdy to slight, a foam toy in a washing machine. The shafts from the engines are the only things holding us together. Fish are flying out of the waves. We're ducking as they fly by and hit the boat, torpedoes from the deep. It was brutal, and we had become the target.

The aerial for my radio went down, my radio went out. Our communication is lost. We've gone deaf, nothing but static. The compass flies out and hits the deck. It breaks and all the alcohol runs out. It's useless. Now we're blind. We're in a hell of a mess, deaf, blind, the boat crippled, and in the worst seas I've ever experienced. At that point I knew, I knew our lives were on the brink.

The only thing I had that was working was this little transistor radio. I know we're about an hour out of Cuba, and I took that transistor and started fiddling with the dial, fighting to keep it dry, away from the unrelenting waves. Turning the dial back and forth, finally I picked up a Havanna radio station. The reception's poor, just enough to know it's Havanna, all in Spanish. Then I moved the radio slowly to the southeast until I picked up Matanza. Matanza is halfway between Havanna and Camaroica to the southeast.

Camaroica is a tiny fishing village with a little inlet. Not much there, but it is where my country has told me to go, to get the answer to Castro's promise of asylum for those wishing to leave. I knew I had to go to the east of Matanza, as far southeast as Matanza was southeast of Havanna. Fighting the seas, I listened to the static on the radio trying to get a clear signal. Havana first, then the static broadcast from Matanza. Pointing my little aerial, I'd get Havanna, move across the horizon until I hear Matanza, then glide the antenna that much farther southeast. I used that to guide us, the level of the static from Havanna to Matanza, an equal distance to Camarioca.

Using that static, I estimated the angle from Matanza to Camarioca. Static was my navigational guide. It was my ears and eyes, hearing and seeing our way through the raging seas on a crippled boat toward Camaroica.

"It was bad, Brad, and we never should have survived." There was still a glint of fear in his eyes, respectful fear in a face of confidence. "I thought I was going to become *The Third Man,* lost at sea never to be found again." Then the captain grinned.

But I hit Camarioca almost on the fucking number. My crew was amazed. It was a fabulous bit of navigation and a miracle that we made it alive, but we sailed right into that little port like we were on a little fishing trip enjoying a day in the sun and calm seas. My transistor radio and me, we proved to be eyes and ears enough to beat the raging storm and sail into the heart of Communist Cuba.

When we docked at Camarioca, it's clear Cuba is Communist. The Russian TV was there, Russian weapons, the military presence was everywhere. It's a Communist state, there's no doubt about it, and I sailed into Camarioca with the American flag flying high as I always fly it. It was a face off, the Cubans with their Communist weapons and me with my American flag. It was Ali against Frazier before we even knew who they were. I flew my country's flag proudly, and never thought about taking it down. Why would I? International law allows me to fly my country's flag. It was my right.

Remember though, Russia hated us as much as the United States hated Communism, and now Cuba is Russia's ally. A Cuban military man comes to me, he salutes and demands, "The flag comes down." I tell him, "No sir, I'm not taking the flag down. I have a right. It's international law that I can fly my flag on my stern." The Cuban gets angry, his face all red and demanding, saying in Spanish, talking fast and loud. "I don't care. You're in Cuba. Take it down or I'll be forced to get the commandant." I can't understand all of the words, and my little Spanish interpreter is telling me this, fear laced in her eyes.

I'm thinking, 'to hell with you and the commandant. International law says I can fly my American flag.' The reporters on board, they've got their own orders, so they're telling me, "Tony, look at all the Russian influence here, the military. Let's not start something. This is not the time or the place for this battle. For all of our sakes, take the flag down."

I'm angry now. I've just sailed through the worst seas of my life. By all rights, I shouldn't even be alive, and some little Communist son-of-a-bitch is not going to tell me I can't fly the American flag. I stand my ground firm and American proud saying to them, "I don't give a damn. I have a right to fly the American flag. It stays up."

It's stupid of me, I know that now, but I was stubborn, exhausted, and determined. I believed in my right to fly my country's flag. I refused to be pushed around by these Communist sons-a-bitches. So the Cuban military man spews some angry words in Spanish, and marches off. A few minutes later he returns with the commandant, an officer with all kinds of medals dangling over the pocket of his uniform.

Impressive in his presence, an officer in action, I almost shit when I saw him. Not because of my fear for him and his military support, but because he used to be an orderly in our hospital in Key West. The connection between Cuba and Key West was only a few miles of Caribbean Sea. I knew him as a nice young man, helpful and compassionate as a hospital orderly. Now he's grown and carrying guns in his holsters, weapons of power. Big military uniform, and he's all proud and charismatic.

In this strong, authoritative voice he gives an order in Spanish through an interpreter. I'm thinking, what's he doing, he speaks English. I've had conversations with him before, but he ignores me, continuing to speak in Spanish. The interpreter, the young Spanish girl says to me, "The Commandant says to go with him."

With that, his military escort turns and begins walking. The Commandant points to the ground beside him, signaling for me to walk with him. He's glaring, anger in his face, but his eyes are locked on me, and they say something different. So I step to his side, and we're marching toward this building, and I'm being led like a guilty man to the gas chamber. I'm their prisoner, a little guy being escorted by all of these Cuban military carrying lethal, high caliber weapons.

As we're walking, the Commandant allows for a little separation between the guards leading the way and us. When there's enough distance, he leans over and whispers so nobody else can hear, "Tony, cut the shit will you? Just take the flag down. I'm asking you as a personal favor. You're going to get in a lot of trouble. This is serious stuff, and I'm in a serious spot here. Take the flag down and make me look good. You'll save us both a lot of trouble. Please, as a favor to me." I can hear it in his voice and see it in his eyes. He's a good guy, a friend from Key West, a friend asking a favor.

I stop and shout for my interpreter. She comes running to me, and I make this big, bold statement in English. She listens, turns to the Commandant, and in a very formal and fearful voice says,

"The Captain, out of respect for you Commandant, will take the flag down." He smiles at me, I smile back, and we march back to the boat where I lower the flag.

Tony is sitting tall in his chair, staring off toward the ocean. "These are the breaks of my life. Knowing that guy probably saved my life. That day I survived the fatal seas and the hatred of the Communist for Americans. It was one of those breaks that has me sitting here talking to you today."

For that I was thankful.

So I let the reporters sneak off and do whatever they're really doing, and I spend a couple of days sitting with the Commandant telling Key West stories, learning about his life in Cuba, eating his officer steaks, and smoking the best Cuban cigars. My job's easy. I'm doing what I'm supposed to be doing. Finding out if Castro is sincere in his offer to release American's friends and relatives. Nobody said I couldn't enjoy myself while I'm doing it, visiting with my old friend, the Key West hospital orderly.

The orderly-turned-Communist-commandant explained that there was a little hotel in Camarioca, and if you took the name of the person you wanted to the hotel, they would find the person, and then release them to you. I had orders from the government not to bring any refugees back, just to verify the information that Castro was doing what he said he would do. That's when things got complicated again.

My radio man, John, his father's still in Cuba, and he tells me, "Tony, I'd love to get my father out." I say, "I don't know how we'd do that. I'm not supposed to take any refugees back." But this is his father who has lost his homeland to Communism, lost his freedom. How can I not help John help his father? I tell him, "Maybe we can pretend he's part of the crew."

I work some magic with the Commandant, and he arranges for John's father to come to Camarioca. He's a little old man about the age I am now, and he's shriveled up, you know, old like me. So we make a deal with the Commandant to pretend that John's father is part of the crew, and we're to take the father back with us. All the arrangements are made, and we're all ready to go. Nobody suspects anything, and the military is overseeing our departure under the Commandant's orders.

We're making all of the preparations to leave, sneaking John's father down to act like he's with us. We get the boat prepared, the Commandant giving us some provisions and a box of Cuban cigars. We're finishing everything and ready to go when the old man bends down. Feeble in his motions, he reaches pressing his palm to the ground, and picks up a hand full of dirt. Rising slowly on his wobbly legs, the old man takes the dirt to his face, and smells it breathing deep into his lungs. Breathing full, he holds his hand out to his son, and opens it with the palm up. The small pile of Cuban dirt is resting there, and his father is staring at the earth in his hand. Lifting his eyes, he says to his son, John, "Does it smell like this in Key West, in the United States? Does the dirt smell the same in America?" My radioman John answers in Spanish, "It's a different country, Papa. Things are different in America." The old man looks up at his son and says, "But America is not my homeland."

The crew has the lines off the dock, and we're ready to shove off. We're ready, but the old man is standing there holding the dirt. We're all getting on board, getting anxious to get out of Cuba and head for the safety of Key West, but the old man just stands there. Small and shriveled, he seems helpless as if he's unable to go on. He can step on the boat and leave his homeland, and by stepping on the boat, earn his freedom, but he just stares at the dirt in his hand.

John's begging his father, "Come on, Papa. We've got to go." He's pleading over and over again knowing this is his last chance to save his father. But the old man remains unmoved until in his frail voice the old man finally spoke, "No son." He says, tears growing in his aged eyes. "I can't go. This is my home. When I die, I want to be buried in my soil, Cuban soil."

We're all pleading, time has run out, but the old man is adamant. Cuba has been his home all of his life, and it's as if leaving now is giving his home to the Communists. He just can't do it, standing firm and unwilling to step onto the boat. The Cuban's are yelling at us, the boat lines are off. John is begging his father to take that one step onto the boat. We've got to leave, but no matter how much we pleaded, the old man wouldn't step off Cuban soil. He wants to die in Cuba, to be buried in Cuban soil, in his homeland.

We have no choice. Russian equipped Cuban military are yelling at us, and the boat is beginning to drift from the dock. We have to go before the tensions gets worse, more dangerous. John is pleading with his father, but his old man just stands there unable to move. He is a solitary figure, standing alone on the dock as his eyes begin to pool watching as his son drifts from him. As much as we didn't want to, we had no choice. We had to leave.

The lines are on board, and we're drifting farther away from the docks. The old man is watching us, his hand still open with a small bit of Cuban dirt resting there. John's crying, his father's crying. They're staring at each other with tears running down their faces knowing they'll never see each other again. His father will never be able to leave Cuban soil, and the Communists will never allow John to return. They know this is the end, this is goodbye forever. Everybody's crying-the entire crew-as the engine began to churn and move us out into the bay away from the old man. As tears stream down my checks blurring my vision, I'm guiding us back to freedom.

As we step out into the open ocean, we're watching the old man get smaller and smaller standing on the island with Cuban soil in his hand. My heart aches with the pain of a son losing a father as I watch John standing on the stern and his father in the distance. The old man is slowly getting smaller as his son's going to America and he's chosen to stay in his homeland. I wanted to do something, but there was nothing we could do. Communism had torn this family apart.

We left Cuba as ordered two days after we'd arrived and without the reporter passengers we'd taken over. Before we left, one of the reporters had snuck back to the boat and given me eight rolls of 16-millimeter film in a burlap bag. In the dark of night, he'd told me, 'When you hit the docks at Key West, there'll be a guy with a red baseball cap. He's the one you must give these to. It's important. No matter what you do, make sure the man in the red baseball cap gets this film.' I don't know what the reporters were really there to do, but I did my job. I left with the film, and I never saw them again.

We get back to Key West, and everybody's waiting for us. The docks are full of people waiting my return because the headlines in the *Key West Citizen* had read 'Captain Tony goes to Cuba.' *Maggie, my girlfriend editor had published the story, too much reporter in her to keep a secret.*

Tony glanced up smiling with a glimmer in his eyes. "Damn reporters."

The TV crews were there. This is a big deal, going to Communist Cuba. People are gathered all around, and all these officials are arguing about who had authority over this situation. I went to Cuba without official permits, no passports, so these officials were doing their duty. Whoever hired me to go to Cuba and paid me $20,000 never notified the locals, the sheriff, the Coast Guard, didn't notify anybody. So when Maggie made my trip the headline of the Key West Citizen, it alerted the government officials. When I came back, these officials only knew what they'd read in the paper, and they knew I'd broken the law.

As I step off the boat all of the sudden I'm taken into custody. They've got me handcuffed and have arrested my whole crew. They gave us chicken pox shots, and began to search the boat. While this is happening, I'm searching the crowd, searching for the man in the red hat. Finally, I see a guy with the red cap, but he's holding the bill of his cap and shaking his head a subtle 'No.' He understands the situation, knows the timing isn't right, isn't safe. I read the signal, and turn away as if I'd never seen him.

I've got the burlap bag of film gripped tightly in my handcuffed hands, and a guy in a government uniform comes forward all official and taking control. In his intimidating bravado, he announces, "Immigration has full authority here." He grabs my arm, gripping a large hand hard over my bicep, and takes me to his office. When we get inside away from the crowd, his demeanor turns angrier. He demands, "I want that bag." Pointing at the burlap bag in my hand, he reaches for it.

I'm getting pissed off now, so I swing away, my eyes never leaving his, and say, "I want a receipt for it, then I'll give it to you. I want a receipt." He pulls out his .38, and points it at me, square between the eyes. His hand is shaking with anger, as he pressed his finger against the trigger. "Give me a reason, and I'll blow your fuckin' head off," he yells with this uncontrolled anger.

I don't know this guy or why he hates me, but he's pissed off and looking for an excuse to shoot me. He's acting unstable, like logic doesn't matter, but I repeat, "I'll give you what's in the bag. Just give me a receipt." Those are my demands.

He grabs a tablet and begins to write out a receipt. As he does this, I lay out the eight rolls of film. When he's finished, he glares at me, not even looking at the paper as he writes his signature. That's when the telephone rings.

It's a call from Washington, somebody important, somebody he must listen to. The caller gave the immigration officer his orders. It's pissed him off, I can tell, his face turning red as he slams down the pen.

His orders are to let the Captain go, let his crew go, return his boat to him, forget this ever happened, and allow Tony to walk out the door with the film. He's angry like you can't believe, a pit bull provoked, but those are his orders. He has to let me go. He waves his hand telling me to get out, so I scoop up the film, dropped it into the burlap sack, and push out the doorway.

As I leave the immigration office, the man in the red hat is waiting in the crowd of people. I push through the crowd, never *making eye contact, and as I pass, I slipped the burlap sack with all eight rolls of film into his hand. With that smooth exchange, I keep walking and get the hell out of there.*

I sat there on the balcony of Rick's, listening spellbound, and shocked. Tony just looked at me like he'd finished another story. Such is life. But I wanted more.

"So what happened to the reporters?"

"Don't know," Tony shrugged as if he had no clue, then his eyes shifted. "But I did hear this story."

I lifted out of my seat, leaning to the story-telling Captain, my mind churning for more details. "What story?" My voice fought to draw more from him.

With that, he smiled a self-satisfied grin of an old man sharing his memoirs as an international spy.

Every weekend morning, Castro would come out on to his palace patio, and he would smoke his cigar as he walked back and forth. It was his morning ritual, and we knew it. Our government had planned to kill him, kill him for betraying our support and bringing Communism to our back door. Assassins were sent with a plan to knock him off while he's standing alone on his palace patio smoking his morning cigar. The rumor was three guys had been deployed to Cuba to assassinate Castro. They had found their way onto the palace grounds, hidden in the shrubbery, and were there ready and waiting for him when he came out for his morning cigar.

It was all set up, and Castro was going to be killed, assassinated to end the great Communist threat to the United States. But it turned out that one of the men sent to assassinate Castro was a Cuban sympathizer, a Communist who had infiltrated our government years before. Instead of assassinating Castro, he killed the other two guys and saved Castro's life.

"Were those the reporters?" I asked, anticipating, leaning in.

Tony just watched my eyes, stared at me with an unmoving expression, without giving me any clue. It was his poker face. As I watched his eyes without any response to mine, I thought *what a great secret spy story.*

"Is that the truth Tony?"

His grin and eyes both slowly transformed from his poker face to one beaming confidence. "I told you I was going to bring you into my world. I told you I was going to tell you the truth. And I told you I'd throw in some bullshit for fun." He stared directly into my eyes. "Brad, the reality of some stories is so intriguing, bullshit would only weaken the truth."

As we left Rick's going down the wooden stairs, Tony bounced like a teenager just called for dinner.

"Going down's a lot easier," he told me, full of breath.

On the street, he waved at Marty and stepped to the car. When I held open the door, Marty grinned a happy hello, relieved that Tony had made it up and down. Tony slipped carefully into the passenger seat, his oxygen supply on the floor between his legs.

"That was good, Brad," he reached out his hand, and I put mine in his. "Let me get some rest and let's meet for dinner. Can you find the El Siboney Restaurant?"

"I'm sure I can." I couldn't wait.

"It's a Cuban restaurant, wonderful authentic food. I'll meet you there at six o'clock," he squeezed my hand. "I want to tell you what I've learned from gun-running. What I've learned about the way our world has changed."

I nodded, and as Tony pulled away, I stood for a long time watching he and Marty disappear down the mile long length of Duval Street.

CHAPTER 11

Late that afternoon, I felt a bit harmonic taking my guitar poolside where inspiration would encourage me to work on Captain Tony's song. Moving from the cool breeze of the room air conditioning to the tropical heat wave, I succumbed to the call from a guesthouse lounge chair and found that it formed perfectly around my body like a feather bed in a sauna.

Settling in, I visited with a highly tanned couple who had worshiped the sun much more than I, though their glistening bodies told me they had learned the value of UV protection. Escaping from the strain of his medical software business, my new friend Steve toasted the solitude of a quiet afternoon while his wife, Lisa, replayed her vision of the ocean's shades of blues reflecting off the coral reef. They'd been snorkeling the day before, and she couldn't get over the brilliant colors and aqua aliveness of the shallow waters.

"Peace, quiet, and the island life." Steve lifted his glass, and our ice teas clanked in the off tone of thick plastic. "And the rowdy fun of the nightlife," he added.

Grinning sedately, I felt the escape. "That's Key West. A heck of an adventure where you can blend in to tropical escape from real life."

A nice guy with unnaturally dark hair and a bold body only slightly impacted by time behind his computer, his talk of escape turned when he asked the inevitable conversation starter. "What brings you here? You a singer?"

I glanced at my guitar case, wishing I could acknowledge the label. "Just a hobby. Actually, I'm here writing a book with Captain Tony."

He lowered his sunglasses to stare wide-eyed over the top. "Captain Tony? Like the saloon?"

"The one and only."

Steve's wrinkled forehead deepened. "I thought he was dead."

Laughing, I sat up from my towel-covered lounger. "Common mistake," I told them both. "He probably should have been time and again, but right now he's very much a living legend."

"What's your book about?" Lisa's voice spoke but she was unmoving from her spot in the sun with trendy sunglasses shading her eyes.

"It's about understanding him, figuring out why he's a legend, and the lessons we can learn from his life."

Her head tilted sideways from the sun to me. Pretty with a well-kept figure, her real blond hair was cut short to highlight her high cheekbones. "Interesting. I heard he was a legend because he had a ton of kids."

I reached down for the complimentary pitcher of sun brewed ice tea and filled both of their glasses before refilling mine. That is most people's image, the belief that Tony's simply a fertilizing machine, a Casanova who planted seeds like that Johnny Appleseed.

"Tony is a lady's man, no doubt about it," I laid back, the conversation made as words floated to the air above us where they caught in the humidity and floated back down. "That part of his reputation often precedes him, but his life has been much more important than that, much more legendary. It involves gun-running and being Key West's mayor. There's his relationship with Jimmy Buffett and his flight from the New Jersey mob. But most of all what I've learned is that he has a great love for people, cares deeply for this island, and that's why he's become a legend."

There was silence for a moment as I let the words sink in like the heat beating into our pores as we all stared eyes closed into the sun.

"Tony lives his life based on three premises," I took a long breath, honored as if sharing my grandfather's wisdom. "Compassion is the most important word in the dictionary, and Tony's taught me to allow it to be my guide." I shifted toward them, turning slightly sideways. "Tony's reminded me that there's a jewel in every person, and if you don't connect with the people, you'll never find their treasure. Like right now. Meeting you, seeking the jewel that you each have in you, the jewel you can share that will mean something enriching to me once I've discovered it."

As Steve sat upward in his chair, Lisa reached her hand out to his arm. "Oh, you're so kind. I like that," she told us both. "A jewel in every person."

"And Tony believes that you should share a word of kindness." I gave my own slight shrug. "Simply put ... well, do you mind if I share in my own way?"

Their shaded eyes both glanced toward me as I opened the guitar case, pulling my Taylor from its safety felt enclosure.

"This is something I've been working on." I spoke as I plucked each string, tuning. When I had all six steel wires in perfect blend, I began to play, first the intricate notes of the introduction building to the casual strumming harmony.

> *I met him at a bar in a pirate town*
> *Living his life out by the sea*
> *With his knowledge of time*
> *He spoke his wisdom to me*
>
> *Life lessons of a legend*
> *Captain Tony's wisdom to us all*
> *Fill your heart with compassion*
> *Seek the jewel in every soul*
> *Share a word of kindness*
> *Simple life lessons that make us whole*
>
> *From a life lived teetering on the edge*
> *Sailing high on hurricane seas*
> *He's lived his life without fear*
> *The immortality of a good buccaneer*
>
> *Life lessons of a legend*
> *Captain Tony's wisdom to us all*

Fill your heart with compassion
Seek the jewel in every soul
Share a word of kindness
Simple life lessons that make us whole

As I fiddled with an instrumental blend of A minors and E minors with open chord notes, I talked over the music. "That's what I've got so far, a tribute to Tony and his lessons." I picked through a G chord. "I'm thinking about a bridge with something focusing on *It's the people* and ending with a verse that includes *He knows he won't live forever, but his lessons live on and on.*"

"What simple but true lessons," Lisa freed her face from the sunglasses to share enlightened eyes. "That's the key to our business, Steve. If that's what we'd do, if that's how we approached people … Steve's already created a great product, but the connection with people is our key. If we'd focus on those three lessons, we'd open the doors to so many more potential clients."

I grinned upward, laughing. "You'd be software legends."

Lisa's eyes danced a little, one of those happy dances of a confident woman feeling playful in Key West. *"Fill your heart with compassion, seek the jewel,"* she hesitated, her head turned toward me, her cheek on the terrycloth towel.

"…And share a word of kindness."

"Yes, of course. *Share a word of kindness.* Perfect," she declared. "What's the name of the book?" Lisa asked.

"Life Lessons of a Legend," I told them.

"Oh, I like that."

"And good lessons they are," Steve added. "And a good song."

"Thanks," I grinned happily, my mind fiddling with the perfect words for the song's bridge.

On the island map, the El Siboney Restaurant is in the middle of Key West, nestled quietly within a residential neighborhood. I rented a bike and rode lazily along the weather worn streets, taking the long route circling here and there but always moving in the general direction of the restaurant, enjoying the sense of being within the maze of the residences inhabited by the locals.

The decision to ride to El Siboney was not one of transportation or wanting exercise or even a chance to see the beautiful homes or the interior real life of the island. It was a decision of a renewed spirit feeling strong and capable and wanting to go out and get some fresh air because I was full of energy. Comfortably cruising along in my cotton hiking shorts and a Buffett inspired tee-shirt adorned with a ring of dancing parrots circling the chest and back, I felt a renewed sense of self. I had refocused on the important things in life, and had been rewarded with the strength and enthusiasm of a good bike ride.

Arriving at the restaurant, I learned that El Siboney is an unobtrusive white structure with a parking problem. On a residential corner, it was already busy with cars parked up and down the street, but I rode right to the front door, gliding in with one foot on a pedal as I lifted my other leg over the seat. I leaned my bike against the white siding of the building. A reward, feeling renewed and active, had given me the perfect parking space.

Tony was waiting for me at a quiet corner table with a pleasant surprise. T.J. was with him. Tony stood with a big wave and open grin, his white dentures gleaming. T.J. stood too, slightly taller than his father with the same slender build and kind smile. As I stepped to them, I reached out my hand to T.J., and he nodded a quiet, respectful greeting, the understated personality of his mother. Tony took my hand too, but he did so with enthusiasm and warmth, his left hand covering the back of mine in an envelope of caring.

As we sat down, Tony pointed at the menu. "You order anything you want. Tonight is on me."

"Oh, that's not necessary." The vinyl chair felt cool in the air conditioning.

"It's my honor," he pointed softly. "Your last night in town. It's my honor to buy you dinner." *Share a word of kindness.* "This is true Cuban food. Excellent. I've known the owner for years," Tony acknowledged. "Beautiful Cuban people, and they really know their authentic food. El Siboney is a Key West favorite."

I scanned the menu and the selections all looked wonderful, but it also all looked Cuban. Not being a Cuban connoisseur, I didn't know one item from the other.

"T.J.," I said, "are you having your favorite?"

"Yep."

"Why don't you order the same thing for me," I nodded, tapping the corner of his menu. "I'm sure it'll be great."

As the restaurant dinner guests walked by the table, Tony waved and acknowledged their hellos. Tourists stared and whispered to each other asking if that was "Captain Tony," while locals just called out his name greeting an old friend. "How you doing today, Captain?" And Tony would answer. "Great, and you look great yourself. It's good to see you looking so healthy."

With all the notoriety, Tony turned to me. "I'll tell you something I haven't told anyone else," Tony said as he placed his tiny Cuban coffee cup on the table. "If I had the financial backing, I'd run for mayor again."

"Why's that?" I asked, lifting my soda.

"Because when you're running for office, you can say things you can't say otherwise." His eyes bore down on me. "In our country, we can't openly express ourselves anymore. There was a time when you could say things like *I don't agree with the president. I think his ideas are all messed up*, but not anymore," he truly looked distressed. "After our talk this afternoon, I think it's important that you know these things, know what I think about our country, our decisions, because I've learned so much in my life. You can't live as long as I have and do all of the things I've done without learning."

He took a moment to put things in order in front of him. His paper placemat, the napkin rolled silverware, and cup of Cuban coffee.

"I'm disturbed at the recent events of our country. If this were the 70s you could stand up and say *I don't agree with this war in Iraq.* President Bush led us into a war of religion and oil and a family feud with Saddam Hussein. Bush used the words *weapons of mass destruction* to scare us to the point of supporting an unjust war. Now that we know the truth, you might want to say what you believe, but you can't say that. Twenty-five years ago was the last time we respected our right to speak freely."

"You don't think we can speak freely now?" I pushed for more.

His passion seemed to explode like a dozen 4th of July bottle rockets. As Tony leaned in over the table, his long finger pointing outward sharp and direct, intensity in his deep frown, his eyes were penetrating needles, absolutely determined to inject what he was saying.

"We've learned not to say anything publicly. The damage is so complete. Every word is dissected in the press, meanings manipulated by mind-reading talk show hosts with no experience except to turn your thoughts from your truth to theirs. Look at what they did to the Dixie Chicks. Nice girls, entertainers, Americans who have a right to say what they believe. That little blond one, the cute one, she stood up and made an impassioned statement from the heart on what she believed about our president and his war with Iraq. She might not have said it in the best way or used the right words, but she had the right to say it.

Instead of appreciating the right to speak freely, we attacked the Dixie Chicks for speaking out. The press and politicians went after them. She didn't say anything against our troops or not supporting them. She was just angry at her president, but we turned her statements against the President's war into anti-American words of disrespect for our troops. It had nothing to do with not supporting the troops. It had everything to do with her opinion of the President's decision to go to war with Iraq, yet we shunned them, burned their records, and called them un-American."

I had not seen such animation as the Captain's arms began to swing about directing the orchestra of his conscience. "Instead of attacking the Dixie Chicks, we should have been celebrating that girl's right to say what she did. Isn't that why President Bush said we went to war with Iraq anyway, to give the Iraqi people the same freedom we were denying the Dixie Chicks?" T.J. smiled as the passion of Tony's resolve flowed. "It confuses me that we've lost that right. I feel bad for T.J. that he can no longer speak freely, truly say what he believes. If I was running for mayor, I could hide protected behind the political campaign and say what I believe."

Tony was quiet for a moment, almost solemn before he went on, staring harshly at the table as if his long, hard stare would somehow change what he saw as an injustice. He looked up grinning with his stare of clarity, his mouth falling slightly open.

"You know," the old man announced, "keeping your mouth shut is a form of constipation. Our whole country needs a good enema."

While my laughter burst out, T.J. let loose with this slight chuckle that told me he knew better what to expect from his father. T.J. was used to such pronouncements, but to me, I was just getting acquainted with the color of Tony's blunt honesty.

"I got you with that one, didn't I?" So glad he made me laugh. "But it's true. Sometimes you just have to take the risk, you have to say what you believe, otherwise you're full of shit."

I pushed for more. "How would you teach your children, Tony, about freedom of speech? What do you teach them, teach T.J.?" I reached out touching his son's shoulder.

He sat back in the chair, his eyes diverted as he shook his head with the frustration of one who'd lost something precious and could not get it back.

"Ten years ago, I'd have taught my children to stand up for what they believe." He grew emotionally charged with sad determination in his eyes. "I can't say that now. People who disagree with you attack your right to express yourself. If you're talking to ten people, one is your enemy. They don't want to debate you or challenge your position anymore. There's no respect for freedom of speech. They want to attack you personally. An enemy today is dangerous and can destroy you because they will twist your words. They get it on T.V., some reporter picks it up to sell papers, or a kid puts it on the Internet and other people will believe what they read. And people remember. They hold those thoughts for so long and use them against you. I can't teach my children to speak out for what they believe in anymore. The damage is too complete."

"How's that all fit with compassion?" I asked.

Tony's blue stare shot outward. "The Dixie Chicks. What's that girl's name, the little one?"

"Natalie." T.J. and I said at the same time.

"You think Natalie is a bad person? You think Natalie has lived an evil life?"

"No," I answered, "the Dixie Chicks even did that song, that song about the soldier."

"Travelin' Soldier," T.J. said.

"Yes," I pointed his way, "about a boy dying in a war."

Tony's wrinkled hands pressed flat against the Formica tabletop. "They're good people, Americans who have brought many good things to the world. Good lessons in the words of their songs, music with compassion in their lyrics. They're nice girls. The world loves them, then one statement is made, and the press grabs on to it and puts it in the headlines. People, important people, comment on it with harsh, damaging words. They turn the Dixie Chicks into hated anti-Americans." Tony stared straight into me. "Do you think that it's compassionate to ruin a life, a career because of one statement made in the name of freedom of speech? Freedom of speech is no longer a freedom in our democracy. There are too many consequences."

I looked right back into his patriotic eyes. "So you'd run for mayor to have that right to speak again?"

His clear eyes turned downward with large bags of tired skin hanging full below as his thoughtful stare searched to understand. When he looked up, his eyes turned haunting. "I love my country, and I want the right to judge it. I want all Americans to have that right once again."

We ate a traditional Cuban plate full of overflowing shredded beef, potatoes, and a little banana-like cinnamon sweet dessert.

I pointed at the creamy miniature bananas, my eyebrows questioning.

"Cuban bananas," answered Tony. "Plantains."

"Ah, yes," I held my thumb and finger a couple inches apart.

As we savored the wonderful food, the table had grown quiet with the Cuban delicacies. Tony nibbled at his plantains before he set his fork aside.

"Brad," he said, looking up at me, "I saw Haiti and Cuba. They weren't that much different than Iraq, but our world is different now. I've lived a long life through so many wars. Wars fought in Europe, wars with our own weapons of mass destruction, war in the jungle of Viet Nam, and wars live on T.V. What I've learned in my long life is that I hate war."

"Isn't that a contradiction?" I asked. "Gun-running to Cuba and now denouncing war?"

"Much of my life is a contradiction," stated like a man with a grip on a lifetime of learning. "When you've lived as long as I have, lived from a time of learning to fly to landing rovers on Mars, your thoughts are going to change, your beliefs change. It's okay for knowledge and experience to change our beliefs. The press doesn't accept that. Hell, they go searching back to what somebody said a lifetime ago and hold it against them without respect that a person can learn, grow, change, and become better." T.J. sat quietly listening to his father. "Here's what I believe now, after all of my time on this earth."

I've told you that I learned a long time ago that life is just people. I've lived a lot of years, and I've loved every president, I love President Bush, and I love my country. At the same time, I realize what we're doing today in this war. It started with a crock about weapons of mass destruction and turned worse from there.

In my lifetime our world has changed, war has changed. We're a world of communication, a global society, yet we still preach to young men that the answer to disputes is to carry the flag into battle and become a hero. We forget that the guy carrying the flag is a father with a couple of kids. We live in a time of communication, a time of negotiations, yet we fight wars using hand-to-hand combat. There's got to be a better way than all of these young people dying. Our young soldiers are killed. Then they give the widow and the children a little medal on a ribbon, there's a flag over the casket, it's folded and handed to the mother of his children, and they call him a hero.

What's it worth, this father being a hero? Wouldn't the children like to have him tuck them in as they grow up, his wife wanting him to say goodnight every night as they hold each other tight? Would their lives be better with days at the beach with their father instead of him being a fading hero's picture on the mantel. These young men and women go out and die, leave their families to survive on their own, their children to grow up without their guidance, their husband or wife struggling to provide for their children, and our government rewards them by calling him a hero.

They are heroes, young men and women who give their lives because our country asks them too. We should stand up and honor them as heroes, but we'd be better off, their families would be better off, and our world would be better off if they were alive because we chose diplomacy instead of the violence of war. Instead of showing compassion, instead of seeking the jewel in all men, instead of offering words of kindness, we send our young men to fight, and when they die 40, 60 years before their time, calling them a hero is supposed to make it all okay.

President Bush has got us fighting a 20th century war in a 21st century world. I'd rather we'd have focused on diplomacy and communication, made a greater effort to connect with the people, talk to them, and help them make better global decisions than to see our young soldiers die as heroes leaving their family with only a medal and a flag.

With a slight sag in his shoulders, Tony's words quieted. "I don't know if I'm right or wrong. I just know we have sacrificed too much, too many American soldiers, and too many Iraqi lives. I think if people really want peace, if they live with compassion in their hearts, they can find a way. In this war, I don't think peace was the objective." Captain Tony looked up into my eyes, his gaze distant and filled with sorrow. "From my experiences in Haiti and Cuba, from watching our world grow and gaining knowledge, I've learned that there's a better way than killing."

The bags under Tony's eyes hung fuller against his cheeks as he cast his stare downward fiddling nervously with his fork.

The rest of the meal was a slow, quiet reflection, and we tasted each bite while thinking, absorbing Tony's wisdom. It was seven o'clock when we finished the last of the seasoned, shredded beef and sweet baby bananas. T.J. was sitting back with a big smile of satisfaction rubbing the slight bulge from his skinny belly, and Tony was sipping coffee from a tea-sized cup.

"So," he set the clay cup on the saucer, "your last night in Key West. Has your visit been everything you hoped?"

Easily, I wiped the last bit of cinnamon sweetness from my lips, folded the white cloth napkin into a smaller square, and placed it on the table before me. "More," I smiled, and Tony smiled too. "I came here to learn about you, and I learned about me."

"I learned to," Tony said. "You're a good man, and you've made me a better man, Brad."

I'd found the treasure in Tony, and rediscovered the jewel in myself. *The people are what it's all about.*

"So it's your last night in Key West," T.J. said. "What're your plans?"

Smiling again, this time with a little laugh, I answered. "Start at the saloon, and have some fun with new friends."

I rode my bike without using my hands as I glided through the residential streets, leaning slightly into the turns to weave right and left down blocks lined with quaint homes and tropical retreats. I was like a carefree kid with no worries because I'd quit thinking so much and instead found myself doing what felt right, and riding with no hands felt right. There was a whole lot less second-guessing and a whole lot more personal honesty. I'd found a comfort in the integrity of believing in my own good instincts.

On Duval Street I grabbed the handlebars once again and rode weaving among the cars of tourists who were trying to figure out how they'd gotten trapped on this busy street. At the Women's Society house I stopped to listen to the five-string guitar player. He pounded steel wires into music like a man on a mission to release both anger and energy too long confined. His beard was tangled with slight dreadlocks of long hair twisting from his chin. Through his straggly mustache, I could see his unhealthy smile as he sang the words to some made-up song. Words of determination and belief, words of optimism and joy, words that must have been of his past or maybe they were of his future. I dropped a five-dollar bill in his guitar case.

I was walking my bike a block later when I passed the Flying Monkey. During our last visit to Key West, Denise had been on a mission, a mission to find the best Piná Colada in Key West. She went on a vacation diet plan *of eat seafood sensibly and drink all the Piná Coladas you want.* She tried them everywhere. A Piná Colada in one restaurant, then another in the next bar, and at six bucks a pop, I might add. With my protests of the cost, she'd waved me off like an insignificant fly buzzing around her head. Then she'd raised her glass, and in a high-pitched revelation, told me to have some fun and just spend the silly six bucks, reminding me once again, *We're on vacation!*

With each icy cream treat, she'd fought off the brain freeze attacking the top of her mouth, and evaluated her enthusiasm for the coconut flavor, sweetness, and libation blend. After cruising like a treasure hunter scanning the island tourist map for the X, she kept coming back to the Flying Monkey. At the Flying Monkey, Piná Coladas were a treasure.

"This place freaks me out," she'd roll her eyes. "Flying monkeys freak me out. Since I was a little girl and watched the Wizard of Oz, flying monkeys have freaked me out." Then she'd raised her frosty plastic glass covered with graphic flying monkeys, smiled innocently with her sweet enthusiasm and said, "But the Coladas make me forget."

From a stool at the bar of the Flying Monkey, I ordered a Piná Colada, pulled out my cell phone, and spoke her name into it. She answered quickly.

"Hey." Her voice was a sweetened surprise.

"Guess what I'm doing." I said with a laugh.

"I don't want to know." There was jealousy in her snicker, always supportive yet unable to hide her disappointment that I was in the Caribbean and she was in the land of corn.

"That's right, you don't," I told her taking my first sip of the sugary coconut.

"What are you doing?" She demanded with that teasing tone, that tone I knew even better than the words.

"Drinking a Piná Colada."

"Augh!" The breath flew from her throat in mock irritation. "Are you at the Flying Monkey?"

"Best Piná Coladas in Key West."

"Well, I'm glad I'm not there," her tone turned stubborn. "Flying monkeys freak me out."

It was good to hear her voice, and I wished she were with me. I'd love to spend six bucks to buy her the best Piná Colada in Key West. Hell, after a week with Tony, I'd spend twelve bucks, twenty-four bucks. I'd seriously shock Denise by putting a fifty on the bar and spend freely without remorse saying *keep'em coming.*

As I talked to her, I wished I could share her beautiful eyes and feel that slight touch of her hand that was always reaching over to rest lightly upon my thigh. Denise is part of the jewel in me, part of what keeps me young, lively, and not so wrapped up in my seriousness that comes with being an educational task hermit. She is the side that reminds me it's okay to play.

We talked while I drank, and then I ordered another Piná Colada.

"For you," I told her.

She didn't answer.

"Are you there?"

"Yes," she said hard and short but there was happiness in her tone.

Then we slipped back into our conversation as I told her about dinner, and she made me promise to take her to El Siboney on our next trip south. I talked about my time with Tony and the things he'd reminded me about. When I talked about compassion, she interrupted me.

"Honey," she said softly. "Wayne called last night." As her voice mellowed there was a slight pause. "Thank you. You don't know how much it meant to him."

"I do," I told her. "But it might have meant more to me."

After the quiet, we talked about my flight home the next day, about her picking me up at the airport. I was missing her and looking forward to her smiling green eyes, the gentle touch in the way she held me, and her playful belief that life is meant to be lived.

When I stepped into Captain Tony's Saloon, Tony had already arrived. He was in his corner leaning over a scrumptious, tight-bodied beach lover who blushed at the tickle as the old man autographed her swimsuit-swelled bosom. Then he leaned forward and pressed his lips into the gentle slope of her neck. As he did, a dozen camera flashes illuminated them both and the poster behind them.

I reached across the counter as Randy's hand caught mine in a firm shake. As I did, I heard my name.

"Brad," Tony was pointing at her bikini, "can you believe how beautiful she is?" As he said it, Tony lifted his own imaginary bikini top, and the blushing girl, laughing freely at the playfulness of the old man, quickly pulled him closer giving him a great big hug and huge smacking kiss on his stubbled cheek. "87 and I kiss more beautiful women in one night than most men do in a lifetime. It's great to be

Captain Tony." Then he danced a little side to side before giving the young woman one last sweet kiss on the soft cheek she offered back.

I went to the bar and ordered a free beverage, and stood there a minute listening to the guitar player, Craig, pound out magic in all six strings. Talented, I couldn't help but admire the coordination and speed of ten digits all working in perfect harmony. When he finished, he spoke into the mic talking history with the people, history of the bar and Captain Tony.

"He's like a grandfather to me," He told the crowd. "You should go back and meet him. He'll change your life."

Some big guy in a cowboy hat with boot cut jeans and snakeskin dirt kickers swayed sideways at the corner of the bar. "Can't hold a candle to my granddaddy."

I thought, *Who the heck wears jeans and snakeskin boots in Key West?*

"I'm sure your granddaddy was something special," Craig spoke kindly. "But Captain Tony is a legend."

"He ain't nothing to my granddaddy." The big man's words were bold for being slurred slippery from his mouth.

Craig ran his fingers over the strings causing sweet sounds to vibrate as he lowered his head down to hide his irritation. Looking up with a jolly grin, he said. "Did your granddaddy ever run a gambling scam on the mob and live to gamble with them another day? Did your granddaddy ever have a shark he caught displayed in the Smithsonian?

Was your granddaddy ever a spy for the United States, a covert gun-runner battling the high seas?"

The cowboy slopped beer from his souvenir cup as he waved it at the guitar player. "My granddaddy could kick your granddaddy's ass."

Craig could not hide his annoyance. "While your granddaddy's trying to kick somebody's tail, Captain Tony'll be lovin' a beautiful woman. You tell me." Craig smirked toward the big, stupid drunk. "You want to try and kick somebody's ass or make love to an island beauty?"

"I'd kick ass." His chest puffed up until from behind him a rather plump girl, with a beefy chest and a giant silver belt buckle pulling her waist tight punched him hard in the arm. The cowboy in the snakeskin boots yelled "Ouch" as he rubbed his tender bicep with a pouty look.

Craig's irritation disappeared with the irony. "Was your granddaddy the Mayor of his town?"

"No sir." The oversized cowboy was still rubbing his arm and slurring his words.

"Well here's a song Jimmy Buffett wrote about a true legend, Captain Tony." With that Craig started the familiar intro to *The Last Mango in Paris*. As he did, he leaned back toward the cowboy, nodding. "You go back and meet Captain Tony. He'll change your life. He changed mine."

I thought about Tony's relationship with the purveyor of fun, Jimmy Buffett. Earlier in the week he'd shared with me a special memory.

You know how life goes, the challenges. We all get ourselves into situations that we have to work through. Years ago, Jimmy came in here as just another kid playing his guitar. I liked him, liked his spirit and his connection with people. As Jimmy's popularity grew, we stayed close. He'd made it big with his 'Changes' album, but his personal life was going the wrong direction. Just like you or me in our lives, it was Jimmy's tough time to work through. People were worried about him, and a friend of ours told me, 'Tony, you've got to talk to him. He respects you, and he'll listen to you.' So I sat Jimmy down and like a father to a son, we had a serious talk. I don't know if that's what turned his personal life around or not, but I tried to help, and after that, he seemed to get his life going the right direction again.

With that, I listened as Craig sang Buffett's lyrics speaking of his respect for Captain Tony. I lifted my beer toward the singer, and he gave me a jovial nod as the song flowed with the perfect pitch of suave devotion.

Tony was surround by a group of women, one pushing him with verbal banter like somehow he'd irritated her. Randy pointed toward them wanting me to listen.

The short-haired stocky woman with a bull-dog demeanor growled at the Captain. "So you knew Hemingway?"

I already knew the answer.

Tony waved his hands back and forth. "I knew him, but not well. We'd say hello when we saw each other around town. You know, a wave, a nod. I knew him, yes, because

Key West was a small island back then, but we weren't close friends."

Her stare turned to a glare, challenging him, "So what's your favorite Hemingway book?"

I recognized the challenge, the assumption that Tony was all talk. The bulldog before him wanted proof.

Tony's eyes lifted, surprised at the question, "He wrote at a different time, about a different time. It was a time I lived, that's why *Old Man and the Sea* is my favorite."

Her glare pressed into him. "So you read a lot?" Her assumption showing strong, how could a man of Tony's history be an intellectual, a man well read?

With a slight, dignified nod, the politician answered, *"Then must you speak of one that love'd not wisely but too well."*

As she stepped back, I could almost see a smile on her lips, "Shakespeare?"

"Othello," Tony's head tilted with a slight, dignified nod.

I could see it in her eyes. He had won her over, and they fell into a discussion of literature, she being a teacher of literature from Ohio. They talked of Shakespeare and Hemingway, the magic of words, and the impact of a great story. It was a lively conversation, one I'm sure she had not expected. Yet, it wasn't long before I heard him say, "You know, in my experience teachers are great lovers."

Instead of glaring irritation for what she had assumed, she gave him a little hug. Drawn to him, she was enlightened that the *Salt of Key West* was more than she expected, yet in the end it came back to exactly what she'd expected. It's just that she hadn't planned on liking it.

When I felt the hand land firmly on my shoulder, I turned to see the cheesy grin of my new friend Steve. Lisa was beside him, exquisite in a flowered sundress and understated heels.

"Hey guys," I gave them both a hug, not sure if the affectionate reaction was because of Tony's lessons or the free beer I'd been drinking.

With Lisa's little squeeze, she stepped back, "We came down to meet your Captain."

"Tony," I waved to him, he motioned for me, and we stepped between the many admirers where I offered an introduction. "My new friends," I told him as Steve and Lisa shook his hand.

"Down here on vacation?" he greeted them like he was president of the Chamber of Commerce. "Welcome to Captain Tony's."

"Brad told us about your book," Lisa moved closer to be heard over the crowd.

"He's a great writer," Tony put his arm around me. "Better than that. He's a good person and a true friend."

"Thanks Tony."

"It's the truth," he told Lisa. "He's made me think about how I think, the things I think. He's helped me understand myself even better. It's been a great week getting to know him, and tomorrow when he leaves, I'll miss him."

"We can't wait to read the book," Steve stood between Lisa and me. "Brad shared your life lessons with us."

"Oh," Tony lifted his eyes, his arms waving in the air like skinny goal posts, "the life I've lived. Who'd have thought a little WOP from New Jersey would do what I've done?"

They broke up with their own laughter as did those behind them listening in.

"It's true," his hands reached to each of their forearms. "I've done more in my life, survived more. You can't believe it. And with it all, there's been some great bullshit too. You'll love the book. The lessons, the stories I've lived, and the color added for fun."

Tony lifted his finger, pointing upward above the bar. "I used to take so many women up the ladder. That's where I lived, above the bar. I'd love to do it just one more time. You know." His hand flipped a couple of times toward the trap door in the ceiling. "Go up the ladder one more time and make love to a beautiful woman. Just one more time for old times shake. A woman of blond beauty with eyes of the sea, slender like a sail in the wind."

With that he winked at Steve and took both of Lisa's hand in his.

"Like you," he squeezed her hands. "Oh, what soft hands. I bet you know how to love a man. If you'd go up the ladder with me, grant an old man a simple wish, you could have my last baby. I'd make you famous. How about it?"

The entire crowd was leaning in laughing, straining to hear the old man's words, wanting him to make them laugh. And laugh they did.

"You know," Lisa was blushing like a new bride, all blond with laughing sea eyes, "I'm half tempted."

"Damn," Tony blurted, playfully nudging Steve away. "Don't put that in the book, Brad. Only half-tempted. I must be loosing it." He turned back to Lisa, lifting her hands as he leaned forward kissing them. "If you went up the ladder with me just once, the second time there'd be none of this half-tempted stuff. You'd be begging me."

I patted Steve on the back. "He's a man of both great compassion and great passion."

Steve lifted his shoulders, unsure of what else to say. "I can't believe it, but she's loving this. How's he do it?"

Before I could answer the unanswerable, Tony pulled Lisa to his side, his arm gently around her waist, as he drew Steve's attention with a kind hand to his square shoulder.

I learned compassion from so many people in my life. My father was a master of compassion, a tenderness that came from deep within his heart. I saw that in the gentleness, the attentiveness as he cared for my mother before she passed away. The women I've loved, they've all taught me compassion, taught me to open my heart. But there was a time, a special time with some special people who sought the jewel first, teaching me to truly understand compassion.

My second wife, Mae, she and I were struggling financially to make our way in Key West. We were hustling people on to our charter boat, taking them out fishing, telling stories, selling sodas, being the best New Jersey hustlers we could to make a living. We made a few bucks off each customer, but, of course, much of that went to pay our overhead before we took money home to support our family. We weren't rich, but we provided for our family.

Back then, back in the lean times, we had some friends who were also struggling to find their way in the world, but their struggle wasn't so much about money. Some of them were well off, wealthy even. Money didn't challenge them, but they hadn't found their way in the world because the world wasn't open to them. Our world lacked compassion, so each week we'd get together.

These good people would come to my home, each bringing something for a meal, bread or a nice bottle of wine. Not cheap stuff, but good wine because money was not an issue to these individuals. They had money, but they lacked compassionate friends who focused on the jewel within. They'd bring the vino, and Mae would cook up a big stove-top pot of spaghetti, swirling noodles in boiling water. On the other burner was her special Italian sauce, a secret recipe from the old country.

It was a wonderful time of sitting around together, eating heaping plates of saucy spaghetti, spicy meatballs, breaking bread and drinking fine wine as we shared good talks. Stories were told and there was much laughter, laughter among friends. Good people, kind people who we shared our home and our dinner table. Those talks with those friends taught me so much about compassion because they understood compassion, and they understood the lack of compassion in others. It was an emotion they lived with each day in their lives.

There we'd be, a little wine and our close friends with Mae and me. Wonderful people. There was Tennessee Williams, Jamie

Kirkwood who wrote 'A Chorus Line,' Jamie Hurley — you remember the Academy Award winning movie 'Midnight Cowboy,' and Captain Tony; three gay writers and this straight hustler from New Jersey. Those gentlemen understood compassion because of the prejudice they lived, the unearned hatred they faced each day of their lives. From them, I learned so much about compassion. I learned about caring for the quality of each individual, and discovering the jewel that exists in each person. For me, these good friends defined compassion.

"You knew all of those people?" Lisa's eyes were wide open.

Tony nodded slowly with a dignified, gentle smile. "They were my friends, and they taught me lessons that I want others to learn. I want people to learn compassion from this book. I want people to learn to be good to their fellow man. We've got so much to give. We're all born good, and if we could just be good to each other, if we just understood compassion and lived with it as our guide, our lives, our world would be so much better."

Louie stepped into the bar just as the band was finishing their set-up on the back stage. It was about to get much more noisy, and he motioned for his Dad that it was time to leave. As Tony stepped out onto the street, he thanked Steve and Lisa for their friendship, and patted me on the back.

"Last night in Key West," Tony grinned. "Why don't you go chase one of these beautiful Key West women?"

"Don't think so, Tony." In ways, our worlds were still far a part. "Thinking more about getting home to Iowa."

"Ah yes, the beautiful wife," as Louie opened the car door, Tony smiled at me. "You're just lucky I didn't meet her first."

With that I patted him on the back, my head shaking. "Believe me Tony, I know."

Steve, Lisa and I wandered down to the Conch Republic seeking seafood and libation. A pretty woman of my age, still caught a bit in the sixties with straight grayish hair down to the slight curve in the small of her slender waist was playing familiar songs on the acoustic guitar. With her crystal blue eyes, blue like the singer Crystal, Adrienne had a familiarity, a vision of my past that I could not bring from the clutter of my life-filled mind. We listened for a while longer, but Steve was excited wanting to explore more of Key West. As we left, I stopped to stuff a twenty into her cigar box, lifted a CD from beside it, and nodded to her sincere smile of thanks.

As we walked by the memorial at the end of Greene Street next to the Conch Republic, a group of homeless people sat on the steps leading up to the permanent bronze plaque.

"Just one moment." I told my friends, and stepped toward the group where a couple of drunken yuppies were having their picture taken as they posed with the downtrodden.

When I approached, the rail thin man with the pirate's bandana looked up at me grinning. "Hey, you got any money." Causing us both to laugh.

"How you guys doing?" Two other familiar faces looked my way, and I reached out to shake their hands. When I took the girl's with the familiar spider web tattoo on her neck, I pulled gently and she stepped to me. "You," I squeezed her palm, "you could make a difference in this world. You understand compassion."

She looked straight into my eyes, "Maybe I'm just waiting for my time to come."

"Why wait?" I asked.

Her deep brown eyes brightened. "Yes," she answered, "why wait?"

I reached into my pocket and pulled out some money, handing bills to each of them. "Eat something good tonight."

The man in the pirate bandana took the bills I handed him. "Mind if I drink something good tonight?"

I only smiled.

The dark girl pushed her hair out of her eyes, "Thanks. Maybe I'll get a job so I can buy your book."

"Better yet," I encouraged her, "write your own book. You've lived a life people need to understand."

With that she gave me a little hug.

A short time later, I found myself in the contrast to homelessness that is Key West. I was dancing in the middle of a jam packed crowd of rich people singing to music about living a Corona-enriched life as Hugo Duarte and The Full

Sail Band played their songs of beach life shenanigans. The Hog's Breathe Saloon had been transformed from an afternoon acoustic bar into a rowdy late night buccaneer dance-a-thon, and I was in the middle of the expensive flowered shirt mash pit with Lisa and Steve as we danced the dance of island freedom.

Time seemed to fly by with song after song of escaping to the land of palms and never returning to the cold, barren north. While we swayed to the rhythm, the stars sparkled in the late night hours, and I was feeling like life had just begun. Trouble was Lisa wasn't on the same soul discovering high as Steve and me. Despite our protests, as our energy flowed like lava from the volcano hot and unstoppable, we reluctantly followed her away from the fun and down Simonton Street back toward our guesthouse. That's where we found ourselves talking when my cell phone rang.

I looked at the number, didn't recognize it, but answered anyway.

"Brad."

I could hear the noise in the background. "Yea," I almost had to yell.

"It's Marty. Tony wanted me to call you. He wants you to come join us."

"Where you at?" I yelled back.

"The Chart Room," when I didn't respond, she added. "At the Pier House."

I recognized the name. Smiling to myself, I yelled back into the phone. "I'll be there in a few minutes."

"Tony wants you to bring your guitar."

"My guitar? Why?"

Marty laughed out loud, that optimistic laugh of a happy woman. "Trust him on this one." She directed me, not giving me a second chance.

Slipping the phone back into my pocket, I turned to Steve. "I'm going to meet Tony for a beer. Want to come with me?"

His eyes grew big and happy ready for pirate seeking adventures in a night too young to end.

Lisa rolled her eyes, "You boy's go on and do your male bonding rituals. I'm going to bed."

Steve gave her a luscious kiss good night, as I slipped away to retrieve my Taylor acoustic. A minute later, Steve was waiting for me, rubbing his hands together and ready to head happily off toward 1 Duval Street, two boys unleashed on the night.

"We're going to the Chart Room," I told him.

"What's the Chart Room?" Steve asked.

"New one on me. Somewhere at the Pier House Resort," I shrugged. "I guess we'll find out."

With our flip-flops flapping, we weaved through the maze of the parking lots and walkways of the high end Pier House Resort, following the ornamental road signs pointing at goofy angles yet directing us to the Chart Room. In the middle of the upscale hotel complex, we pulled the Chart Room door open and stepped into history. It had a Captain Tony's feel to it with the friendliness of down home island locals that seemed completely out of place in the middle of a chic Caribbean spa resort.

Twelve feet ahead was the bar that squeezed in all of six stools set firmly on a floor carpeted with peanut shell dust. There were a few worn wood top tables with initials, symbols, and dates carved into them and old vinyl covered chairs with the plastic picked away. In the corner was a statue of a painted bar room lady as if frozen in time, dancing with a high rolling customer who would surely tip her two-bits. Tony was sitting with Marty between the sensuous plaster lady and weathered wooden door, only separated by 15 feet of old plank floor worn by too many years of drunken shuffling.

"I wanted you to see this place," Tony said, his hand sweeping the slight room in one slow-motion acknowledgement. "This is the first place Jimmy Buffett played when he came to the island, then he met his wife Jane here and the rest is history. I want this to be the first place you play in Key West."

I swung my guitar case between us in absolute denial. "I'm just learning this thing."

Steve elbowed me, "You play better than you think."

"I think, even if I play better than I think, I don't play very good."

Marty smiled, and I sensed my slight surrender. "Oh, Brad, I'd love to hear you play." Her freckles were laughing, as Tony pointed toward the bar. "One beer and you'll be great. Liquid courage." Something I surely needed.

The beers were cold as an artic night and the cheapest I'd paid for in Key West. As Steve and I leaned on the bar corner, the brunette barmaid introduced me to the General and his friend, a high flying man of enthusiasm and grins with a rousing laugh that could serve as the Chamber of Commerce for Key West's gay community.

"You going to play for us?" He pointed at the guitar case left sitting by the door.

I rolled my eyes. "I'm pretty bad."

His laugh exploded with a loud exclamation and a rosy-cheeked beam. "Anybody want to hear this guy play bad guitar?"

All twelve people filling the joint called out a rowdy *Yes* as if on cue, while Tony only laughed and Marty waved me toward the bar corner where a chair sat next to the lady-in-waiting.

The General patted Steve on the back. "Buffett used to come in here with his friend Jim Croce, and they'd sit in the corner back there and play, sing, laugh, drink, and they'd be paid with free hotdogs."

"Will Brad get a free hotdog if he plays?"

"Sure," The barmaid flipped her hand freely toward a bubbling crock pot with a plastic wrap of buns beside it. "Hotdogs are free to everybody except people who don't play when Captain Tony requests it. They get nothing 'till they play a Buffett song."

My vivacious friend leaned his shoulder into mine, laughing even louder. "Guess you're playing." His cheeks grew bright stop-light red. "And singing too. I hope you don't suck." His laughter made the crack seem like a compliment.

I knew I wouldn't suck, and heck, it could be fun. Besides, what would Jimmy Buffett do? I looked at all of the encouraging faces, pointing, laughing, and coaxing me to the musician's corner. As Tony would say *It's all about my ego*.

I grabbed my guitar, pulled up a seat under the watchful eye of painted Matilda, and strummed the strings into tune. All twelve people were looking my way when I announced. "This is my first time playing in public."

Then my tall, lanky red-faced friend yelled from the bar, "That's okay. It's our first time hearing you in public." Then he nudged the General, "He's got to be pretty good. He's as bald as Buffett." This was followed by more rousing laughter.

"I heard that."

Of course, he laughed some more because by now it was clear that one of the great things he did in his life was laugh.

"Quit caressing that thing like she's your high school prom date, and play us a song." He was an outlandish personality, no doubt about it.

Tony gave me a broad toothed smile and swinging fist of encouragement, and I did what a person should do who's sitting with a guitar in his hand, hungry for a hotdog, and wishing he were Jimmy Buffett. I sang *Come Monday* with animated mediocrity, gained confidence when I picked smoothly through the intro of *Changes,* and then belted out *Cheeseburger* like it was a free hotdog song. As if prompted by the last Bm – A – D chords, Steve handed me a wiener covered with relish, ketchup, and mustard 'cause that's the way I like mine.'

My friends at the bar cheered loudly with too much enthusiasm to be real, only to be interrupted as our heads all whipped toward the squealing of a short-haired blond in a too-tight tank-top who appeared rushing through the door toward the good Captain, her toned arms flapping as if in super flight.

"Captain Tony, Captain Tony!" She sang better than I. "You're alive. I thought you were dead, but you're alive." And she wrapped her arms around him in a death grip, her lips to his temple with a pressure lock of over-eagerness. "I've always wanted to meet you, always." Then she yanked downward on her top, exposing more cleavage like a peep show ready to happen, exclaiming, "Can I have your autograph!" Thrusting her chest inches from his face.

Tony looked at Marty who rolled her eyes and waved him on. Magically, a permanent Sharpie appeared, and he tattooed his name across the top of revealed cleavage.

She giggled with the tickle, asking, "How old are you anyway?"

Tony looked from her chest to her eyes announcing for all who could hear. "I'm 87. I was born in 1916, the same year the Model T Ford was produced. Like the Model T, I'm a classic." Then Tony winked at her make-up rich face and pointed at his ears. "The horn's shot..." He called out filling the room with his powerful voice as his finger reached for his eyes. "The headlights are dim." Moving his legs rapidly as if running in place, he grinned. "The tires are worn out." Then he lifted his fist pumping it up and down with great vigor and announced. "But the clutch is still pumpin'."

Laughter roared from the room, men and women alike, as Tony had enlightened the small but vibrant crowd, and the girl who could be his granddaughter admired her chesty memoir, leaned forward, and laid a big smacker firmly on his wrinkled, puckered lips.

There was nothing else to do but keep playing for it was a Captain Tony party in need of acoustic music. I broke into *Brown Eyed Girl* with the General, Steve, and our vibrantly colorful friend singing the *sha-la-las* with infectious off-key enthusiasm, then, the mighty crowd became sharks to my *Fins*. Not quite 35,000 people doing *Fins* at a Buffett concert, but from it I gained the confidence to play my own *One More Piná Colada* when to my surprise, they sang right along in a rousing rendition of chorus echoes *One More, one more, One More, one more, One More Piná Colada!*

While it was the far side of my life, I was glad to be there with my buccaneer friend, the legendary Captain Tony, his kind and gentle wife, and a bar of misfits fitting perfectly into this hidden historical corner of Key West. Steve, the bar maid, the General, and my laughing gay friend were sharing a great time at the bar. Marty was now in conversation with the flighty woman whose cleavage her aged husband had just autographed. Grinning, I found myself completely lacking in judgment at the variety of

CHAPTER 12

Life has its unique moments, those unexpected twists of fate that guide you down a less cluttered path toward understanding the goodness in yourself, those who touch you, and those whom you have the fortune to be touched by. Ten days with Tony Tarracino was one of those unique twists of life toward the goodness and wisdom of *filling your heart with compassion, seeking the jewel in every soul, and sharing a word of kindness.*

I was meeting Tony at the tourist flush corner of Duval and Front Streets, by the Conch Train connection and a souvenir jewelry kiosk run by the young tropical beauty Nikki. It was our swan song, Tony and me in our final moments together. In a couple of hours, I would fly off toward the less wild blue yonder of the more conservative Midwest, leaving behind a legend, but taking his lessons with me. Away from the sunny sand beaches, swaying palm trees, Tony's womanizing escapades, and his university of life lessons, I was returning to my focused job as an educator of children with a renewed enthusiasm to connect with people and lead with compassion.

Slipping between the slow churning of cars and annoying buzzing of mopeds, I carried my guitar as I weaved across the concrete by-way toward Nikki, her tropical allure of rich brown skin and sweet fascination radiating as she waved my way. She was working in the shade of her canopy umbrella selling coconut bracelets like the one now worn on my wrist, a symbol of the person I am, of the honesty discovered in Key West, and a subtle reminder of Tony's life lessons.

"I like it," I told her, spinning the bracelet I'd bought a couple of days before.

She smiled warmly in her sweet, sultry way, "It's got a tropical flair that suits you, Brad."

How nice that she remembered my name.

As we chit-chatted, I saw Tony standing at the crosswalk light waiting for the signal that would allow an old man time to shuffle through the congested traffic. Dressed in his usual soft, gray polyester slacks, casual shirt unbuttoned at the cuffs, and worn black house slippers, in his hand hung a tattered plain brown grocery sack. From a distance, I could see him breathing deeply his morning energy boost, inhaling the pure oxygen that made him stronger, healthier, and more able to free his natural enthusiasm. I was thankful for the oxygen and Doc Mike.

"Tony," I waved as he lifted his leg onto the curb near us. "This is Nikki."

Graciously, Tony stepped forward to reach out his hand taking hers. As he did, his eyes popped wide open as did his mouth of glistening dentures. "So beautiful. Lovely. You are a beautiful girl, Nikki. Gorgeous," he gave me a smile and that knowing head nod. "Do you know you're talking to a great writer?"

"Brad," her own eyes opened with impressive surprise. "You're a writer?"

I scrunched my forehead and gave a shy shrug.

Tony released her hand with a slow, gentle touch, his other hand waving me off with his oxygen bag. "He's too modest. We're writing a book together. He's going to tell the world about my philosophy," he grinned confidently "And you, oh, you remind me of the beautiful Conch women when I first came to this island. Such good hearts and kind eyes with beautiful sun-kissed skin."

"Thank you Captain Tony," her rich, brown eyes never left his.

Tony's finger jumped outward at the name recognition, pointing as he turned to me. "See. All the beautiful girls know me. It's my reputation. It always precedes me."

Fiddling with my bracelet, I rolled my eyes upward toward the mid-day sun before reminding myself of the opportunity to offer a compliment. "She's a walking advertisement for all that's beautiful about Key West."

Nikki curtsied a polite thank you, pulling slightly to parachute her tropical sarong.

"You and me." Tony elated. "We should be on a poster together, one of those tourist advertisements."

"The contrasts of the Conch Republic." I laughed out loud.

"A Conch island beauty and *The Salt of Key West* proclaiming *The island is all this and everything in between.*" Swinging his hand in a celebration of the idea, Tony announced, "They'd love it. We'd make millions."

Nikki batted her coconut eyes, blushing, flirting, and waving him away all at the same time, and I realized that sensuous charisma was a jewel she shared with the Captain.

We strolled at a healthy 87-year-old pace down to the spot where Duval Street drops into the gulf, then meandered onto the deck along the aqua waters where every evening a crowd gathered to bid the sun goodnight. Tony stood for a moment, a short, quiet moment to watch the sea. After a time, he silently turned, and we walked side-by-side along the wooden path to Mallory Square.

Open with its pattern of decorative bricks and benches, at mid-morning Mallory Square is a quiet spot in the midst of a tourist-congested island. Pointing toward one of the wooden benches, Tony moved to it motioning for me to join him where I leaned my guitar case against the decorative metal armrest.

We sat together, Captain Tony and me, on the bench in the solitude of Mallory Square as sailing ships drifted before us on the coral calm waters in the Gulf of Mexico. When I'd first met Tony, I was intrigued because Jimmy Buffett had written a song about him. Now, as I sat next to him, I felt rewarded that I had been given his gift of time. I now understood compassion better, I knew how to more purposefully seek the jewel in every person, and I better realized the important impact a simple word of kindness can have. The gift of time and knowledge from the *Salt of Key West* had reawakened a craving to focus on people and the connections we each have. In that, I had no doubt. Marty was right. Tony had changed me.

Sitting on the bench beside him there was none of the hesitation of a few days before. There was trust, caring, and the conviction of friendship. With the exception of Denise, I'd not sat in such a way for a long time, not sat with such comfort in a relationship. My friend Captain Tony, my trusted, caring, compassionate friend shared this bench with me, and I was honored.

"My father was a man of great compassion," he said drifting back to our first conversation. "I think that's where I got my appreciation for compassion, from my father, but my mother was the one with the power. She ran the family. It's like that with me and Marty. It's like that with you and Denise. Women are the ones with all the power."

"You think?" I asked sarcastically as I surveyed the sailboats heading out to sea. I thought about how much Denise loved sailing, and how much I'd like to give her a life where we could sail away. Chuck it all and sail off into the sunset toward tropical adventures and unique people of simple lives and afternoon naps in swaying hammocks under the shade of a listing palm tree.

Tony put his hand to his chin covering his white beard, his fingers tapping his time-creased lips.

"Let's say you tell your wife you want to go to a movie," he spoke as his fingers slid down over his chin, the bags under his eyes large, almost looping. "Your wife wants to go to the PTA meeting." Lifting his leg, he crossed it over the other, the atrophied slenderness of his thighs clearly evident. "You both say what you want to do, and neither says anything else. An hour later," Tony pulls his fingers from his chin reaching out toward me as if holding the answer in his hand, "you're going to the PTA meeting."

We sat together, side-by-side, laughing at the reality of being both the stronger and the weaker sex. Denise is a great salesperson. The first one to speak loses. In that hour of decision-making quiet, I am always the first one to speak.

"Compassion has been so important to me." His hands rested folded in his lap now as our shoulders touched side-to-side. "The great influences in my life have had great compassion. My father, Tennessee Williams, and Shel Silverstein." There was softness in his voice as we sat on this bench in this quiet spot watching the ocean he had sailed most of his life. "Our families always had Thanksgiving dinner together, every year, me, Marty and our kids with Shel and his family. I miss Shel."

Once again, my thoughts turned to Wayne. "Shel's poems, I used to read them to Wayne when he was young. Wayne and I would sit together on the couch or in his bed at bedtime, and I'd read Shel's poems. I'd have Wayne explain what Shel meant." I leaned back on the bench thinking of my son, feeling good to be his father. "It was a game of thinking and learning that we played together. It didn't matter what Wayne's answer was. It only mattered that he was thinking, analyzing, and creating an answer."

As I turned toward Tony, I had that sudden realization of whom he was. For an instant I'd forgotten that he was an old man, forgotten that time had caught up with him and rushed onward while he moved at a slower pace. As I stared, a wave of sadness swept through me.

There was the impact of time in the sagging of skin long absent of elasticity. His face was much longer than it had been in his youth, dominated by the large bags hanging like small puffy balls beneath his blue eyes. There's something about an old man's skin, the quiet demeanor of having known life and not needing to force it any longer, to be able to sit and reflect. As I sat next to Tony, I looked forward to that day of calm, that day when my own skin would be wrinkled, and I'd found the peace that time and knowledge can bring.

"Did you know Shel wrote the song *A Boy Named Sue?*"

"The Johnny Cash song?"

Without looking my way, his eyes on the sea, he nodded decisively.

Classic country. "No," I said, "I didn't, but it fits perfectly."

"It's all about compassion." Tony said. "A father's misguided compassion in naming his son Sue, and a son's determination never ever to name his own son Sue junior."

Shifting on the seat, my arm was over the wooden railing resting comfortably against Tony's shoulder. "I've never looked at it in that way before."

"My father never raised a hand to me, and I never raised one to my children," Tony said still thinking about *A Boy*

Named Sue. "Shel was a brilliant man even with the fight at the end of the song being a statement of compassion. A father and a son coming together."

A few yards off shore, a charter boat was passing by, a fishing charter with two men sitting leisurely watching four large rods supporting jumbo reels dangling in the ready off the stern. One man was older and one younger, a father and a son. Late this afternoon, when my plane landed in Miami, when I got to the terminal and was twiddling my thumbs waiting for my connecting flight, I needed to call Wayne to check on the details of his house loan, and make sure everything was going as he hoped.

"Life's just people," Tony announced. "I've told you that so many times, but it is just people. The things don't matter. It's the people that matter, and we have choices about how we treat people. I always try and take something bad and make it good. I always make excuses for people, to accept the weaknesses in people, and focus on their good intentions. It's easier that way, to assume the good and look for the jewel in others."

In an unexpected moment, Tony's hand reached over to rest gently on my thigh. "So many people have come to me, wanted to do stories, articles, documentaries, things about my life. They wanted to hear my story and profit from it, but Brad, you're the one who's greater intent was to know me, and I'm honored." With a slight pat of affection, his hand lifted from my leg as our eyes connected. "I'm honored to call you my friend."

Our eyes brought the emotion from somewhere deep in my heart, and at that moment I realized I'd found an understanding. Contentment flowed through me like a gentle sea breeze so strong that I wanted to hold it as an endless moment. I wanted to sit on this bench with my friend, Captain Tony, and watch the sailboats drifting by. I wanted to feel the sun hot against my shoulders while my arm rested on the back of the bench, Tony leaning against it with his eyes to the sea. I wanted to hold this time and never let the warmth slip away.

"I'm going to write a good book about you," I told him. "You'll like it."

"Oh," Suddenly his voice gained strength, resounding with determination. "Don't make me perfect, Brad. I want people to know me, and I'm not perfect."

"I know," I laughed, patting his shoulder with an untroubled hug. "You're a crass, horny, womanizing pirate with a history of coloring outside the lines. At times your life hasn't been a pretty picture."

"Exactly," Tony laughed at first until his demeanor changed and his eyes turned serious.

"You know that Frank Sinatra song *My Way?*" He was having a great time, talking and watching the ocean. "Well, I did it my way, and I'm not ashamed, so don't sugar coat my life. Tell the sorted truth. It's my life, and I'm not ashamed of it. Yes, I've slept with a lot of women, run guns, gambled. I've done a lot of things most people wouldn't do, but I've always had compassion, and I always knew it's the people that matter."

"And that's your jewel?" I told him.

"If people always lived with compassion, and because of that sought the jewel in others, we'd have a better world," he answered. "It's the people who don't have compassion that should live to be 200 years old."

Oh, what now, I laughed. "What do you mean?"

"The son-of-a-bitches in the world, those living without compassion." Tony explained. "They deserve to live to be two hundred years old. They should have to live with their miserable selves that long. Dying's too good for them. They should suffer what those around them must suffer living with them."

"Not very compassionate." I chuckled.

"Of course it is. What's not compassionate about wishing life on one who's self-serving?"

With that, he had me thinking and laughing again. As my brain waves danced, I was reminded that my good friend was 87, on oxygen, and his heart pumped with the rhythm of a pacemaker. Life has its limits, and surely Tony would not live to be 200 years old.

"So is this your last mountain, writing this book with me?"

Tony slipped his hands back into his lap, his eyes returning to the ocean. Boats moved in and out of the bay and a flock of pillow white clouds drifted between the blues as the sun warmed our backs. Searching the horizon, once again he began to talk. That's when I realized how to end the song I was writing, the simplicity of the dramatic ending as I watched him absorb the ocean view.

"I hope to leave this world a little better place. I've got my wounds and have wounded others, but I've tried to do good and to live with compassion. I hope when I leave here I've left behind a little better world. You do that when you connect with people. And now it's this book that gives me another chance. That's how I'll continue to connect with people, continue to preach compassion."

"What about the wounds?" I turned to face the aged Captain. "Are there any unhealed wounds?"

"Only Lorenzo," he answered with a quiet breath. "And now, we're writing this book, and with it, I'm putting my house in order." In his own noble way, he lifted his chin, the sun warm around him. "When I die, I want it to be on my terms. I don't want to be deprived of knowing I'm dying. I was dead once, my last heart attack. I was dead for seven minutes, but the EMT kept working on me. He said *We can't let this man die,* and he didn't. He brought me back to life. I see him all the time on the gambling boat. He gave me the chance to die on my terms."

"Why's that so important to you, dying on your terms?" I asked.

Captain Tony looked up at me, looked me in the eyes with his own clear thought. "I don't ever want to be a burden to anyone, but I do want to thank them for caring so much for me," his head lifted slightly. "I always wanted to be the best I could be. I'd like to be the best in death too, first class, to die on my terms, and say goodbye to you and all of my friends. It's all ego, to be able to do it my way."

My arm shifted to rest against the slender shoulder of the aged legend. "You've lived an amazing life, Tony. What's the best part of it? What was the best time of your life?"

He nodded as his blue eyes lifted to mine one more time. "This moment here with you. Every moment of life is the best moment of your life, and I'm so thankful for this time with you," his eyes shifted to the ocean. "The best moment of my life is right now, here with you."

"It's great for me too, Tony." Reaching for my guitar, I pulled it from the case and began the slight strums of tuning. "May I play a song for you, a song I wrote inspired by our week together."

"You wrote a song for me?" Tony's hand pressed to his heart, his eyes grateful. "I'm honored, Brad."

"I wrote this for us, for you Tony," I shared as I pressed each string of the introductory harmony. "I finished it last night after we left the Chart Room." Then I moved smoothly into the melody of open chords.

> *I met him at a bar in a pirate town*
> *Living his life out by the sea*
> *With his knowledge of time*
> *He spoke his wisdom to me*
>
> *Life lessons of a legend*
> *Captain Tony's wisdom to us all*
> *Fill your heart with compassion*
> *Seek the jewel in every soul*

Share a word of kindness
Simple life lessons that make us whole

From a life lived teetering on the edge
Sailing high on hurricane seas
He's lived his life without fear
The immortality of a good buccaneer

Life lessons of a legend
Captain Tony's wisdom to us all
Fill your heart with compassion
Seek the jewel in every soul
Share a word of kindness
Simple life lessons that make us whole

You can be a concrete mogul
An investor with a billion bucks
But you must know it's the people
The people's what it's all about...so
Fill your heart with compassion
Seek the jewel in every soul
Share a word of kindness
Simple life lessons that make us whole

As I played the rhythm of the instrumental interlude, Tony sat in self-satisfaction, his eyes closed, his ears listening, and his arm around my shoulder with a gentle rub of his hand.

> *He sits on the dock watching passing ships*
> *The days go by one by one*
> *He knows he won't live forever*
> *But his lessons live on and on*

The song built with the intensity of his life, and the importance of his lesson.

> *Life lessons of a legend*
> *Captain Tony's wisdom to us all*
> *Fill your heart with compassion*
> *Seek the jewel in every soul*
> *Share a word of kindness*
> *Simple life lessons that make us whole*

Then I strummed slightly the blend of a G chord, my voice quieting to the softness of compassion when I sang with loving respect in a slow, soulful ending.

> *I met him at a bar ... in a pirate town*
> *Living his life out by the sea ...*

We sat silently for a time as I watched Tony, watched his gaze drifting out and over the sea, and the large puffy bags beneath his eyes.

"You know, Brad. I like that better than the song Jimmy Buffett wrote for me."

"Better than *Last Mango?*" I grinned at his overt kindness.

"Yes. I believe I like it better."

"Thank you, Tony," I set my guitar to the side. "Like Jimmy, it was my privilege to write it."

He nodded knowingly, his eyes turned to mine, bright blue with the age of time surrounding them. That's when I knew, when I understood the large fluid bags of skin hanging below his gentle blue eyes, those full hanging puffs of age were a testament to a long, long life of compassion.

In Memoriam

CAPTAIN TONY TARRACINO
AUGUST 10, 1916 – NOVEMBER 1, 2008

Authors Capt. Tony and Brad Manard at Lower Keys
Medical Center book signing on October 28, 2008

We sat in the quiet of Key West's Lower Keys Medical
Center ICU, my wife Denise and I, Tony's wife Marty, and
his daughter, Little Toni. He had been anxious for our
arrival, sitting among the heart monitors and oxygen tubes
watching the big clock on the wall. Now that we had come
to join him, Capt. Tony was holding court.

With feeble hands, he passed out Kleenexes, handing one gingerly to Denise, saying with a wink, *You're going to need these.* Then he teared up, apologizing as he dabbed his own eyes and said, *In my old age I'm a lot more emotional.* His hand reaching out pointing to me, smiling with his handsome blue eyes on mine, and spoke, "The book. I can't tell you what the book means to me. Brad, you're the Michelangelo of Key's literature." We all laughed and cried at the same time as Tony *shared a word of kindness.*

Tony had received his copy of *Life Lessons* three weeks before, and on the official book release date, October 28, 2008, he was unable to leave the hospital, so the hospital helped him celebrate. In the Board Room, they held a book signing. Three of his children Alicia (43), Little Tony (48), and Louie (73) were there, and for an hour and a half, the aged man was the legendary Capt. Tony. He autographed seventy-three books purchased by hospital employees. Doctors, nurses, and volunteers, they all came to get their copy, and Tony thanked them kindly, offered to bed the pretty girls telling them *You'll love it,* told stories like no other, and laughed freely as he celebrated his life turned to literature.

Four days later, on Saturday afternoon, November 1, 2008, as I sat at Captain Tony's Saloon signing books, Tony, surrounded by family and with Marty at his side, passed away. When Marty reached me with the news, she told me *Brad, this book made his last month one of the best months of his life.* Overwhelmed with a sense of loss, I cried for my friend wanting to hear just one more story, one more narrative to keep the adventure alive. He had become my grandfather, a man of historic tales, of a deep heart, and an advisor that had become so much of my life.

An hour later, at the family's request, I arrived at the Casa Marina Resort as the Cedar Island Band played the main stage for Meeting of the Minds. After sharing the news with MOTM Director Bill DeWalt, he stepped on stage, raised his glass with honor, and announced through sensitive words of respect the passing of Captain Tony. From the thousand who loved him and the spirit of his life, glasses were raised as tears flowed freely through the grief of admiring eyes. With heartfelt emotion, the Cedar Island Band played *Last Mango in Paris,* and lead singer Doug Rassler sang the verses in perfect harmony, tears streaming down his cheeks.

That night, in Captain Tony's Saloon, glasses were raised again as his children Louie, Tonia (72), and Richard (64) honored their father. Then, in a craziness Tony would have loved, Denise began dragging us all into the women's head to read upon the dingy walls the words authored by an anonymous soul: *11/1/08 - On this saddest of days, we all celebrate the life he lived, the life we wished we lived, and the possibilities of the life before us....*

The writing of *Life Lessons of a Legend* was a personal journey, and the release and successful sales that followed were a surreal experience. Through it all, I learned so much more about Tony, so much more about how he lived his life philosophy and drew others to him. It was my joy to have shared his stories, my honor to call him friend. Through it all, I learned that the title *legend* did not do his good heart justice.

On November 8, 2008, at the funeral, his son, Keith Famie (48), and friend, Al Kelley, spoke eloquently with humor and honor of the man who had lived such a long life yet had left us all too soon. In a post-funeral celebration on a crowd-filled Greene Street outside of Captain Tony's Saloon, 21 doves were released. As her children Josie (25) and T.J. (23) looked on, Marty released the last dove who flew up into the blue sky, circled around in the current of the soft ocean breeze, and settled onto the peak of Captain Tony's Saloon. From there, for the longest of time, the dove gazed down on all those who came to honor the legend, and then, as if it was time to fly away, he did.

So, as Jimmy Buffett sings, *Our lives change like the weather, but a legend never dies* ... sail on, my friend, sail on.

Brad Manard

About The Authors

With a doctorate in educational administration, Brad Manard is a school superintendent and educator serving communities in Iowa and Nebraska for twenty-eight years. A former English teacher and high school principal, in 2001 he playfully shared with his wife, Denise, that he had decided to *become Jimmy Buffett.* That interest led him to Captain Tony Tarracino and the valuable life lessons shared in this story.

Made in the USA
Lexington, KY
24 February 2014